MEMO FROM DARRYL F. ZANUCK

THE GOLDEN YEARS AT TWENTIETH CENTURY–FOX

ALSO BY RUDY BEHLMER

Inside Warner Bros. (1935–1951)

Behind the Scenes: The Making Of . . .

Memo from David O. Selznick

Hollywood's Hollywood: The Movies About the Movies
    (with Tony Thomas)

The Films of Errol Flynn
    (with Tony Thomas and Clifford McCarty)

THE UNIVERSITY OF WISCONSIN/WARNER BROS.
SCREENPLAY SERIES:

    The Sea Hawk (editor/annotator)

    The Adventures of Robin Hood (editor/annotator)

MEMO FROM
DARRYL F. ZANUCK

The Golden Years at Twentieth Century–Fox

SELECTED, EDITED, AND ANNOTATED BY

RUDY BEHLMER

WITH A FOREWORD BY PHILIP DUNNE

GROVE PRESS · NEW YORK

Published by Grove Press
A division of Grove Press, Inc.
841 Broadway
New York, NY 10003-4793

Published in Canada by General Publishing Company, Ltd.

Library of Congress Cataloging-in-Publication Data

Zanuck, Darryl Francis, 1902–1979
    Memo from Darryl F. Zanuck: The golden years at Twentieth Century–Fox / selected,
edited, and annotated by Rudy Behlmer ; with a foreword by Philip Dunne.—1st ed.
        p.   cm.
    "A selection of Darryl F. Zanuck's letters and memoranda during
the glory days of 20th Century–Fox (1935–1956)"—Introd.
    Includes index.
    ISBN 0-8021-1540-3 (alk. paper)
    1. Zanuck, Darryl Francis, ,1902–   —Correspondence.   2. Motion
picture industry—United States—History.   3. Twentieth Century–Fox
Film Corporation—History.   4. Motion picture producers and
directors—United States—Correspondence.   I. Behlmer, Rudy.
II. Title.
PN1998.3.Z36A4   1993
791.43'0232'092—dc20   92-32865
                                                                CIP

Manufactured in the United States of America
Printed on acid-free paper
Designed by Debbie Glasserman
First Edition 1993

10 9 8 7 6 5 4 3 2 1

TO MY WIFE, STACEY

ACKNOWLEDGMENTS

The correspondence from Darryl F. Zanuck contained in this book is housed in the following archives (in alphabetical order).

Academy of Motion Picture Arts and Sciences Center for Motion Picture Study, Margaret Herrick Library (Linda Mehr, Sam Gill, Robert Cushman, Howard Prouty, Stacey Behlmer, and Patrick Stockstill): Lloyd Bacon Collection, George Cukor Collection, Valentine Davies Collection, Alfred Hitchcock Collection, Hedda Hopper Collection, Henry King Collection, Milton Krims Collection, Ranald MacDougall Collection, Lewis Milestone Collection, MPAA Production Code Administration Files, Charles Schlaifer Collection, Darryl F. Zanuck Photographs (from various collections).

The American Film Institute, Louis B. Mayer Library (Alan Braun): Charles Feldman Papers, Edmund Goulding Papers.

Bison Archives (Marc Wanamaker): Darryl F. Zanuck Photographs.

Boston University, Mugar Memorial Library (Howard B. Gotlieb and Charles Niles): Nunnally Johnson Collection.

Columbia University, Manuscript Library (Bernard R. Crystal): Earl I. Sponable Papers.

Indiana University, The Lilly Library (Saundra Taylor): John Ford Manuscripts, Darryl F. Zanuck Manuscripts.

The Museum of Modern Art/Film Stills Archive (Mary Corliss): Darryl F. Zanuck Photographs.

Stanford University Libraries, Special Collections (Maggie Kimball and Carol Bickler): Delmer Daves Collection.

University of California, Los Angeles, Research Library, Department of Special Collections (Anne Caiger): Kenneth Macgowan Papers, Preston Sturges Papers.

University of California, Los Angeles, Theater Arts Library (Brigitte J. Kueppers): Twentieth Century Fox Archives, Jean Renoir Collection.

University of Southern California, Cinema-Television Library (Steve Hanson, Anne G. Schlosser, Robert Knutson, and Ned Comstock): Twentieth Century Fox Collection, Philip Dunne Collection, Alfred Newman Collection, Jerry Wald Collection, Jack L. Warner Collection.

University of Southern California, Warner Bros. Archives/USC School of Cinema-Television (Leith Adams and Stuart Ng): Warner Bros. Papers.

The University of Texas at Austin, Harry Ransom Humanities Research Center (Prentiss Moore): David O. Selznick Archive.

The University of Wyoming, Special Collections (Gene W. Gressley and Emmett D. Chisum): David Brown Collection, Lyman Munson Collection.

Wesleyan University, Cinema Archives (Jeanine D. Basinger and Leith G. Johnson): Elia Kazan Collection.

In addition, the following individuals (again in alphabetical order) were helpful in various ways: John Belton, Brenda Berrisford, Julian Blaustein, Walt Bode, David Brown, Abigail Cheever, James V. D'Arc, Ken Darby, Mrs. Valentine Davies, Joyce Drzal, Diana Jones Dunnahoo, Philip Dunne, Alan Gevinson, Bebe Goddard, Mel Gussow, David Y. Hanelman, Miriam Hurewitz, Elia Kazan, Don Keller, Max Lamb, Otto Lang, Bill La Vallee, Arthur Lewis, Lorraine LoBianco, Connie M. Lopez, Janet Lorenz, Clifford McCarty, Dottie Morey, James Pepper, Victoria Rossellini, Diane St. John, Thomas Schatz, John Schultheiss, Daniel Selznick, Alexander Sesonske, Eileen Shanahan, Charles Silver, Anthony Slide, Maynard T. Smith, Aubrey Solomon, A. M. Sperber, Tom Stempel, George E. Stephens, Jr., Susan Tillack,

Mel Tormé, John Trotti, Malvin Wald, Alan D. Williams, Steven W. Workman, Jack Yaeger, and most particularly Richard D. Zanuck, whose generous cooperation made this project possible.

Jim Moser, my editor at Grove, strongly believed in the manuscript at first reading and continued to offer counsel and support.

CONTENTS

Photographs follow pages 104 and 216

FOREWORD BY PHILIP DUNNE

Philip Dunne started working for Darryl Zanuck in 1937 and subsequently spent twenty-five years at Twentieth Century–Fox as a writer and later a producer and director.

In publishing a selection of Darryl F. Zanuck's letters and memoranda during the glory days of Twentieth Century–Fox (1935–1956), Rudy Behlmer has gone far beyond assembling the correspondence of a major executive. His book also presents a vivid picture of how movies were made in that so-called Golden Age of the midcentury, as well as a gripping account of the ups and downs of the studio from its inception until Zanuck, disenchanted with Hollywood and the changes within the industry, moved to Europe as an independent producer. Most of all, it is a character study of one of the dominant characters—and in my opinion the most talented producer—in the history of the movies, told in his own words.

No Hollywood personality has been so maligned, in history and fiction, as has Darryl Zanuck since his death in 1979. He is usually described or portrayed as an arrogant and tasteless boor, a sadistic bully who, in one worthless "biography," enjoyed torturing various nameless "writers of the day" in an imagined hot seat. Nothing could be further from the truth. Writers had names, and were treated with the same respect as all other professionals—perhaps even more so because, unlike star-rich M-G-M, Zanuck's new and relatively star-poor studio depended upon good screenplays.

Perhaps he could push over individuals intended by nature to be pushovers. I twice heard him berate with the tongue of an angry drill sergeant world-famous directors who, by no coincidence, were themselves notorious bullies on the set, but he never raised his voice to a Nunnally Johnson or a Lamar Trotti.

In this wise and thoughtful selection of Darryl's written communications we get an accurate picture of the producer and the man. Buffon's aphorism perfectly applies: *Le style est l'homme même*.

What comes through is a great creative executive: intelligent, decisive, totally in support of his subordinates as he was totally in charge of their work. No great screenwriter himself, he was an excellent editor. He recognized the strengths and weaknesses of his staff writers. Among mine are verbosity and impatience. He sent one script back to me with "Come to the point" scrawled on its cover, another with "Dig in!" and a third, when I was also directing, with "Shoot it." When he asked me to rewrite the script of *The Robe*, a project for which I had no enthusiasm, I asked rather glumly: "What do you want me to do with the damn thing?" "Put it in English," he said. Brevity is another executive virtue.

Still another is the power to create enthusiasm, and at this Darryl was a past master. Every assignment would become the greatest picture ever made and remain so until, in the drafty forecourt of some preview theatre, a subordinate would dejectedly remark: "Well, we got a great *woman's* picture."

On most of my assignments we exchanged very few memoranda. On such productions as *The Rains Came* and *Stanley and Livingstone*, on which I collaborated with Julien Josephson, we were usually well in accord before work on the script had begun. Julien was a veteran of the silent days, and I still have a vivid memory of the tyrant Zanuck pleading with the stubborn old gentleman: "You can't *always* be right, Julien. Sometimes even *I* can be right."

On *The Ghost and Mrs. Muir*, far from occupying a hot seat, I wrote the entire screenplay at a desert resort, without interference from either Zanuck or the staff producer.

In this book, the most important memo concerning the writing of *How Green Was My Valley* is a sharp critique of an early screenplay. When, later on, this screenplay was sent to me for comment, I wrote a critique which bears an uncanny resemblance to Zanuck's own, which I had not seen. But I blamed not the screenplay but Richard Llewellyn's novel, which I hadn't read, wondering why the studio had bought the rights to it. Zanuck's characteristically laconic reply was to send me the book, with which I promptly fell in love.

More often than not we saw things in the same light. The movies we made during his reign emphasized courage, self-reliance, honor, and integrity. These are the Victorian virtues, and Darryl's mind-set, like my own, was essentially Victorian. Consider the characters in his great movies: the valiant Okies in *The Grapes of Wrath* and coal miners in *How Green Was My Valley*, the courageous airmen in *Twelve O'Clock High*, and *Pinky* choosing dignity and pride over personal happiness. It is significant that his personal hero was Woodrow Wilson, a man of whom it could be said that he destroyed himself with an overdose of integrity.

The memoranda concerning *Wilson* are particularly poignant, as what Darryl hoped would be his greatest success was gradually transformed into a cruel disappointment. Yet there was always room for humor, and Darryl Zanuck was a witty man. When *Wilson* was released in 1944 I was still on leave of absence from the studio for my government war service. I ran the picture and sent him a pro forma telegram of congratulations. Years later, a group of us in the executive dining room were discussing *Wilson*'s failure. Darryl suddenly pointed his finger at me and said: "And there's the man that talked me into making it."

Another poignant set of memos concerns Somerset Maugham's *The Razor's Edge* and Darryl's attempts to understand the character of Larry, the book's central figure. As Lamar Trotti, who wrote the screenplay, told me at the time: "Darryl can't bring himself to understand that his and Maugham's concepts of life are as far apart as the North and South poles."

Every set of memoranda records the ups and downs of the movie in question, its crises and continuing drama. For me, to read them today is to relive the triumphs and disasters of events long forgotten, now recalled with affection.

If I may conclude on a personal note, there was one little set of memos that clearly had no place in Rudy Behlmer's collection but which perfectly illustrates the nature of my own working relationship with Darryl F. Zanuck.

I will set out the three brief memos in dialogue form. They covered a line I had written in 1948 for Tyrone Power, playing a writer in *The Luck of the Irish*.

DFZ

With this line, are you saying that all writers are frustrated egomaniacs?

PD

All writers are frustrated egomaniacs, and in this category I include the entire personnel of 20th Century–Fox Studio—with the possible exception of Sam Silver.

(Sam Silver was Darryl's personal barber.)

DFZ

It is not generally known that Sam Silver is the author of *Carnival in Costa Rica*.

Need I add that *Carnival in Costa Rica* was the previous year's biggest flop?

Following a long battle with cancer, Philip Dunne died in June 1992—shortly after writing this Foreword. His 1980 memoir, Take Two, *has recently been reissued in an updated edition.*

PREFACE

The correspondence in this book covers the period between 1935 and 1956 when Darryl F. Zanuck was vice president in charge of production at Twentieth Century–Fox. Earlier he had the same position at the independent Twentieth Century Pictures and before that he was in a similar capacity at Warner Bros. for several years. But the Fox span has a long continuity and reflects the gradual modification of the studio system as practiced during that time.

The years 1935 to 1956 were the period at Fox of such pictures as *Young Mr. Lincoln, The Hound of the Baskervilles, The Grapes of Wrath, Down Argentine Way, The Mark of Zorro, How Green Was My Valley, Laura, My Darling Clementine, Miracle on 34th Street, Boomerang!, The Ghost and Mrs. Muir, Kiss of Death, Gentleman's Agreement, Unfaithfully Yours, A Letter to Three Wives, Twelve O'Clock High, All About Eve, Viva Zapata!, The Day the Earth Stood Still, Gentlemen Prefer Blondes, The Robe, The King and I*—to say nothing of little Shirley Temple, Betty Grable, Marilyn Monroe, directors John Ford, Joseph L. Mankiewicz, Elia Kazan, and others.

Except for a relatively brief time during World War II, Zanuck was in complete charge of the Fox studio and product. There were no committees to decide what to produce; no frequent games of top-executive musical chairs. Zanuck ran the show. Naturally, he had to answer to the president of the company and the board of directors, most of whom were in New York, but generally they left the business of *making* the movies up to him. The vast majority of the people on the lot, including the actors, writers, directors, art directors, cameramen, composers, and so forth, were under contract and/or were full-time employees. Zanuck had to make a large number of pictures every year to feed the Fox-owned theatres prior to the time in the late 1940s and early 1950s when the government's antitrust act broke up the film companies' ownership of production, distribution, and exhibition.

It is particularly revealing to note how many of his associates from those days later talked about Zanuck in their own autobiographies, oral histories, and interviews. David Brown, his story editor in the early 1950s, commented in his book *Let Me Entertain You* (1990): "I thought he was a brilliant analyst of scripts and stories, and I loved his enthusiasm. The simplest story, if he liked it, became the Second Coming. He infused his associates with his excitement."

Writer-producer-director Philip Dunne often has said that "writers at Twentieth never wrote 'for' directors, as most critics and movie historians assume; they wrote for Darryl Zanuck." Another longtime Zanuck staff member, writer-producer-director Nunnally Johnson, pointed out in his 1969 UCLA/American Film Institute oral history with Tom Stempel that Zanuck "was a great editor of a script. . . . He was far and away the most valuable man I've ever been associated with in the business. One of the very few who really made contributions and was a collaborator." Johnson left Fox in 1943 for a more lucrative deal and part ownership in a new independent company, International (before it merged with Universal). In 1973 he told Aubrey Solomon for Solomon's book *Twentieth Century–Fox: A Corporate and Financial History* (1988): "I remember when my contract at Universal-International terminated [a few years later], L. B. Mayer invited me over to have lunch with him and talk about signing with M-G-M. I was planning to go back to Fox where I'd been for so many years. Mayer mentioned all the stars on the lot, but I still didn't want to sign. He asked me what Fox had that they didn't—and I said 'Zanuck.' "

Writer Mary Loos, who in the late 1940s and early 1950s collaborated on scripts with her then husband Richard Sale, said at a February 1981 USC Zanuck tribute: "He had this great affection and understanding for people who worked with him. Sometimes it was difficult, and we had our discussions and arguments, but . . . it was a very kind thing to have somebody say to you, who was absolutely in control of your life's work, 'Well, I disagree with you; I think it should be this way, but if you feel that much, if it's that dear to you to make it the way you think it should be, you try it your way, and if I like it, it'll go.' "

Writer-producer-director Joseph L. Mankiewicz was quoted by Robert Osborne in the November 13, 1984, *Hollywood Reporter* as saying that Zanuck "seemed to instinctively, and immediately, know what was wrong or right about a project or a scene. I always thought he was at his best at the very first reading of a new screenplay, the first time through. . . . I was very happy at Twentieth Century–Fox, and I can't think of another studio I ever felt that way about."

Veteran director Henry King stated in a 1974 interview with Scott Eyman for *Focus on Film*, No. 26: "Zanuck's got an open mind. . . . He was never anything but a model producer." Director Elia Kazan from his 1988 autobiography, *A Life*: "Darryl . . . was the best executive I've ever known. . . . He wasn't afraid of anyone. . . . The important thing for all of us who worked at Fox during those years was that the man heading our studio didn't back off when he was challenged."

Even director John Ford, who apparently had a particular aversion to producers and studio heads, told Mel Gussow in 1970 for his biography of Zanuck that he "was head and shoulders above all other producers. . . . I had this tacit agreement that he would cut the picture. . . . He was a great cutter, a great film editor."

Philip Dunne says in his 1980 autobiography, *Take Two*, that "Zanuck was happiest when he was sitting in his projection room alone with his cutter, molding the picture closer to his heart's desire." And film editor William Reynolds noted in *American Cinemeditor* (Summer 1991): "Back then, editors didn't cut each film for the director; they cut for Darryl Zanuck."

Writer-producer Casey Robinson in his 1974 oral history with Joel Greenberg: "He was not a hog for credit; I'm not speaking of credit on the screen, I'm speaking of giving credit to people. I never heard him claim the credit for a successful picture. I never heard him lay the blame for a bad picture on anybody but himself. Now this is remarkable."

And naturally there are those ex-associates who did not join in the hosannas for Zanuck.

This book is not a biography. Its focus is on the myriad elements that made up the production of a feature picture under the command of one of Hollywood's greatest moguls during the colorful days of the old studio system.

Zanuck, having been a writer, was a strong believer in story conferences following the completion of each draft of an outline, treatment, and screenplay. It was his custom to have his script coordinator—for many years Dorothy Hechtlinger and then Molly Mandaville from 1943—attend his conferences (he did most of the talking), make detailed notes on what was said, type the notes, and then distribute them to each person at the conference: usually the writer(s), staff producer under Zanuck, and later, when the final shooting script was being prepared, the director. Fortunately, these notes were kept along with the various drafts of the script, and they provide an excellent record of the evolution of a piece of material and Zanuck's strong input regarding story construction and script detail.

Molly Mandaville wrote in an interoffice memo in late 1951 that Zanuck "never reads things after he's dictated them; this refers not only to my work but also to the work done by the secretaries in his own office. . . . When Mr. Zanuck gives a person something to do he assumes that you've done it, and done it correctly. Hence the need for a sense of responsibility. . . . We usually have story conferences in the afternoons; sometimes we will have one every afternoon during the week. . . ."

In addition to reading drafts of the scripts and making his own notations in pencil directly on the pages prior to the conferences, Zanuck was responsible for casting decisions (key roles) and producer, writer, and director assignments. He also looked at "dailies" or "rushes" once or twice a day and would make comments to the producer and/or director if he felt they were warranted.

One thing he decidedly did *not* do (with rare exception) was to visit the set, back lot (now Century City), or location while a picture was shooting. He was a firm believer—during this period at least—in the director functioning as a director when the film was in production without any second-guessing by the production executive pacing on the sidelines. However, after the feature was cut, Zanuck concentrated on editorial changes. The screenings and modifications of the edited work print usually took place at night in the projection room at the studio.

Most of the time he let Alfred Newman, the head of his music department from 1940, function with very little interference, but he would on occasion request a specific composer (usually Newman) for a particular film.

Zanuck, of course, attended previews and presided over postpreview discussions with his associates. He generally left the advertising, selling, and distribution of the films to Fox's New York corporate office, but occasionally he would communicate his observations to those in charge. (And they in turn would communicate *their* observations about the finished films.)

As did every studio at the time, Fox ground out reams of assembly-line "product," including formula films and their "disguised" variations, remakes, and sequels; but Zanuck himself rarely made series films or sequels. The "B" unit, completely under Sol M. Wurtzel for several years in the 1930s and 1940s, took care of the series films (Charlie Chan, Mr. Moto, the Jones Family, etc.). So there is no correspondence herein regarding that separate operation.

===

The papers for this book have been gathered from a good many archives and individuals throughout the United States—as reflected in the Acknowledgments. There is no "Zanuck Archive"; virtually none of his papers (from this period) had been saved by him. Fortunately, an unusual number of people who worked with and for Zanuck did save *their* correspondence to and from Zanuck. The search went on for several years, with a few choice entries turning up at the eleventh hour.

All inclusions were written or dictated by Zanuck, and the only change I have made with regard to altering words is in some of the story conference notes: "Mr. Zanuck says" has been silently modified in those instances to the first-person "I."

I have tried to select correspondence on different aspects of the filmmaking process, as well as Zanuck's discussion and analysis of overall industry problems through the years. Also, there are a few communications to executives at other studios, such as Jack L. Warner, Hal B. Wallis, and David O. Selznick. And when he felt it absolutely necessary, Zanuck would personally write to the Production Code Administration (the industry "censors" or self-regulatory body) about a rejection by that office of parts or all of a shooting script or edited film submitted for the mandatory approval.

For the most part, personal correspondence, corporate papers, and military communications are outside the scope of this book, which is specifically devoted to creative and administrative matters.

But inevitably there are gaps. Certain personalities, favorite films, and milestones in the history of the company will be conspicuous by their absence in these pages. If you miss revealing documents along some of these lines, so do I. What is represented here are bits and pieces tracked down from a multitude of sources throughout the country, rather than from a single, reasonably definitive collection. This is a record of the drama of the moment, recorded when it was happening, rather than recall from a later perspective.

Often the reader will find a great many ellipses within a piece of correspondence indicating that material has been eliminated by me along the way. The words have not been deleted in order to hide some highly charged revelations, but rather to eliminate redundancies, digressions, and in many cases—particularly with regard to story conference notes—specific lines of dialogue or plot points relating to indicated page numbers of the script that would only be of interest to a person conducting an in-depth study of a particular film or series of films.

Although there is some Zanuck correspondence in my book *Inside Warner Bros.* (Viking, 1985), that volume primarily deals with the period from 1935 to 1951 when Zanuck was at Fox. After weighing the possibility of starting with "prologue" memos from Warners—and perhaps from Twentieth Century before the company's merger with Fox—I made the decision to stick to the time, place, and action unities when he was in charge of production at Twentieth Century–Fox. This doesn't mean that there is not an interesting story to tell via paperwork from these other periods; it only means that it is not the story I have chosen to tell.

I decided to let Zanuck's resignation in 1956 as production chief to become an independent producer, working mostly in Europe, conclude the book. At the Fox studio he had his office, secretaries, script coordinators, and various associates who were around him on a regular basis; when he became an independent producer, the papers, or at least those that survive, are relatively sparse. And the next phase, after he returned in 1962 as president of the company, based in New York, is an entirely different story—a story that really does not fit with the one told in these pages.

Although Zanuck's son Richard has accurately quoted his father as saying "Success in movies boils down to three things: story, story, story," actually Darryl Zanuck went a step further. The choice of subject matter precedes the actual story, and in a 1940 memo to Fox executives, Zanuck said: "I would rather have a bad script on a great subject than a great script on an ordinary subject. Star power is valueless unless the subject matter in the story stands the test. . . . Audiences . . . go [to the movies] only when there is something playing that they definitely want to see." There is certainly nothing dated about the pronouncement.

Obviously, there were then (and are now) different approaches to running a studio. Louis B. Mayer, to cite one obvious example, did not function at all at M-G-M as Zanuck functioned at Fox. Jack L. Warner had yet another modus operandi and so did Harry Cohn at Columbia, and so on. Zanuck, like David Selznick and Hal Wallis among a few others, was strictly a hands-on, totally absorbed in day-to-day production type of executive.

And again, there was no question about who was running the show at Fox in those days.

ONE

TWENTIETH CENTURY-FOX: OFF AND RUNNING

April 28, 1936
Mr. Ernest Pascal [Fox contract writer and president of the Screen Writers Guild]
2010 La Brea Terrace
Los Angeles, California

Dear Ernest:

In reply to your letter of April 26th, I can only repeat the ideas expressed in my original letter to you. . . .

In your article [in the Screen Writers Guild paper] you continually speak of abuses. What are these abuses? Let's be specific. What has any producer done to create a situation that calls for unionism among the ranks of creative talent? You admit, in your letter, that if all producers were like me there would be no cause for complaint. As yet, no one has been able to give me any concrete or substantial evidence of abuse to any writer from any producer. It is also quite obvious, despite your denials in your letter to me, that your article definitely promises the screenwriters that eventually they will be able to control the screen destinies of the stories they work on. I can imagine nothing that would kill this business any quicker. Moving pictures are not made by any one individual. Many minds are essential if success is to be desired. Many contributors are required. . . .

In the last paragraph of your letter of April 26th, you state that if I had "confined my extraordinary talents to screenwriting" I would be the President of the Screen Writers Guild today. I have thought about this last paragraph a long while. I have tried to consider myself both as to failings and virtues, and I have gone back to that period when I was a screenwriter.

For four years I drew wages as a writer in this business. I wrote twenty-one produced feature scenarios, sixty-five produced two-reel scenarios, and made thirty-one produced adaptations. I remember when the first writer in the business was given five hundred dollars a week. At that time, I was receiving, under contract, $125.00 a week. Before this prosperous period of my career, I had walked on many occasions from Hollywood to Culver City and from Hollywood to Universal City because I didn't have carfare, in an effort to "peddle" my stories. I lived, at the time, in the back room of a bungalow with two other "almost writers." When I finally got my first job I was indeed happy, as it gratified a great ambition. I remember the first time Jules Furthman sold an original story for $1,500.00. This was an unheard-of amount. He was the toast of every writer in Hollywood. He had at last elevated the screenwriting profession. I remember Bess Meredyth when she was raised to $500.00 a week. Writers throughout the industry were absolutely amazed; that anyone could receive this amount of money for writing scenarios on a weekly contract was unheard of. There was no talk then of unionism or any ism. We were all happy in the thought that we were delivering something every week for which we were being handsomely rewarded.

When I think back on those old days (fourteen years ago) and look at the screenwriter's situation as of today, when salaries are what they are, when there are at least one hundred writers in this business receiving $1,000.00 per week or more, when working conditions are pleasant and profitable, I can only come to the realization that this certainly is Utopia for those of us who were here on the job with our pencils in the days when a screenwriter had a guilty conscience unless he turned in an "original" once a month. These are the thoughts that went through my mind when you said in your letter that in all probability if I were a writer today I would be the President of the Guild. I could never accept that position knowing what I do about the history of screenwriters as a body. . . .

In closing, let me say that as an old writer who has "strayed from the fold," I urge you, Ernest, to publicly abandon a policy which will cause more pain than it can ever remedy and which, in the long run, will only bring you misery because of your failure to effect a cure on a patient which is already strong, healthy, and normal—to wit: the moving picture industry.

Sincerely,

DARRYL ZANUCK

═══

During this trying period, the Screen Writers Guild was seeking to be recognized as the collective bargaining agent for writers in the film industry. Naturally, all the studio executives opposed this. (It finally came about in stages a few years later.) Philip Dunne, actively involved in the Guild and a contract writer at Fox at the time, years later said: "It was the first time I began to hear the word blacklist. There were several people whose options were dropped, but both Pascal's and mine were renewed [at Fox]. Ultimately, his [Zanuck's] interest was in writing." Pascal and Dunne had refused to resign from the Guild.

═══

TO: John Cromwell [director]   DATE: July 3, 1936
    Kenneth Macgowan [producer]
    SUBJECT: THE MCKINLEY CASE [retitled *This Is My Affair*]

We are making one of the most stupid mistakes that a producing company can make. We are running around in circles frantically endeavoring to get somebody with a name to play the part of "Lily" in *The McKinley Case* [*This Is My Affair*] and we have right here on the lot a girl who is climbing to stardom so rapidly that we are unable to keep up with the demands of exhibitors in connection with her. I am speaking about Alice Faye. I have just come from the projection room and saw three cut dramatic episodes of her from *Sing, Baby, Sing*; I have never seen her look so gorgeous, her new hairdress has changed her into a new girl; she is glamorous, exciting and is certainly a young Mae West in physique and attitude. . . . You can bet your last dollar that Faye will be a star. . . .

The same thing is true of Loretta Young; I had her under contract for three years at Warner Bros. before I could get anybody to agree that she could do anything but look beautiful. . . .

[Faye] is going to be co-starred in the biggest musical we have ever attempted—Irving Berlin's *On the Avenue*. . . . After seeing her in the one dramatic scene in [*King of*] *Burlesque* [Fox, 1935], Berlin begged for her and wrote the part for her. . . .

DARRYL ZANUCK

≡

Zanuck had inherited Faye with the merger of Fox and Twentieth Century in 1935. By 1938 she was a top star at the studio. Loretta Young signed with Zanuck in 1933 and in 1935 her contract was revised after the merger. (Because of scheduling conflicts and Faye's illness, when This Is My Affair *was finally produced in 1937, Barbara Stanwyck played the role.)*

≡

July 30, 1936
"WEE WILLIE WINKIE" CONFERENCE ON TREATMENT OF JULY 25, 1936
I feel that the only way to make this [Rudyard Kipling] story is to disregard the formula of all the previous pictures Shirley Temple has appeared in to date. . . . My idea about doing this picture is to forget that it is a Shirley Temple picture. That is, not to forget that she is the star, but to write the story as if it were a *Little Women* or a *David Copperfield*. . . . All the hokum must be thrown out. The characters must be made real, human, believable. Only then can we get a powerful, real story.

The role must be written for Shirley as an actress, and nothing sloughed over because Shirley is in it and therefore it will be good. We don't want to depend on any of her tricks. She should not be doing things because she is Shirley Temple, but because the situations—sound and believable—call for them. In other words, write a role and let Shirley adapt herself to the picture. . . .

And it must be told from the child's viewpoint, through her eyes. . . .

≡

Zanuck inherited Shirley Temple with the merger. She was the top box-office star in the United States in 1935, 1936, 1937, and 1938. Wee Willie Winkie was a very "loose" adaptation of Kipling's story (which was about a boy). In general, Zanuck's ideas were followed.

≡

August 3, 1936
SONJA HENIE STORY [*One in a Million*] CONFERENCE ON TREATMENT OF AUGUST 1, 1936

. . . I feel that Sonja Henie will be perfect in this story. She has very few actual acting scenes. Be sure she has as little and as simple dialogue as you can get by with. Give her only questions and answers; questions which are questions, answers which are direct statements. We presume that both she and her father are speaking English with an accent, to accommodate the other characters. . . .

≡

Norwegian ice-skating champion Sonja Henie set world marks in three consecutive Winter Olympics—1928, 1932, and 1936. Zanuck signed her in 1936, and with her first two starring roles in One in a Million *and* Thin Ice *she became a major Fox star through the late 1930s and early 1940s.*

≡

April 28, 1936
Mr. Neil McCarthy [attorney]
510 West 6th Street
Los Angeles, Calif.

Dear Neil:

Yesterday Mr. William Goetz, my executive assistant, had a conference at the studio with Miss Loretta Young in regard to the role of "Lady Clementine" in our production *Lloyd's of London*. You are no doubt aware of the fact that on two specific occasions recently, Miss Young has failed to appear at our studio wardrobe department for fittings in connection with *Lloyd's of London*, and you are also aware, no doubt, of the fact that she wrote me a letter refusing to play the role of "Lady Clementine" [changed to Lady Elizabeth] in *Lloyd's of London*.

Today Mr. Goetz received a letter from Miss Young as follows: "Dear Bill—I want to confirm what I told you yesterday. Any business you wish to discuss with me, please get in touch with Mr. Neil McCarthy. Best regards, Loretta." Apparently, Miss Young has engaged you as her agent or business manager or attorney, at least we have come to this conclusion from her letter.

Now you know, Neil, we are friends and I can imagine nothing more pleasant than a conversation with you about polo, but I cannot conceive of what possible assistance you could be to us in connection with Miss Young's wardrobe fittings or any other details of production. I will be perfectly willing to discuss with you any matters pertaining to negotiations for future services of any person or persons you may represent, but the policy of 20th Century–Fox Film Corporation is to reserve the right to discuss all matters of production, or future productions, with our employees directly, as provided for in our contracts with our employees. . . .

If it is true that you are now the agent or business manager or attorney for Miss Young, I think it would be only fair for me to advise you of our past and present relations with Miss Young, as I am certain that someone is giving her a considerable amount of bad advice, and so that the facts be known, I refer to the following history:

Shortly after I left Warner Bros. [in April 1933], Warner Bros. failed to exercise the option on Loretta Young's existing contract with them because, apparently, she refused to remain at the same salary and they did not think she was worth any more. In any event, she went on the free-lance market. . . . At that time we had formed 20th Century Pictures and we successfully negotiated a long-term contract for Miss Young's services [June 1933]. Since that date Miss Young's popularity has steadily increased.

I know of no artist in the moving picture industry who has received more consideration from a studio than the consideration that has been shown Miss Young. True, there have been times when we differed on various roles which she was scheduled to portray and at times it was necessary for us to compel her to play certain roles; such compelling, however, was handled on a very friendly basis and until very recently Miss Young has always publicly professed that the portrayals which were most beneficial to Miss Young's career, were, in several instances, the very roles which she did not wish to portray: *The House of Rothschild* [1934] being one shining example of this. While we were still 20th Century Pictures, Inc., we did not have a great number of productions and, therefore, Miss Young's roles were somewhat limited, but after the merger with Fox I knew that I would have ample opportunity to further develop Miss Young's career in the interest of herself and in the interest of 20th Century—Fox.

At this point, I should bring to your attention the fact that immediately after the completion of Miss Young's role in the Walter Wanger production *Shanghai* [1935], we permitted Miss Young to go on a vacation to Europe and we kept her on the studio payroll for a total period of approximately three months while she was on vacation, although, because of her ill health at the time, we would have been within our legal rights if we had suspended her contract and compensation. This, of course, does not include many, many other shorter periods of time when Miss Young has not been assigned to a picture. When Miss Young returned from her vacation we had scheduled our production *Ramona* for her and we had held this particular story and production in reserve knowing that it would be an ideal vehicle for Miss Young. At this time Miss Young again suffered an illness and we were forced to postpone our production of *Ramona* although many thousands of dollars had already been expended. I needed stories desperately at that time and I had the opportunity to borrow several female stars from other studios to portray the role of "Ramona," but inasmuch as I wanted to give Miss Young every possible consideration, I declined the offers and held the production until Miss Young recovered. . . . In due time she appeared in our production *Ramona* [1936] and at the conclusion of *Ramona* we assigned her to the role of "Susie" in our present production *Ladies in Love*.

At this time Miss Young complained again of illness and stated that her physician had ordered her to take a complete rest, but because she was so enthusiastic about the role of "Susie" in *Ladies in Love* she wanted to play it regardless of her physician's orders, providing we would take her illness into consideration and prepare our shooting schedule in such a fashion which would enable her to have various periods of leisure during the production. We were only too glad to accommodate Miss Young and we have religiously abided by this concession on our part. . . .

Shortly after the commencement of production on *Ladies in Love*, Miss Young was advised that she had been selected for the coveted role of "Lady Clementine" in our most important production on this year's schedule, *Lloyd's of London*. At various times she discussed the production with various of our employees, including the director, Mr. Henry King, who told her the story of *Lloyd's of London* in detail and explained the excellent possibilities of the role. It was unimaginable for us to conceive that Miss Young would balk at this selection of a role for her and you can well understand how amazed I was to receive a blunt note from her telling me that the part of "Lady Clementine" was not suitable to her and that she definitely refused to portray it, particularly after the conference I knew she had with the director, Mr. King, in which she expressed herself to be most enthusiastic over the role of "Lady Clementine."

At this point I would like to bring out the following facts for you to discuss with Miss Young if you so desire. . . .

When I assigned Miss Young to *Ramona* I was severely criticized by my associates as well as by the newspaper columnists for mis-casting Miss Young as "Ramona." It was inconceivable to many people that she could possibly play, with her limited experience, such a powerful, tragic story. I was also criticized for imagining that Loretta Young could play a half-Indian. Our production of *Ramona* has been finished and I am certain Miss Young more than justifies our faith in her and our selection of her for this role. Miss Young did not select the role of "Susie" in *Ladies in Love*. She had never heard of the part or read it until she was assigned to it. I have already told you earlier in this letter how much Miss Young wanted to play this part, after we assigned her to portray the role.

Several times during the production of *Ladies in Love* Miss Young came to see me about production matters, asking that certain favors be done for her, such as adding certain scenes or incidents which she thought might improve her role in *Ladies in Love*. I went out of my way to accommodate Miss Young and personally saw to it that these scenes were included. We have three co-stars in *Ladies in Love*: Miss [Janet] Gaynor, Miss [Constance] Bennett and Miss Young, and if Miss Young will tell you the truth and the facts, you will know how careful I have been to personally protect her interests in the production for which, at the time, she profusely thanked me.

This leads me up to the moment of her refusal to play in *Lloyd's of London*. Doesn't it seem most peculiar to you that anyone, after receiving the treatment that she has received, after receiving the roles that we have given her in her last three productions, after accepting the lenient working conditions that we have given her, could now suddenly decide that she no longer desired to discuss production matters with us.

I am frank to say that the entire situation bewilders me, and so, as before stated, I can only come to the conclusion that someone is giving her a lot of bad advice as certainly nothing has been done by us which in any manner or form justifies her present attitude or her refusal to play in our production *Lloyd's of London*, or any attitude except one of absolute cooperation and unquestioning compliance with our every request.

Miss Young has been assigned to play the role of "Lady Clementine" in *Lloyd's of London*. We do not intend to withdraw or cancel this assignment. . . .

I trust that this explains the entire situation. With kindest regards,

Sincerely,

DARRYL ZANUCK

≡

Of course, the above represents Zanuck's (and Fox's) side of the story. Loretta Young was suspended for not playing the role (given to Fox contract star Madeleine Carroll), with the suspension time of a few weeks added to her contract, as was the custom at the time. She went on to do several additional pictures at Fox—many of which were successful—but in early 1939 after completing The Story of Alexander Graham Bell *she did not want to renew her contract. In a 1987 interview with James Bawden in* Films in Review, *Loretta Young stated: "I blame that on [my role as] Mrs. Alexander Graham Bell. . . . She was a deaf-mute but I was only allowed to play her as a deaf person. The real story wasn't told. . . . The studio treated you as a child. . . . Darryl never really understood his female stars. . . . I decided to free-lance. I thought I was stalled. My pictures were not getting any better. . . . Darryl was furious. He had me blackballed from the industry." At the time she left Fox, Young had commented that in all the years she'd worked at the studio Zanuck had "never once sent me a bouquet of flowers." In the late 1940s, when she returned to Fox to star in three films, Zanuck sent flowers.*

≡

February 25, 1937
"HIS MAJESTY'S CAR" [retitled *Thin Ice*] STORY CONFERENCE ON TREATMENT OF FEBRUARY 25TH, 1937
 . . . I caution you against giving Sonja Henie too many lines. You should work it like we did in *One in a Million*, where we get the impression that she is carrying the whole thing, whereas if you analyze it, you will see that everything is happening around her, and only occasionally does she speak a line. And, when she does, it is always a very effective one. . . .

≡

Twentieth Century–Fox was the defendant in a plagiarism suit regarding the story basis for Irving Berlin's Alexander's Ragtime Band *(1938). Zanuck gave the following deposition (excerpted) on June 13, 1944, and Berlin supported what Zanuck related.*

. . . I had engaged Mr. Irving Berlin to write the score and collaborate on the story and production of a picture called *On the Avenue*—Irving Berlin's *On the Avenue* (1937). During the making . . . of this particular film I was naturally anxious to try and secure the services of Mr. Irving Berlin for further productions. I had been interested in doing the life story of Irving Berlin. Mr. Berlin objected for personal reasons. He did not feel that it would be proper or good taste to present his more or less colorful life on the screen. Of course that was a private and personal objection and I saw his point. . . .

Here is the one songwriter . . . who has set styles in music, who started from very humble beginnings in a ragtime age and whose songs over a period of twenty years have consistently been the most popular American music. . . .

I thought of the idea of doing a picture called *Alexander's Ragtime Band*, which was the most popular song that Irving Berlin had written. . . . I told Mr. Berlin that the title, in my opinion, *Alexander's Ragtime Band* would be the basis for a tremendous musical and that we could, without violating his private life, invent a fictitious story but we could include certain definite incidents from his life and that it did not have to be the story of Irving Berlin, it could be the story of an imaginary character, "Mr. Alexander," who could start humbly with an idea about music and who could finally end up after a number of years in the highest musical temples. This immediately appealed to Mr. Berlin. I recall the conversation on this point because . . . it has been a prideful point with me that I originated the piece of material . . . that literally changed the destinies of Twentieth Century–Fox.

Mr. Berlin was enthusiastic and immediately said, "We can make this man a combination of Paul Whiteman, George Gershwin, Irving Berlin, anything that we want. We can take this character and we can open, instead of the Bowery [in New York] where I opened, we will take the Barbary Coast in San Francisco, where I have never been. But it will have the same dramatic equivalent" . . .

We talked further, most enthusiastically about the idea and he said, "Look, . . . we can do that whole episode that happened to me when I was in the Army as a sergeant and they asked me to put on a big show and I did put on a Broadway show for the Army called *Yip, Yip, Yaphank* [1918] that ran for many months at the Century Theatre in New York.

We will take some of the famous things from that show such as the number, 'Oh, How I Hate to Get Up in the Morning' that can be the middle section of our picture."

We talked further, and, I might say that this was not one conference. This was a series of many conferences. Mr. Berlin became most enthusiastic. We saw ways of dropping in fifteen or twenty of his famous songs and working our story so that these songs could come in. Then he came along with the idea of having the climax be in Carnegie Hall.

We immediately realized that we faced a very difficult situation as some of the rights of his old music were out of his hands. In the passing of years some of the foreign rights on some of his songs had gone to other publishers and we would be in a very difficult spot if we wrote this story expressly to fit these particular songs and then found out that we had to buy off or make most difficult deals with publishers, some of whom might still be in existence or out of existence. That problem came up. So we made a new deal with Mr. Berlin in which he took over the job of particularly buying up all of his old material in that connection. At that time we started to talk about production plans and writers. . . .

Alexander's Ragtime Band was Fox's biggest success up to that point. Supported by depositions, outlines, scripts, and story conference notes, the studio was acquitted in the plagiarism case.

≡

June 24, 1937
"REBECCA OF SUNNYBROOK FARM" CONFERENCE
. . . Characters—Rebecca [Shirley Temple]: . . . Whereas in *Wee Willie Winkie* she was always asking questions, in this one she knows all the answers. She should not be brilliant. . . . She has merely absorbed certain knowledge and information from association with her father. . . .

≡

TO: MR. HENRY KING [director]   DATE: February 3, 1938
     SUBJECT: IN OLD CHICAGO

Dear Henry:

[Director H. Bruce] Lucky Humberstone's advertisement [in the trade paper *The Hollywood Reporter*], in connection with *In Old Chicago*, which appeared some time ago [January 18], has only today been brought to my attention.

I think I owe you an apology for putting his name on the picture in the first place, and I think that his advertisement adds insult to injury. The main part of the fire was directed by you and by you alone, and the scenes that he contributed to the picture were well done, but I don't think they total 100 feet [approximately one minute] of used film.

I want you to know that I feel Humberstone stepped way out of line.

Regards,

D.F.Z.

=

As part of a special In Old Chicago *multipage advertising insert in* The Hollywood Reporter, *the full-page ad, taken out by Humberstone, stated: "H. Bruce Humberstone directed The Fire." It went on to thank Zanuck and various special-effect technicians, then concluded with "and congratulations to Henry King for his achievement."*

King replied to Zanuck's memo by saying that "Humberstone's advertisement has caused considerable discussion that has practically shut me out of the Academy nominations, and I would like your permission to make a one-page advertisement of your letter."

Zanuck responded on the same day (February 7):

=

Dear Henry:

My advice is to print nothing. It will only cause discussion which may put you in the position of being "sore." I am really to blame for the whole situation, and I only wish someone had called the screen credits to my attention before we previewed the picture. I have written

Humberstone my opinion of this ad, and despite the fact that I know how you feel, I urge you not to run any further advertisement.

D.F.Z.

≡

The official credits stated: "Directed by Henry King. . . . Special Effects scenes directed by H. Bruce Humberstone." The matter was dropped. Henry King was not nominated for an Academy Award for In Old Chicago, *but he was most assuredly the director of the film— with the exception of some of the fire sequence.*

≡

Mr. John Ford [nonexclusive Fox director]   DATE: March 2, 1938

Dear Jack:

Last night you gave me a great thrill in permitting me to see [Jean Renoir's] *The Grand Illusion.* It is one of the most magnificent pictures of its type that I have ever seen. . . .

I think that it would be a criminal injustice to attempt to remake the picture in English. The most wonderful thing about the picture is the fine background, the authentic atmosphere, and the foreign characters, who actually speak in the language of their nationality. Once you take this away, I believe you have lost 50% of the value of the picture.

I don't know whether you are aware of the fact that three English companies have already endeavored to make an English version of this picture, including [Alexander] Korda, and eventually gave it up. Also, I have investigated and found that this picture has been released all over Europe, which would make a remake a very dangerous proposition— but, in spite of all this, I still feel that we could never get anywhere near this picture. . . . I honestly feel that I am right in this and I hope that you agree with me.

Again, many thanks for a most enjoyable evening.

D.F.Z.

≡

An English-language version was not made.

≡

April 15, 1938

"LUCKY PENNY" [retitled *Just Around the Corner*] CONFERENCE ON TEMPORARY SCRIPT OF APRIL 12, 1938

. . . Both [director Irving] Cummings and I are concerned about Shirley's [Temple] dialogue. At times, it seems too precocious and, at other times, it seems too boyish. Please watch this carefully throughout. . . . We are taking out many of the "Little Miss Fix-It" scenes; you will find that Shirley's lines will almost write themselves in the natural style that we want from her. I would like you to give her *questions* to ask as often as you can. Shirley is most effective when she asks the kind of questions to which there are no answers one can give a child, like "Why is the Depression?," etc. . . .

≡

No date; circa late September, 1938

TO: MR. HENRY KING [ON LOCATION IN MISSOURI]

AFTER REVIEWING EVERYTHING THAT HAS BEEN SHOT TO DATE [FOR *JESSE JAMES*], I AM DEFINITELY CONVINCED THAT THE ENTIRE LOCATION TRIP [TO MISSOURI] WAS, TO A GREAT EXTENT, A FINANCIAL MISTAKE. I FULLY REALIZE HOW YOU HAVE BEEN MOLESTED AND HAMPERED BY CROWDS AND OTHER DIFFICULTIES, BUT THE FACT REMAINS WE ARE NOW SIX DAYS BEHIND SCHEDULE WITH NO PROSPECTS OF IMPROVEMENT. I ALWAYS OPPOSED THE ENTIRE IDEA OF EXTENDED LOCATION TRIPS AND NOW CERTAINLY REALIZE THAT I WAS RIGHT.

EVERYTHING I HAVE SEEN HAS BEEN FINE, BUT THERE IS NOTHING IN THE WAY OF SCENERY OR BACKGROUNDS THAT WE COULD NOT HAVE PHOTOGRAPHED NEAR HERE AT FAR LESS EXPENSE AND TROUBLE. THE UNIVERSAL [STUDIO] WESTERN STREET OR OUR OWN STREET COULD HAVE SERVED JUST AS WELL AS WHAT I HAVE SEEN ON THE SCREEN, AND PHOTOGRAPHED TWICE AS FAST. THE RAILROAD STATION IS VERY INTERESTING AND EFFEC-

TIVE, BUT COULD HAVE BEEN BUILT ANYWHERE IN THE SOUTHERN PACIFIC BETWEEN HERE AND SAN BERNARDINO. CERTAINLY THE FARM EXTERIORS WERE NOTHING IN THE WAY OF SCENIC BEAUTY TO JUSTIFY THE TRANSPORTATION AND LIVING EXPENSES THAT WE ARE BEING PENALIZED WITH, TO SAY NOTHING OF WHAT YOU ARE GOING THROUGH WITH AN EFFORT TO TRY AND GET A FULL DAY'S WORK.

WHEN I REALIZE THE WASTING OF TIME AND MONEY SHOOTING CLOSEUPS . . . IN THE TRAIN CAB, WHICH SHOULD HAVE BEEN DONE HERE WITH PROCESS [REAR PROJECTION] BACKGROUND, THEN I REALIZE MORE THAN EVER THAT WHAT WE SHOULD HAVE DONE IS WHAT WE DID ON "KENTUCKY" [1938]. AND THAT IS TO HAVE SENT YOU BACK WITH CAMERA CREW FOR LONG SHOT DOUBLES OF THE ESSENTIAL EPISODES, SUCH AS THE VARIOUS HORSE CHASES AND A FEW SCENIC SHOTS. . . .

I HAVE DEFINITELY DECIDED TO PROCEED AS FOLLOWS: WE WILL CANCEL ALL FURTHER INTERIORS AND WILL CONCENTRATE ON LONG SHOTS OF HORSE CHASES AND ESSENTIAL THINGS THAT YOU CANNOT DO IN THE STUDIO. YOU WILL TAKE YOUR SECOND CAMERA CREW AND HAVE THEM GET PROCESS BACKGROUND SHOTS TO COVER ALL OTHER EPISODES THAT ARE NECESSARY. FROM HERE ON, WE WILL DUPLICATE AND FAKE EVERYTHING THAT WE POSSIBLY CAN AT THE STUDIO. . . . BRING THE MAIN COMPANY AND THE MAIN CAMERA CREW BACK TO THE STUDIO AS QUICKLY AS POSSIBLE. . . . EPISODES LIKE THE LONG SHOT OF THE JUMP OFF THE CLIFF SHOULD BE LEFT FOR SECOND UNIT TO BE DONE WITH DOUBLES AND TO BE COVERED FOR BACKGROUND [REAR PROJECTION] PLATES, AS IT IS RIDICULOUS AND COMPLETELY OUT OF PROPORTION FOR US TO CONTEMPLATE HOLDING THE ENTIRE COMPANY FOR SEQUENCES WHICH ARE STRICTLY SECOND UNIT STUFF.

AT THE RATE WE ARE GOING, THIS PICTURE WILL NEVER BREAK EVEN, NO MATTER HOW SUCCESSFUL IT IS, BECAUSE OF THE EXPENDITURE. . . .

I BLAME NO ONE BUT MYSELF FOR NOT ACTING ON MY ORIGINAL HUNCH, AND REALIZE THAT IN THE HISTORY OF OUR INDUSTRY THERE HAS NEVER BEEN A SUCCESSFUL LOCATION TRIP THAT LASTED LONGER THAN TWO WEEKS. AND I APPRECIATE YOUR DESIRE FOR AUTHENTIC LOCATION, WHICH PROMPTED YOU TO SUGGEST THE TRIP. AND I ALSO REALIZE THAT YOU HAVE NO CONFIDENCE IN PROCESS SHOTS. BUT WE NOW FACE THE SITUATION THAT BECAUSE OF EXPENDITURE JEOPARDIZES A SCRIPT IT HAS TAKEN A YEAR TO PREPARE.

AFTER YOU HAVE CAREFULLY DIGESTED THIS ... TELEGRAPH ME WHAT
SCENES YOU CAN FINISH UP WITH QUICKLY AND WHAT YOU WILL LEAVE FOR
SECOND UNIT.

REGARDS,

DARRYL F. ZANUCK

≡

*The company did return and second unit director Otto Brower stayed
behind with a crew to complete the necessary location shots. Jesse
James was one of Fox's most successful pictures at the time. After World
War II, Zanuck became one of the leading advocates of location shooting
all over the world.*

≡

DATE: September 8, 1938

TO: William Dover [personnel manager]
    SUBJECT: BRIGHAM YOUNG

There is no way that you can conceivably excuse to audiences of the
world the idea of one man having eight or nine bed companions. . . .
Brigham Young has been used as a standard vaudeville joke for years
and it is going to be awfully tough to try to explain to the public that he
slept with more than one woman because of religious or economic
problems. . . .

≡

TO: Mr. Kenneth Macgowan [producer]   DATE: March 24, 1939
    SUBJECT: BRIGHAM YOUNG

I want to do this story for the following reasons:
First of all, I feel that this is a great box-office title.

Secondly, it is the only logical way we can do another *Covered Wagon* [Paramount, 1923]. Plus, the opportunity of doing a *House of Rothschild* [Twentieth Century, 1934], to say nothing of *The Good Earth* [M-G-M, 1937]. The story has the elements that were contained in all three of these pictures and we should strive to develop it for all its opportunities. . . .

≡

Brigham Young (1940), which starred Tyrone Power, Linda Darnell, and Dean Jagger as Brigham Young, muted to a considerable degree the polygamy aspect of the Mormon religion. The emphases were on the elements contained in the pictures to which Zanuck alluded in the above memo: the westward pioneer movement in The Covered Wagon, *religious persecution in* The House of Rothschild, *and the famine and massive plague of locusts in* The Good Earth *(crickets in* Brigham Young*). The relatively costly film was not a big hit.*

≡

October 21, 1938
"HOLLYWOOD CAVALCADE" CONFERENCE ON TYPEWRITTEN SYNOPSIS
. . . There is no doubt that there is a wealth of fascinating material connected with the days of early Hollywood—before that, Edendale. And even more interesting are the lives of the actual characters who made up the pioneers of the picture business—Mack Sennett, Mabel Normand, Thomas Ince, Lew Cody, Raymond Griffith, Mickey Neilan, Marie Prevost, etc., etc. Instead of going out of our way to contrive a story and situations from out of thin air, we should take as a pattern the composite of several of these interesting personalities and adapt them for our story.

You are cautioned not to inject into the piece items that are familiar only to Hollywood people. Remember that all the reminiscent items must be of universal interest. . . .

It is excellent to discuss the first closeup—to show the studios moving to Hollywood for the first time—to show how they nailed down the cameras in those days—the first inside stage—Cooper Hewitts [lamps]—the days of slapstick—the days of spectacles, and so on.

While all of the above will serve as colorful, fascinating background to the story, we do not want it plotwise to affect the lives of our principals. The only time a change in the business will have an effect on our characters is when the talkies come in. . . .

We are not going to use any old film in the picture. Everything that is in the script will be [newly] photographed. We will have our own bathing beauties, our own Keystone Cops, etc., etc.

Later on we might hire Mack Sennett to work with us on the story. There is no doubt that Mr. Sennett can give us endless authentic highlights, as well as supply interesting bits and gags. This will be decided on after the new treatment comes out. . . .

Also, you might give some indication of the . . . rumors going around when Fox and Warners were experimenting with sound. Discussion about it. [Character played by Don Ameche] ridicules it— thinks it a lot of baloney—all right for a musical scoring but not for actors. People want idols to worship—not creatures of flesh and blood. Talking will take away the illusion—they go to the movies to relax, not to strain and listen. Give him a composite of all the reasons which were given at the time against canned music and talk. . . .

Now the big change—talkies appear. Everybody talking about them. *The Jazz Singer* is released. . . .

≡

A great deal of what Zanuck outlined was used in the film. Industry pioneer Mack Sennett was hired as a consultant and made an on-camera appearance as himself. Don Ameche, from radio and the theatre, had been signed by Zanuck shortly after the merger and quickly became one of Fox's biggest stars.

≡

April 5, 1939
"DRUMS ALONG THE MOHAWK" CONFERENCE ON TEMPORARY SCRIPT
OF MARCH 11, 1939

Need foreword and clear explanation . . . so that we know who is
fighting who. Whenever possible, keep British out of brutality. . . .

Be sure and preserve the wonderful domestic relationship between
Gil and Lana [Henry Fonda and—on loan from Paramount—Claudette
Colbert]. . . .

Establish early that Gil is a great runner so that big climax will be
escape from Fort and twenty-mile run. Gil, alone, will make it. It will
be far more exciting to have the run made by *one* person rather than two
[as in the Walter D. Edmonds novel]. What will happen in this portion
will be detailed further on in the notes. This can be whipped into one of
the most unusual and exciting climaxes ever seen on the screen and we
can afford to let it run a thousand feet [eleven minutes].

≡

*The run, directed by John Ford on location in Utah, was extremely
effective (at almost five minutes' screen time).*

≡

December 3, 1938
Mr. John Ford
c/o Walter Wanger Productions
Hollywood, Calif.

Dear Jack:
Happy you are pleased with the Lincoln assignment [*Young Mr. Lincoln*]. We have got a great story and, of course, you know [writer
Lamar] Trotti is practically an authority on Lincoln. He also was east
last week and saw the Lincoln play that is running in New York [*Abe
Lincoln in Illinois*]. Our story, of course, is entirely different, although
on some historical points, naturally, they are the same. It is going to be
a great picture. I am anxious to have you see the test that [Henry] Fonda

made. He looks exactly like Lincoln and he really was immense. I want to start shooting the picture on February 20th, if possible. How does this date agree with you? Will it give you time to do what you want to do? Please let me know. . . .

Best regards.
Sincerely,
Darryl Zanuck

☰

At this point Henry Fonda was not under long-term contract to Fox, but he did sign a few months later.

☰

TO: Mr. John Ford   DATE: March 22, 1939
SUBJECT: YOUNG MR. LINCOLN

Dear Jack:

I have been more than pleased with the rushes. You are making grand progress and everything that I have seen looks honest and real. There are a few things that have occurred to me in watching the rushes that I thought I should drop you this note about. Looking at the scenes from the perspective that I do in the projection room, perhaps a few of these points are apt to become clearer to me than they are to you.

Do you feel that at times the tempo is apt to be a trifle slow? I don't mean that we should speed up Fonda, as it is the slowness and deliberate character that you have given him that make his performance swell, but I have had a feeling that at times we seem to be a little draggy as far as mood is concerned. This may be eliminated when the various sequences are put together, but wherever we can pick up the tempo and give it a little more drive with the characters other than Lincoln, we should do so, so that we don't take the chance of having all of it done in one key. I may be wrong about this, but I wish you would give it some thought.

I feel that we should avoid shooting down on Lincoln wherever possible and shoot up on him. Not only does it give him height, which is essential, but when you look up at him for some reason or other he looks exactly like Lincoln and not Fonda.

The photography has been very good, although I have complained about a shadow they have been getting recently on Fonda's forehead. If his lock of hair were pushed over a little bit more to the right it would keep more of the Lincoln character in his face. I like best the scenes where his eyes seem dark and deep-set and where you can see the cleft in his chin. He looks great in a low-camera setup where you see his whole figure sprawled out or standing, like he was on the porch in yesterday's rushes where he had the end of the scene with [free-lance player Alice] Brady. . . .

All in all, I think we are going to have a sensational picture, and the only thing that keeps coming back into my mind is the thought of tempo. . . .

D.F.Z.

≡

April 19, 1939
[*The Adventures of*] "SHERLOCK HOLMES" CONFERENCE ON FIRST DRAFT CONTINUITY OF APRIL 3, 1939
. . . Mr. [Edwin] Blum's script is a good groundwork, there are many fine incidents contained in it, and the continuity line, as a whole, is correct.

However, the story has none of the deep mystery and tense suspense of *Hound of the Baskervilles* [produced by Fox earlier in the year]. It is, in fact, more of a British cops-and-robbers—a game of wits between a master detective and a master criminal.

It is true that in our set-up it is not possible to duplicate the particular eeriness of *The Hound*, with its strange moor and other unreal elements, but nevertheless there are many opportunities that have been overlooked to develop more mystery and suspense in the story. It is this "plus" quality that we should strive to inject. . . .

The traditional character of Sherlock Holmes [Basil Rathbone] is lost here. He was played and written just right in *The Hound*—the superman of literary history. In this story, Holmes seems to be not quite sure of himself. He is surprised too much. He is not so much the cunning and deliberate master as he is the quick opportunist. Instead of always being one step ahead of his opponents, they appear to get several steps ahead of him at times, and only his personal bravery and ready resource enable him to master the situation—just in time. While he is confronting his brilliant antagonist, Dr. Moriarty [George Zucco], Holmes should never for one second leave a doubt that he is Moriarty's master, not only in action, but in plotting.

However, not only must he be drawn more cleverly, but he must come through as the traditional fascinating Holmes personality—full of wit—nonchalant—confident of himself at all times.

Study *The Hound* and see how he was handled there. Give Holmes pieces of business, etc.

Specific revisions to be made regarding Holmes will be recorded further on in the notes. . . .

The finish is confusing, rambling, and does not give us the opportunity to have Holmes make a brilliant deduction in line with what we expect of him. We need a great twist where Holmes, in a clever and ingenious way, makes the discovery that Moriarty has manufactured the one crime as a smoke screen for the other, and that Moriarty is still in the Tower [of London]. This will be discussed in detail as it appears in continuity. . . .

The opening sequence is dull—mainly because Holmes is drawn in a dull manner—he is neither brilliant nor resourceful, and in his scenes with the court and with Moriarty later, he reveals himself to be unaggressive, also a poor sport. In his plea to the court he should be dynamic—he must tell them in forceful language what sort of fiend they are turning free etc. etc.

Then, with Moriarty, we want to see Holmes clever—sardonic—witty. He tells Moriarty, in effect: "Doctor, I admire your brain. In fact, I admire it so much that I would love nothing better than to present it, pickled in alcohol, to the London Medical Society—and what's more, I intend to do it". . . .

The element of the man with the clubfoot will, of course, be whipped up to more of a menace and a mystery. Play it for all the eeriness and suspense that you can. As stated ahead, we will never see him until much later in the picture. . . .

D.F.Z.

≡

William Drake did the next drafts of the screenplay, incorporating all of Zanuck's suggestions. The plot was not based on any of Sir Arthur Conan Doyle's stories or William Gillette's play but was an original. The 1939 Fox productions were the first to feature free-lance players Basil Rathbone and Nigel Bruce as Sherlock Holmes and Dr. Watson.

≡

June 1, 1939
"THE MARK OF ZORRO" CONFERENCE ON NEW TREATMENT OF MAY 21, 1939

. . . Each gag and each trick, even though contrived, must be contrived to appear logical and honest. We are still overemphasizing heroics. We must soft-pedal the obvious heroics and melodrama and we must never force or reach for anything.

Without going overboard, we can get an epic sweep to the crusade theme of this picture, but every moment must seem reasonable. If an audience ever gets the feeling that the hero is taking unnecessary chances just for the sake of taking chances, they will cease to take any great interest in it. We can probably retain eighty percent of the gusto we have, but we can make it honest and logical and reasonable.

In *Jesse James* and [*The Adventures of*] *Robin Hood* [Warners, 1938], while daring things were done, they were always done to enable the hero to escape from something, or to achieve a point, not just deliberately provoking situations so that he could have the fun of getting out of them. . . .

D.F.Z.

≡

June 20, 1939
"THE MARK OF ZORRO" CONFERENCE ON REVISED NEW TREATMENT OF JUNE 16, 1939

. . . *Jesse James* is an example of a story where there was an impending suspense underlying the whole thing—a man riding to his eventual doom—a situation which gave us a definite emotional feeling about the story. While we have a different type of story altogether, we have got to devise (as I outlined and which will be recorded further herein) an emotional undercurrent which will take this story out of the standard track.

The Prisoner of Zenda [Selznick, 1937] is an example of a picture where an old, familiar, hokey story was saved by superb treatment— where every situation and scene was milked for the best that could be gotten out of it—and it emerged as an excellent, highly successful picture. Our story lacks a definite personal issue. *Gunga Din* [RKO, 1939], with all its spectacular stunts had a personal story, which can be compared to *The Front Page*. There is an issue—a personal element that gave the story the added element that helped to make it a sensational success.

Here is the drastic revision I suggest, which will supply the personal, emotional element which we now lack. Instead of there being just one girl, Lolita [contract player Linda Darnell], there will be two girls. The older girl (I'll call her Juanita) [free-lance player Gale Sondergaard] will be the Governor's daughter [subsequently changed to wife] and Lolita, the niece or ward. . . .

She [Juanita] wants to go back to Spain with its glamour, its court-life. . . . When Diego [Tyrone Power] comes into it, she will fall for him and consequently be less anxious to get out of there. . . .

D.F.Z.

≡

July 13, 1939
Mr. Jack L. Warner [vice president in charge of production]
Warner Bros. Pictures, Inc.
Burbank, California

Dear Jack:

Many thanks for your letter. It certainly took a long time for you to write it, as I had almost given up the thought of expecting a reply. . . .

Twentieth Century–Fox registered the title *Father Duffy of the Fighting 69th*, and you told me at the race track yourself that you did not deem it important enough to protest our registration. Now certainly the title that we registered told specifically and definitely that we were going to do a story about Father Duffy and his career and life exploits in and out of the 69th Regiment. . . .

The fact that you had previously published your intention of doing a story of this subject does not actually mean anything, in my opinion. Every company has repeatedly throughout the years published their intentions of doing almost every subject under the sun. Some of them are done and some of them are never done. I have been announcing the production of *King of the Khyber Rifles* for so many years that I shudder every time I see it in print.★ At this very moment, I find myself in a similar situation with another studio. I own a published story called "Law West of the Pecos," which deals with the life of Judge Roy Bean of Texas. I have three completed scenarios written on the subject and almost $50,000 invested in it. [Independent producer] Sam Goldwyn announces *Vinegarroon* and says that Walter Brennan will play Judge Roy Bean.† He has purchased another story dealing with the same subject, and in the final analysis, I suppose there is nothing I can do to stop it—although I have published my intentions to do the Judge Roy Bean story repeatedly on our program for two years and the announcements of it have even been included in our published advertisements. . . .

Situations of this type must be met with continually. You will recall that a few months ago you made the press announcement that you were going to do a story of the history of Tombstone, Arizona. The minute that I read this article I wrote you a letter calling your attention to the fact that we were already producing our picture, *Frontier Marshal*, based on the published novel by Stuart Lake, which is the saga of Tombstone, Arizona. I didn't want you to go ahead with your picture without first being aware that we were doing the identical story at that time as I thought you might be involved in expense before you learned of the existence of our picture.

More recently I read that you were preparing a story on the history of

★ It was not produced until 1954.

† Released as *The Westerner* (1940) with Gary Cooper (and Walter Brennan as Judge Bean). Zanuck dropped his plans.

early Los Angeles during the days of the Mexican rule. I want to call your attention to the fact that we own the [Johnston McCulley] story and picture *The Mark of Zorro*. We have been working on this story consistently for the past year and it goes into production as a Technicolor feature starring Tyrone Power when he returns from his honeymoon in Europe. *The Mark of Zorro*, as you know, recalling the old [Douglas] Fairbanks picture, deals exclusively with incidents in the city of Los Angeles under Mexican rule. The only reason I am bringing this to your attention is so that you will not be put to any unnecessary expense if you feel that our story by coming first is apt to take the edge off of your proposed production.

If we would all deal with these things more openly, there would be less bad feelings and certainly less confusion. . . .

Kindest regards.

Sincerely,
Darryl

≡

The Mark of Zorro (*1940*), *made in black and white, was exceptionally well received.*

TWO

TWENTIETH CENTURY-FOX:
A MAJOR FORCE

July 19, 1939
"THE GRAPES OF WRATH" CONFERENCE ON SCREENPLAY OF JULY 13, 1939

I am very enthusiastic about the [Nunnally Johnson] script. The changes to be made are few. There are several places where we can heighten the drama and suspense. . . .

Page 76: Before we come to Hooverville, we need a scene in a town. Their [the Joad family's] money practically gone—gas low—and the terrible realization that what they were told is true. The fellow was right.

We come in on them driving in to town and asking somebody where they should go about finding work—maybe showing the fellow the handbill. The man just looks at them and laughs. Someone else comes along and they ask him. We see the fellow look at the car and down on the license plate. "Oh—Oklahoma. There's a camp on the edge of town—maybe somebody there will tell you—"

Their hopefulness and terrible disillusionment. They drive into the Hooverville camp and their hearts drop at the terrible sights. The futility of what has occurred. They just look at each other as the stark truth dawns on them. "Don't seem very encouragin', does it?" "All this and for what?" etc. Ma snaps them out of it—they'd better pitch the tent, etc. and as they start working we FADE OUT and FADE INTO *Scene 142*. . . .

Page 84, Scene 150: Deputy's last speech is too strong—hard to believe. We must give him motivation—a point of view. That the people in town are getting fed up with all of them—there's not enough work for the people that live there, etc. If they don't move on, there'll be more of them there than the population of the town. . . .

Page 124, Scene 231: After this scene, we want to come in on a shot—just getting dawn. Something happens to the car—they pull up on the side of the road and decide they'd better stop and cool her off. They are down to their last straw—where to go from here—no more money—only a gallon of gas in the car—been burned out—chased out, etc. etc. Somebody stands up on the running board and looks up the road—we CUT TO the shot—smoke, etc. They decide it must be a camp of some kind—might as well go there as anywhere. They start off and we come in on *Scene 214*—the Government Camp. . . .

Page 148: Clarify this scene. Now we get the impression Tom [Henry Fonda] is running away, whereas it should be plain that he is making a sacrifice. He should tell Ma [Fox contract player Jane Darwell] that he is going away and the reason is that he's just heard that somebody has come around and is looking for a fellow with a scar. Even if he got by with it this time, it would only be a matter of time that he'd be getting them all in trouble, etc. . . .

I want complete secrecy in reference to *The Grapes of Wrath* script. Instead of having the first script mimeographed as is our usual custom, I want you to make only three copies—one for yourself [Nunnally Johnson] and two for me. A number of more or less unfriendly newspapermen are waiting to grab our first script to actually find out what we have done with this great book. . . .

D.F.Z.

≡

Zanuck's ideas were executed.

The following is an excerpt from an article he wrote for the Los Angeles Times, *November 21, 1954.*

When I purchased *The Grapes of Wrath*, this company was controlled by the Chase National Bank, which was the biggest stockholder. I was told that the chairman of the board of the Chase National Bank, Winthrop Aldrich, would probably raise hell with me because I was attempting a controversial subject that did not hold capital in too high a light.

I was even accused in a newspaper story of having purchased the book from [John] Steinbeck in order to dilute it and take the controversy out of it.

When Steinbeck came out here for the first story conference he was highly suspicious and finally told me that he had been told and warned that the whole scheme was for the purpose of taking the social significance out of the story and he would never have sold the book to me if he had realized this company was actually controlled by big banking interests.

I reassured him and as we worked on the script with Nunnally Johnson he found that I was willing to take any legitimate or justified gamble.

Now here is the pay-off: I was in New York and I saw Mr. Aldrich on business matters. Out of the blue he said, "I hear you have purchased a book titled *The Grapes of Wrath*." I expected the ax to fall but instead he said, "My wife Winnie is crazy about it and I started reading it last night and it was so fascinating I couldn't put it down. It should make a wonderful movie."

To hear one of the tycoons of the banking world express confidence in *The Grapes of Wrath* astonished me, because none of the Hollywood wiseacres shared this opinion. Everyone who considered himself a judge of story values predicted it would flop.

Picture-goers, they said, wanted to see the brighter side of life on the screen, particularly in a period of economic gloom. . . . But the picture was a big hit and made a profit. . . .

≡

In early December of 1939, about seven weeks before it premiered in New York City, the completed Grapes of Wrath *was shown to John*

Steinbeck at the Fox studios. In a letter to his literary agent, Elizabeth Otis, shortly afterward Steinbeck said: "Zanuck has more than kept his word. He has a hard, straight picture in which the actors are submerged so completely that it looks and feels like a documentary film and certainly it has a hard, truthful ring. No punches are pulled. . . ."

≡

October 19, 1939

"THE COME-BACK" [retitled *Young People*] OUTLINE DICTATED BY ZANUCK

Here is an idea for a story for Shirley Temple, temporarily entitled *The Come-Back* or *The Girl Who Came Back*.

Last night I looked at the musical numbers that Shirley Temple did in her old pictures made three, four, five and five and a half years ago. . . . In viewing these pictures, I realized that Shirley has almost tripled in size since her first pictures and it would be sensational if we could see her actually grow up in front of an audience from a little kid who could hardly walk, to the young lady she is at the present time. If we could get a story of this kind, we would have a sure-fire hit for her.

We would open on a vaudeville act composed of a man like W. C. Fields, or Victor Moore, and a woman like Charlotte Greenwood, who can do great drama as well as great comedy. . . . The idea of this is merely to show that the little girl, who is to become Shirley Temple, is reared in backstage dressing-rooms of cheap vaudeville houses. . . .

We next come to the story when the child is about three and a half years old, or the age that Shirley was at the time she made her [screen] debut. . . .

We find that the act has been enlarged and that the baby is included in it. We see the act has been greatly improved by the addition of the child. Here we use all of the early numbers, and of course we can skilfully cut Greenwood and Fields into the wings, and probably use a little double with its back to the camera running into their arms after the act is over.

Now we go to a series of probably three or four of the top musical numbers she has done on a stage, in each one of which she grows older and bigger.

Bookings get better and better and we see them wind up at the Palace, most likely.

After the last number we probably come into a scene where we pick up Shirley at the size and age she is at the present time. She is now ten years old and all of her life has been spent backstage. The folks have saved their money; are well off. Vaudeville has slipped because of moving pictures but they don't give a damn. All they have wanted is to get enough money, . . . get out of the theatre, buy a farm and settle down. . . .

And so they prepare to "retire." Great chance for comedy in Shirley's attitude toward getting away from the theatre—just like a sixty-five year trouper, etc.

We now go to the Farm . . . and gradually the novelty of doing everything for themselves and the life on the farm begins to wear off. . . .

Of course we will eventually have them leave the farm and go back to the city where they are due for a big surprise. In the year they have been away, they find that a terrific change has taken place. Vaudeville is completely passé. Everything is either motion pictures or radio. . . .

This gives us the marvelous situation of a girl who has been a star in the theatre finding herself, at ten, in a position of having to practically start all over again and beg for opportunities. At the end, of course, she will make a sensational come-back in some way—on the radio, in a musical show, or in the movies. . . .

D.F.Z.

═══

Young People (1940) was Shirley Temple's last film under her Fox contract. It did include two numbers from her earlier films. Shirley's career had a resurgence starting with David O. Selznick's Since You Went Away *(1944). She even returned to Fox in 1949 for* Mr. Belvedere Goes to College.

═══

To: Mr. William Goetz [executive assistant to Zanuck]
Twentieth Century-Fox Studio
Beverly Hills, California
From: Sun Valley Lodge, March 3, 1940

Dear Billy:

Please turn the following over to [producer] Harry Joe Brown as it deals with *Down Argentine Way* and the first thirty-five pages of John O'Hara's script on same. I want Harry Joe to show this to O'Hara and discuss it carefully with him. I am generally pleased with what O'Hara has done in the first thirty-five pages. My only criticism comes from feeling that he has gone overboard in his efforts to be modern, casual, and sophisticated. There is such a thing as becoming too casual or too sophisticated. When this occurs we are apt to befuddle our audience, and if we are too subtle we are quite apt to lose entirely the one or two important points it is essential that we make. I feel to a certain extent that this is what has occurred in this first sequence. I, myself, am slightly befuddled about some of the things that come off. . . .

I believe a story of this type must be written with the Moss Hart–George Kaufman technique rather than with the Noel Coward technique. In a Kaufman-Hart show they don't mince any meat. The audience knows where it stands all the time and it does not worry about a lot of things that perhaps takes its mind off of entertainment. After all, *Down Argentine Way* is a musical comedy. It should have the same pace as a show like *The Man Who Came to Dinner* [1939 play]. There is nothing subtle about the treatment of *The Man Who Came to Dinner*, yet there is nothing cheap or common about it either. If O'Hara will go through these first thirty-five pages and make his points clean-cut, I believe that he can put over exactly the same characterizations that he has put over but that we will know what they are thinking and doing rather than being compelled to fumble and guess. . . .

I hope that this criticism does not make it appear that I am condemning everything that has been done by O'Hara because I am not. I think he has modernized the first part of our story and has put some brightness into it, but I think it is not sharp enough. Nobody in this story so far is *frank*. No one says what they mean. Everybody seems to think and talk alike. . . . There ought to be at least one character in the story who says what he or she means, that comes right out with it. . . .

Best regards.

Sincerely,

≡

The story originally was "a disguised remake of Kentucky" (Fox, 1938). The final screenplay was credited to Darrell Ware and Karl Tunberg. Acclaimed novelist John O'Hara occasionally wrote for films, but he received credit on only a few. Alice Faye was set to play the lead, but at the last minute had an attack of appendicitis. Zanuck replaced her with Betty Grable, who became Fox's longest-running leading lady. She had been in many films at various studios, but none with this impact. Grable was in the top ten list of money-making stars consistently from 1942 through 1951. This record has never been equaled by any other female star. At the peak of her popularity she was the highest-salaried woman in America. Carmen Miranda, in her first American film, also made an impressive debut in a specialty capacity.

≡

April 11, 1940
TO: All Producers

. . . Audiences do not go to the movies out of habit or just to pass the time. They *only* go when there is something playing that they definitely *want* to see. We pay entirely too much attention to good scripts—and not enough attention to good *subjects*.

Audiences certainly appreciate fine writing and fine technical qualities but, after all, they do not pay for these things or think about these things when they decide what movie they are going to see. . . . But not the greatest cast in the world can make them go to see a subject that they don't like or a subject that seems slight, empty, or hackneyed.

It may sound stupid to say so, but I would rather have a bad script on a great subject than a great script on an ordinary subject. . . . Star power is valueless no matter how big the personalities or even if they are Clark Gable and Joan Crawford combined [both M-G-M], unless the subject matter in the story stands the test.

What do I mean by subject matter? I mean stories that are about *something*. . . . Stories that deal with something more than the usual formula output of most studios. . . .

D. F. Z.

≡

May 22, 1940

"HOW GREEN WAS MY VALLEY" CONFERENCE ON FIRST DRAFT CONTINUITY OF MAY 18, 1940

I was very disappointed in the [Ernest Pascal] script, mainly because it has turned into a labor story and a sociological problem story, instead of being a great, human, warm story about real living people. . . . There are many fine scenes in it, as far as scenes go, [but] . . . the spirit of the [Richard Llewellyn] book seems completely lost in its transference to a script. . . .

The labor issue should serve only a background against which the story is laid, and we should concentrate on the human relationships— the trials and tribulations and loves of a Welsh family. And we should see how they are split asunder by conditions of which labor happens to be the most important element. This is far from a crusade picture. The reason that this book has become a best-seller is because of its humanness, its sensitive beauty and the sentiment. . . .

This is a very unusual book and we must tell it in an equally unusual way. We want to put the *book* on the screen and not, as has been done, put the book into our standard technique. The method and approach to the subject are entirely wrong and lose the spirit of the book. I miss the great elements of the boy's love for his father, his relationships with the other characters and, particularly wrong in conception is the character of the minister. He is completely changed from the book and he comes through as a violent labor crusader. You should portray him exactly as he was characterized in the book. . . .

Many of the elements of the book come through in the script, but they are there in the intellectual, technical sense, rather than emotionally. We should strive to get into it all the warmth and feeling that there was in the original. And it can be done by being just as daring and unique in our treatment as the book was in its treatment. I feel that our only chance of capturing this mood is to see the story through the eyes of Huw [the boy]. We should do much of the picture with him as an offstage commentator, with many of the scenes running silent with nothing but his voice-over.

This form would permit us to get in many wonderful descriptive passages from the book and also to express the boy's love for his father and his family. It would enable us to understand their viewpoints without a lot of footage, and also it would enable us to get about twenty more sequences into it and still have a shorter script than you have now. Where you now find it necessary to use long scenes, you could get the same point over in silent flashes and it would be even more effective. . . .

We would open with a beautiful long shot of the valley, and the voice of the boy . . . verbatim from the book. . . .

D.F.Z.

≡

DATE: November 15th, 1940
TO: William Wyler [director] and Philip Dunne [writer]
  SUBJECT: HOW GREEN WAS MY VALLEY

Here are the first 150 pages with my cuts marked. . . .

As I told you before, I have tried to be conservative. I think I have helped the story rather than harmed it. I feel certain that from the standpoint of entertainment, the compression will be beneficial. I will work on the new last half over the weekend to be ready for our Monday conference.

I am more than ever convinced that the new idea of keeping Huw a young boy [Roddy McDowall] throughout the story is essential. If we didn't do it, it would mean doing something as incredible as building half of a picture with Tyrone Power and suddenly having him die in the middle of the story and then trying to tell the last six or seven reels with somebody else. In addition to this, it makes our story compact. We gain dramatically and we certainly cannot be criticized for it, because throughout the story the voice of the grownup Huw is part and parcel of our subject, which is the same illusion that you get from the book. . . .

In other words, we will have told the same story and eliminated one-third of the film and footage.

D.F.Z.

≡

Director William Wyler had been borrowed from Samuel Goldwyn for this one film. The New York corporate headquarters of Fox was apprehensive about the subject matter, the script, the lack of box-office names in the projected cast, and Wyler's reputation for slowness and perfection. They refused to authorize the money for the picture. Zanuck was outraged. According to Philip Dunne, "He [Zanuck] informed me that he told them that this was the finest script he had ever had, that somehow, by hook or by crook, he was going to make this movie, even if it meant a deal with some other studio." Wyler went back to Goldwyn in January 1941 to direct The Little Foxes.

A few months passed. Finally Zanuck convinced those in New York to let the picture be reactivated at a cost not to exceed $1 million and with a now available John Ford to handle the direction.

Although originally envisioned by Zanuck as a four-hour Techni-color production to be photographed in Wales, the war in Europe and New York's adamant stand made it necessary to reduce the length of the script, abandon Technicolor, and do the exterior shooting at the Fox ranch in Malibu Canyon.

≡

TO: Mr. John Ford [director]   DATE: April 7, 1941
    SUBJECT: HOW GREEN WAS MY VALLEY

Dear Jack:

Over the weekend I went through the script again of *How Green Was My Valley*, and I think I have come up with some fairly good casting ideas.

You directed [contract player] Gene Tierney in *Tobacco Road* and did a great job with her. . . .

In *How Green Was My Valley*, for the role of Angharad, where could we get a better actress? She has youth—a strange quality about her—and she has sex. We can understand her falling in love with the preacher and we can understand her marrying the miller's son. We can also understand her going back to the preacher at the finish. There is a strange quality about her that might easily be adapted to this picture, and I think that with proper schooling she can master a slight accent.

For the part of Bronwen, who is the eldest of the two girls, what about the great actress, Martha Scott?

If there is some way we can borrow Ray Milland from Paramount, I think he would be great as the preacher. What about [M-G-M star] Walter Pidgeon for this role? He is giving a great performance in *Man Hunt* [Fox, 1941]. Also, there is [Warner Bros. star] George Brent to be considered.

There is also another great actress who could play Bronwen. Her name is Geraldine Fitzgerald.

Sara Allgood cannot be beat for Beth.

Donald Crisp is perfect for the role of Morgan.

In order to get any of these people, we'll have to work far in advance—as you know what the casting troubles are.

We should discuss this sometime tomorrow.

D. F. Z.

≡

Maureen O'Hara played Angharad, Anna Lee was cast as Bronwen, Walter Pidgeon as the preacher (Mr. Gruffydd), Sara Allgood as Beth (Mrs. Morgan), and Donald Crisp as Gwilym Morgan.

≡

TO: Mr. John Ford   DATE: July 10, 1941
     SUBJECT: HOW GREEN WAS MY VALLEY

   Dear Jack:
   . . . In thinking over the whole story, I am sure that all we need now
to get a great picture is a very thrilling and exciting finish. I think we
should absolutely go to town on the mine cave-in episode, not that we
should change or add anything we have already decided upon in these
sequences, but I believe in this type of picture audiences will expect
to see a thrilling and exciting climax that is fraught with suspense
and danger and then winds up with a beautiful scene between father
and son.
   I repeat, I have every confidence that this will be one of the great
pictures of the year, and if it keeps up like it is going it will be the
greatest directorial job that you have ever turned in.
   We may have a trifle too much singing, but I would hesitate to say so
until I see the whole picture assembled. If we have, it will be very
simple to perhaps prune it down—but at the present time I think the
balance is very good. We will never know, however, until we see the
whole thing together with the mine disaster climax and know just how
the relationship of one to the other works out. . . .

                                                             D.F.Z.

                              ≡

TO: Mr. John Ford   DATE: July 16, 1941
     SUBJECT: HOW GREEN WAS MY VALLEY

Dear Jack:
   I never meant to say that we should eliminate the singing. I said that I
felt that the final picture might show us that we had too much singing
in the picture, but I certainly would not eliminate it whenever it is
effective. It is one of the outstanding things in the picture.
   By all means, I would shoot it in every place where you had planned
to shoot it and then when we look at the picture if we feel there is too
much we can drop the least effective places.

                                                             D.F.Z.

                              ≡

TO: Mr. John Ford   DATE: August 16, 1941
    SUBJECT: HOW GREEN WAS MY VALLEY

Dear Jack:

I am more than ever delighted with *How Green Was My Valley* since thinking it over carefully this morning and recalling all of the eliminations we have made and all of the places where we have rearranged the continuity. . . .

The more I think about the necessity of doing a very short scene between mother and son before they go out in the snow to the strike meeting that night, the more I feel it is essential. It is the rock crashing through the window that drives her to go up on the mountain and face the men and warn them. As it is now, the scene on the mountain is practically over before we begin to understand why she is up there or what it is all about, and I am sure, unless we take a brief scene that comes right up on top of the rock crashing in the window, we are going to bewilder our audience for the next fifty feet. . . .

D.F.Z.

≡

How Green Was My Valley *became an outstanding audience and critical favorite in addition to being the recipient of five Academy Awards and other citations.*

≡

September 26 and 30, 1940
CONFERENCES ON "RINGS ON HER FINGERS" [*That Night in Rio*] FIRST DRAFT CONTINUITY OF SEPTEMBER 25, 1940.

. . . Your handling of Carmen [Miranda] was good except that she does not need to talk nearly as much as she does in English. You should confine her English to one or two line speeches, and if she has to explode, she should go into Portuguese—ending up with a denunciation of one or two words in English. . . .

You cannot cut away from Miranda once she starts to sing. Therefore, be sure that you bear this in mind when writing the scenes. . . .

Page 76: Musical number: This is a Carmen Miranda specialty and she will sing a typical Portuguese song from her own repertoire. (Messrs. [Mack] Gordon and [Harry] Warren have a number called "I, Yi, Yi, Yi, Yi [I Like You Very Much]" . . . which we may want Miranda to do in this spot, or somewhere else) . . .

≡

Carmen Miranda had made her impressive American film debut in Fox's Down Argentine Way, *but strictly in a specialty capacity. That Night in Rio* was her second of ten films at the studio, and the one that firmly established her flamboyant screen personality. The roles were tailored for her and in each, songs were composed with her style in mind.

Miranda's contract apparently specified that, contrary to common practice, there would be no cutting away from her to reaction shots and/ or dialogue from other players while her numbers were in progress.

Composer Harry Warren and lyricist Mack Gordon wrote particularly enduring songs for many of the popular Fox musicals between 1940 and 1945.

≡

December 11, 1940
"MOON OVER MIAMI" CONFERENCE DISCUSSION

. . . In making [*Moon Over*] *Miami*, we want to treat it musically in the manner that we treated *Down Argentine Way*. That is to say, we don't want to make any effort to explain the music or prepare for it. The song numbers can be worked in smoothly, of course, but with whatever musical license we want to take.

We will shoot all of the long shots in Miami, laying all the sequences against the local color of Miami. In other words, take full advantage of the racetracks, the beaches, the nightclubs, etc. We will send a Technicolor crew down there and they can get locales against a background of tarpon fishing, aquaplaning, and scenes that are typically Miami.

Be sure to have the writers and songwriters see the color short that we made in Technicolor, called "Land of Flowers."

We will stick to the story that we have [*Three Blind Mice*, 1938], but take the story from the *cut* version off the screen rather than from the script.

[Producer Harry Joe] Brown should have the location boys get plans of the interiors of the spots that they pick, so that we can match the interiors here. . . .

The casting suggestions would be Betty Grable to play the Loretta Young role. . . .

Messrs. [Leo] Robin and [Ralph] Rainger have been assigned to write the music on this story. Be sure that they, as well as the writer assigned to this story, see the short, the original picture [*Three Blind Mice*], and also read these notes.

D.F.Z.

≡

Betty Grable and Carole Landis played sisters arriving in Miami from Texas with their aunt (Charlotte Greenwood) in search of rich husbands. A third version of the story was Three Little Girls in Blue *(1946).* How to Marry a Millionaire *(1953)—a blend of two plays—had a similar premise, as did still other Fox films. It always worked for Zanuck.*

≡

March 3, 1941
Mr. Hal Wallis [associate executive in charge of production]
Warner Bros. Studios
Burbank, Calif.

Dear Hal:

I am writing you this letter rather than calling you on the telephone because there are so many actual dates involved that I thought a letter was the best way to introduce the subject.

I have just read a copy of your script titled *Flight Patrol* dated February

21, 1941. This copy is marked Final Script. I have learned that it . . . has been scheduled by [Bryan] Foy as a minor-budget production.

The script came into my hands in a rather unusual fashion. We, at the present time, are casting our own film *A Yank in the R.A.F.* and our script has been given to various actors and actresses. One of them reported to our office that they thought I should know that your story in many respects is identical with our story. Therefore, I have read your script in full and I am shocked to discover that the theme of your production is identical with the theme of our production—that many of the characters, including the leading character, are identical. There are some differences of course, but the two stories are alike in so many respects that I am compelled to present this issue to you and bring it to a head.

The entire industry long ago knew that we were preparing *A Yank in the R.A.F.* . . . Our production will have Tyrone Power in the leading role and Henry King directing. It is one of the biggest budgeted pictures that I have attempted in a year. . . .

I hate this kind of a mess more than I can tell you as I remember the outcome of *The Fighting 69th* [Warners, 1940]. I sat back at that time and did very little because I was unable to cast my picture, and before I could properly cast it your picture was in production and therefore our picture was abandoned; and the amount that you paid us later for our scenario did not by any manner of means compensate us for the loss we actually took.

In this case I have first and foremost established priority. I publicized priority. I did everything conceivable to eliminate any such tangle. . . .

If you proceed with your film and utilize newsreel and stock material there is no question but what your picture will be released prior to our film. But if you do proceed, I think that you are making a grave mistake—not for your individual company but for the entire industry. If we fail to respect each other in matters of this kind—if it is going to become a common practice that a minor-budget picture shall be hastily concocted in an effort to beat a major production to the punch with an identical theme; and if publicized themes are to be wantonly disregarded—then only retaliation can come into being, which will result in chaos and loss to all involved. . . .

Sincerely yours,
Darryl

≡

Flight Patrol, *retitled* International Squadron—*a partial remake of* Ceiling Zero *(1935) with a bit of* The Dawn Patrol *(1930 and 1938) thrown in—and featuring Warners' up-and-coming Ronald Reagan, was released in August of 1941 to modest acclaim.* A Yank in the R.A.F., *released one month later, was a huge success. Tyrone Power quickly had risen to be one of the top ten money-making stars of 1938, 1939, and 1940.*

≡

May 6, 1941
"SONG OF THE ISLANDS" CONFERENCE ON TREATMENT OF MAY 1, 1941
. . . It was decided to drop the [*Cafe*] *Metropole* [Fox, 1937] angle completely and concentrate on a story based on the *Second Honeymoon* [Fox, 1937] idea.

Just when everything looks perfect for Bill, another guest arrives . . . (Like the fellow in *He Married His Wife* [Fox, 1940].)

I feel that we can get a *Philadelphia Story* [M-G-M, 1940] type of picture out of this, in a Hawaiian setting.

After all, the basis of all three stories, *Second Honeymoon, He Married His Wife,* and *Philadelphia Story* are similar. . . .

D.F.Z.

≡

The final script evolved quite differently from yet other tried-and-true formulas. The result was a lightweight Technicolor musical for contract stars Betty Grable and Victor Mature.

≡

DATE: May 21, 1941

TO: Colonel Jason Joy [Fox public relations director]
CC—Jean Renoir
    Irving Pichel

Dear Jason,

On the first picture that [French director] Jean Renoir makes for us, I have decided to assign Irving Pichel as the dialogue director to aid and assist Mr. Renoir. . . . While Mr. Pichel is a full-fledged director in his own right, I know that he will be willing to sacrifice his personal screen credit and serve with Mr. Renoir in this capacity. . . .

You will recall when I was at Warner Brothers and started both Michael Curtiz and William Dieterle that I used William Keighley as the dialogue director on each of their first American films. This worked out [to be] very beneficial to all parties concerned. . . .

D.F.Z.

≡

The noted French director had arrived in America in February of 1941.

≡

TO: Mr. Jean Renoir   DATE: May 26, 1941
    SUBJECT: SWAMP WATER

Dear Renoir:

Thanks for your note.

Tyrone Power could not possibly play in *Swamp Water*. In the first place, he is not available, and in the second place, I am sure when you learn more about his work you will realize that he has a voice which would never be adapted to this locale. His voice is a quality voice and every effort we have made in the past to adapt it to backwoods requirements has completely failed.

This is a film that must be made for an economical price. It will have to have a tight budget and a tight shooting schedule. There is nothing sure-fire about it from a commercial standpoint. It will make an outstanding film, there is no question about that, but there is also no question but what it is a financial gamble. . . .

D.F.Z.

≡

TO: Mr. Jean Renoir   DATE: July 30, 1941
CC: Mr. Irving Pichel
       SUBJECT: SWAMP WATER

Dear Renoir:

You are going entirely too slow. From day to day you are turning in less completed film than any other company on the lot. We have changed cameramen and now you have a photographer who can keep up to a fast pace, yet we are getting no more film than we did with the other cameramen. I have discussed the matter on a number of occasions and I feel that several things are causing you to fall way behind schedule, which will add almost $100,000.00 to the cost of the picture. We cannot afford this. You will have to speed up and make up this lost time.

1. You are wasting entirely too much time on non-essential details in your background.

2. You are moving your camera around too much on the dolly or on tracks.

3. You should not play scenes two different ways as you did the sequences on the porch in yesterday's rushes. You should decide upon which way you are going to play it and then follow through without compromise.

4. You are worrying too much about background, atmosphere and elements which will not be important in the finished film.

5. The dolly shot of the sheriff in front of the store took over two hours to get in the camera. It isn't worth it.

6. In order to make up time and keep on schedule and budget, it is essential for you to concentrate your attention on the important scenes featuring the principal actors, and on the other scenes find ways and means of covering them as quickly and efficiently as you can.

7. You used four different angles to get over the action with the sheriff on the porch. This could have been covered with one or two angles at the most.

8. The rushes that I have seen in the last two days should have been shot in one day.

I regret that it is necessary for me to be stern in this matter, but after reviewing the budget it is easy to read the handwriting on the wall and see that we are headed toward a price on this picture that we will never be able to get back unless a radical change is made at once.

D.F.Z.

≡

DATE: August 2, 1941

TO: Mr. Len Hammond [associate producer]
    Mr. Jean Renoir
    Mr. Irving Pichel
    SUBJECT: SWAMP WATER

. . . The Camera Report shows that most of the wasted time is because of lack of decision on camera angles. Renoir will give an angle to the cameraman at night that he is going to shoot the following morning, and then when he arrives and the set is all lined up, he has changed his mind. This, of course, can continue to cost us a fortune. . . .

D.F.Z.

≡

TO: Mr. Jean Renoir   DATE: August 8, 1941
    SUBJECT: SWAMP WATER

Dear Renoir:

I have reviewed all of the scenes that you have photographed on the picture to date and here is my summary of same:

You have done an excellent job in handling [Fox contract player] Anne Baxter. She is the most impressive of all the people.

You have done a good job with [Fox contract player] Dana Andrews. His performance is sincere, particularly in his light moments when he is allowed to smile and be relaxed. . . . Try to keep the hat off him as much as you can from here on. . . .

There is too much production in this picture. By this I mean every time we come to the country store it is so crowded with horses and wagons and people that you would think it is the middle of the city. In other words, there is too much atmosphere, which gives it an impression of being artificial.

My greatest criticism is with the manner in which you have handled the minor characters. They all seem to be trying to act. Every bit or small part is trying to be "a character." They are trying to be so typically American—chewing tobacco, smoking corncob pipes, etc. that it becomes unreal and fakey. I don't feel they are the plain, simple backwoods types who react naturally and honestly as, for instance, the characters reacted in *The Grapes of Wrath*. Everybody, including Russell Simpson and the others, seem to be reaching continually. They seem to be trying. The best things you have done on the picture have been the intimate scenes—particularly those between the boy and the girl.

There is nothing you have done that we cannot correct with a few retakes after the picture is over. Right now the important thing is to be sure that everything is good from here on and that we do not fall any further behind schedule. If you plan your work in advance the night before you shoot and do not try to develop *everything* on the set, there is no reason why you cannot keep on schedule. I don't expect you to make up anything, but I don't expect you to go further behind.

You have got to realize that all of us are behind you in an effort to help you—not hinder you or confuse you. No director on this lot has ever been given the support that you have received. Everybody wants to see you come through with a great first [American] picture. Perhaps you have had too much help—perhaps too many cooks spoil the broth. Pichel is the only one you should listen to for directorial suggestions. The cameraman, the unit manager, your secretary, the cutter and [associate producer] Len Hammond can give you what help you want, but in the final analysis—you are directing the picture, and Pichel is your associate. The daily working report shows that a tremendous amount of time is spent each day on discussions. These are things that should be settled the night before so that when you get on the set you know what you are going to do, and go after it.

In closing, I want you to know that I am behind you and I am going to see you through on the picture—but, by the same token, I expect you to play ball my way.

D.F.Z.

≡

Swamp Water, from a novel by Vereen Bell, in the final analysis did very well for Fox. Its relatively modest cost of $601,900 allowed it to be one of the studio's top money-makers of 1941. Renoir's improvisatory methods were the complete antithesis of the American studios' modus operandi. Also, he missed the support of the circle of close associates that had surrounded him in France. This was his only film for Fox.

≡

TO: All "A" Directors and Producers   DATE: June 4, 1941

Recently I have been observing a great number of pictures made by other studios in regard to the length and tempo of the films. I do not pretend to be able, in this note, to solve any problem but I have taken the time to examine certain facts that I feel you should be familiar with.

The average length of a feature "A" film today is ten to twenty percent longer than at any period heretofore in the history of talking pictures. . . .

Now there is nothing basically wrong with a film that runs even 12,000 [feet] if every inch of that film is essential to the telling of that particular story, but when we examine the facts it becomes apparent that in the great majority of cases the additional length has been caused not because we have added more situations and more action to our film, but because we have slowed down the tempo. Stories that we used to tell in 8,000 feet are now told in 10,000 feet, and it is my sincere belief that this additional twenty minutes of time that you put into a film is more harmful to the quality of the film than it is helpful.★

★ One thousand feet runs eleven minutes.

Gone With the Wind [Selznick, 1939] stood up in great and extraordinary length because of the vast number of characters, situations and interwoven climaxes. It did not dwell too long on any situation. It was full of meat and guts, and it did not slow down just because of the desire for a certain mood or casualness in tempo. Therefore, I repeat, there are always exceptions and there always will be.

My feeling, however, is that we as directors and producers are continually making the mistake of reaching for what we term "mood." No one likes "mood" anymore than I do in a film where it is essential—but not always does the audience in the theatre appreciate or relish the fact that we have drawn out situations and slowed down our tempo so that the whole pace has become almost pedestrian.

How many times in the cutting room have you subconsciously said to yourself—"My God, I wish there were some way of speeding up this sequence or some way of getting that man across the room so that he could deliver his lines and get out of the door without it taking all week?"

Sitting as I do night after night in the cutting room working on films, I would rank the lack of tempo as public enemy #1. I cannot ever remember trying to *slow down* a scene. Many directors, who sat with me working in the cutting room, have cursed themselves time and time again over the lack of pace in scenes that they themselves have directed. It is not surprising to go to a preview and then learn that retakes or additional scenes are invariably essential for the purpose of advancing action and eliminating dullness in tempo.

Where does the fault lie? Very frequently its foundation is in the scenario. Frequently we will photograph a sequence that has one important story point in it, and then we will photograph a subsequent sequence that has another important story point. When the film is put together we find that the two sequences have a feeling of drag. Proper advance consideration would probably, in many cases, enable us to find ways and means of placing both story points into one situation—then, when an audience looks at the film, the story moves *ahead* of the minds of the theatregoers and their interest is intensified.

It is perhaps a sad commendation, but I am of the belief that audiences generally do not appreciate pictorial beauty, scenic or pictorial magnificence, splendor of settings, or slowly developed moods *unless* the story itself is actually being advanced while these scenes are on the screen. Audiences love beauty and mood and fine details of characterization, but only when you are telling them something and feeding their imagination. These elements *contribute* to audience interest but they do not *make* audience interest. The only thing that makes audience interest is the development of the story line itself. A story that moves along at a forceful pace will hold and excite an audience, but a story that crawls, no matter how beautiful and magnificent the background, will usually fold up and die while the audience is waiting for the next "thing" to happen.

I recommend that we be completely conscious of this observation— that in scenario and particularly in direction we devise ways and means of keeping our story moving at an effective pace. Every story, of course, presents a different problem, but there is no story that I know of on this lot today that cannot greatly benefit by this suggestion. . . .

I feel certain that *tempo* is the cure for a great many more things than I have even suggested in this memo. Audiences are pretty bright. Many times they are way ahead of us. Many times while we are creating a so-called mood or painstakingly developing atmosphere or a characterization the audience has already supplied these ingredients, and we find that we are taking ten or twenty minutes more to tell a story than the audience itself is taking. . . .

I have yet to hear anyone complain about a film that had fire, punch and drive, but I would be a rich man indeed if I had a grain of rice for every time I have heard people say—"It's a good film, but it was too long—it dragged and I was ahead of the story most of the time."

D.F.Z.

≡

November 7, 1941
"ICELAND" CONFERENCE ON STORY OUTLINE OF NOVEMBER 5, 1941

I feel that the suggested story line, dated November 5th, is much too complicated a setup for a musical. It has five times the plot that *Sun Valley Serenade* [1941] had. In *Sun Valley Serenade* we told an extremely simple story and had plenty of opportunities and footage to load it with music, comedy and skiing routines. Of the 8,400 feet of film in *Sun Valley Serenade*, 6,100 feet were devoted solely to entertainment material. . . .

I suggest that you study the Deanna Durbin [Universal] pictures, which, for the most part, are a perfect formula for Sonja Henie. . . .

D.F.Z.

≡

DATE: November 10, 1941

TO: Colonel Jason Joy [Fox director of public relations]

SUBJECT: THIS ABOVE ALL

Dear Jason:

I want you to send this letter intact to Geoff Shurlock at the Hays Office [Production Code Administration]. It concerns the script of *This Above All* and their objections.

I have spent the entire weekend doing nothing but carefully studying this script. . . .

We took a best-selling novel [by Eric Knight] and eliminated the illegitimate pregnancy sequences and the illicit love story. . . .

In the haystack scene which, after all is not a haystack, but a kind of barn-like shelter, Prue [Joan Fontaine, on loan from David O. Selznick] and Clive [Tyrone Power] fall in love—and nothing else. . . .

Why should we assume that they have consummated an illicit affair? What have they said or done, or what do they later indicate to prove that they have gone the whole way? . . .

And another thing, *This Above All* is a big picture. It will probably emerge as one of the most important pictures of the year, and as such, it should be allowed at least a tiny share of the allowances that were, for instance, given to *Gone With the Wind* and other comparable films. If you like, in *How Green Was My Valley*, you can assume (and there are probably some who did assume) that Angharad [Maureen O'Hara] came in the dead of night to Mr. Gruffydd's [Walter Pidgeon's] bedroom with the purpose of giving herself to him. As a matter of fact, she probably did. However, the scene proves that he did not take advantage of the situation when she said: "I don't want anyone but you—I want you" . . .

In *Arise, My Love* [Paramount, 1940] you had an entirely different situation. . . . It was definitely *proven* to the audience that the boy and girl spent the night together in the bulrushes—and, furthermore, that they were there when dawn came, and they played the scene afterward, which completely convinced you that their romance had been consummated then and there. . . .

D.F.Z.

≡

Compromises were made on both sides and the film was approved by the all-powerful Production Code Administration.

≡

TO: Mr. Joseph Schenck [executive]   DATE: November 27, 1941

Dear Joe:

As per our conversation today about Howard Hawks—I never at any time agreed to have Howard Hawks Productions. As a matter of fact, I never discussed billing with him.

We should definitely stand pat as I see no reason why we should break our rule in this case. He isn't coming here as a producer, he is coming here as a director.

D.F.Z.

≡

For whatever reason, Hawks did not go to Fox at this time. There were no combination producer-directors on the Fox lot until Ernst Lubitsch arrived in early 1943. Otto Preminger was next, and Preston Sturges signed in 1947. But these were exceptions. Later, when Hawks came to Fox to do some films in the late 1940s, Zanuck always had a Fox producer (Sol C. Siegel) assigned to his films.

≡

April 23, 1942
TO: Milton Sperling [producer]
> SUBJECT: CRASH DIVE

I like *Crash Dive* very much as a basic springboard for another exciting and unusual Technicolor service picture. It will be the first submarine picture that uses color and I think that we can get some very effective underwater shots as well as [Fred] Sersen miniature shots.

Basically, it is a formula story but we have found out in *To the Shores of Tripoli* [Fox, 1942] that if the background and atmosphere are interesting, if the theme is patriotic, if the action is exciting, and if you have good comedy values, the fact that the plot is A-B-C doesn't make the slightest difference. *Tripoli* is continuing to make a bum out of every picture we have made in the last three years [at the box office], including *How Green Was My Valley*, and nobody can accuse us of any great originality as far as plot or characters are concerned. . . . The picture was filled with good writing by Lamar Trotti. The characters, while formula, were honest. . . .

D.F.Z.

≡

America had entered World War II a few months earlier.

THREE

WORLD WAR II: BUSINESS IS FINE, THANK YOU

Early in 1941 Zanuck was commissioned a lieutenant colonel in the U.S. Signal Corps (later being promoted to a full colonel). He was assigned to supervise production of U.S. Army training films. During this period he continued to function at Fox in between army assignments, which on occasion took him out of California (and out of the country). Then in September 1942 he resigned from Fox and was granted leave from the studio to devote full time to military affairs. For nine months he was overseas most of the time, but by the end of May 1943 he received permission to go on inactive duty.

While he was away his executive assistant, William Goetz, filled in. Goetz's modus operandi was the complete antithesis of Zanuck's. He was essentially a businessman who activated deals and purchases of properties and handled overall administrative functions in a quiet, nonflamboyant manner. Fox staff producer William Perlberg, who worked on several films at Fox during Zanuck's absence (The Song of Bernadette, Claudia, Coney Island, Sweet Rosie O'Grady, etc.), stated in a memo to Joseph M. Schenck in October 1943: "I never had one story conference with Goetz in my life. I never consulted Goetz about one phase of the making of pictures, except as it was his due as head of the studio, and these instances could never come

within the definition of producing pictures . . . [but would be] certain
okays on budget, actors, or the purchase of a story I would present to the
company."

When Zanuck returned, Goetz left Fox shortly thereafter to form
(with Leo Spitz) his own independent company, International Pictures, which later merged with Universal.

≡

August 13, 1943
Mr. David O. Selznick
David O. Selznick Productions, Inc.
9336 Washington Blvd.
Culver City, Calif.

Dear David:

. . . On *Jane Eyre*, as you know, I have left the decision [on what to do
with the film] entirely to Mr. [Spyros] Skouras [since 1942, president
of Fox]. I understand that they are going to finish the picture up as it is
now and that they are going to immediately prerelease it in three
selected locations, ahead of the national release date. If the picture goes
over and actually does business, and gets good reviews, they will put it
out in its present condition. If it does not, they will take it out of
national release and make extensive retakes, to try and salvage the
investment.

I did not want to deliberately pass the buck on this, but, insomuch as
I never wanted them to buy the property in the first place, I felt no
desire to take the responsibility for it at this late date. It is, however, my
opinion, as I told you the other night, the picture will do business and,
because business is phenomenal, it will recoup its cost. But, that is no
fault of anybody at the studio.

≡

Jane Eyre (1943), *starring Orson Welles and Joan Fontaine, was*
purchased as a package from Selznick by William Goetz while

Zanuck was away in the service. Apparently, the film went into release without the extensive retakes requested by Selznick. Jane Eyre did reasonably well commercially, but it was a relatively expensive project ($1,705,000). Zanuck's reference to "business is phenomenal" had to do with the boom at the box office during World War II.

===

DATE: August 19, 1943

TO: Julian Johnson [head of story department]

Last night when I was thinking about musicals I happened to re-member that about seven years ago I prepared a musical script on *The Mark of Zorro.* [Arthur] Schwartz and [Irving] Caesar did the score and they had a couple of great numbers. We were to make the script with [opera star] Lawrence Tibbett. He was a flop at the box office [in Fox's *Metropolitan,* 1935], so we did nothing with script or score. . . . I wish you would get the original musical script on the picture, also the music itself, investigate, and give me a report.

===

Johnson replied that there were six songs written by Schwartz and Caesar for The Mark of Zorro *on file in the music department (some of the titles: "My Saddle Is My Throne" [Zorro's song], "The Night Has Lost the Moon," and "Lolita Love Song"). The early 1936 outlines written by Bess Meredyth for Fox were more or less based on the Douglas Fairbanks nonmusical scenario of 1920.*

At that time, according to his notes scrawled on the lengthy 1936 outlines, Zanuck envisioned the project "as a delightful romantic com-edy drama of adventure and song," "must treat like Rose Marie *[M-G-M, 1935]," "Jeanette MacDonald or Irene Dunne. . . . Tech-nicolor? . . . Grand Canyon?" Zanuck's thoughts about reactivating the musical approach in 1943 did not materialize.*

===

DATE: August 20, 1943

TO: Mr. Alfred Hitchcock [director, on loan from David O. Selznick]

SUBJECT: LIFEBOAT

My dear Hitchcock:

. . . You are making excellent progress, and certainly no one could complain about the amount of film you have exposed in the last few days. . . .

It still remains my opinion, however, that our story is repetitious in places, and monotonous. I am certain that the cuts we have made in the last few days have not harmed the quality of the production one iota. As a matter of fact, I feel that they have been helpful. . . .

I do not make a habit of interfering with productions placed in such capable hands as yours. Any interference in this case comes from an emergency problem, which I inherited. On all sides, I have been advised to call off the production. The picture was devised originally, so I understand, to be a million dollar cost project. Suddenly its cost has doubled, and no one could possibly dislike the idea of butting in any more than I do. I have plenty of worries on my own personal productions, and nothing would give me greater joy than to forget all about *Lifeboat* until the night I go to the preview.

You felt you could make the picture in eight or nine weeks. . . . We took into consideration this fact, and arrived at a fair budget. We were all wrong. It would be folly now, in my opinion, to butcher the story in an effort to save a penny here and there, but it is also folly to fail to study each scene, each line and each episode, and see if we cannot find ways and means to eliminate nonessentials.

≡

The final cost was $1,590,000. The project was activated by William Goetz while Zanuck was away in the service. It was not a commercial success. This was the only film Hitchcock did for Fox, although the original deal called for two films.

≡

November 16, 1943
NOTES ON "SOMETHING FOR THE BOYS" SCREENPLAY

It has always been my belief that the reason we have made a successful series of musical comedies over a number of years is because we have used several formulas effectively. Regardless of whether it is the formula like *Springtime in the Rockies* [1942], *Down Argentine Way* [1940], *Moon Over Miami* [1941], or whether it is the formula like *Tin Pan Alley* [1940], *Coney Island* [1943], *Hello, Frisco, Hello* [1943], etc., we have always stuck to certain fundamentals. The reason our musicals have successfully topped all musicals made elsewhere is, in my opinion, because we have consistently eliminated the stage or theatre technique.

While it is true that we have had certain variations of this, in *Down Argentine Way* and others, we have generally adhered to the rule of keeping our musical numbers logical and having them arise from situations.

Likewise with certain comedy ingredients. I believe in comedy but I do not believe in farce, and I have been notoriously unsuccessful with it. I know I have at some times lost a great many laughs by eliminating certain farcical situations or exceedingly hokum routines but at the same time I believe these very eliminations have been responsible for the success of the pictures from which they were eliminated.

I do not believe in the "anything goes" type of technique in a musical. I think that while this is often productive of certain outstandingly funny episodes, it destroys the picture as a whole, and I emphatically believe that legitimate comedy-drama results in more successful pictures than does farce. . . .

If you remember *Down Argentine Way*, we had certain musical numbers develop before your eyes where there should not have been musical numbers, if you want to take it on a logical basis, yet they developed so easily and so naturally that you were not aware of it until you were into them. . . .

D.F.Z.

≡

DATE: November 1, 1943

TO: Messrs. Bryan Foy [executive producer]
   Otto Preminger [producer]
   SUBJECT: NOTES ON "LAURA" FIRST DRAFT CONTINUITY OF OCTO-
   BER 30, 1943

This is a very good first draft as far as the continuity is concerned. As a dialogue job, I find it very ordinary. Waldo is the only well-drawn character throughout, and even his lines can be punched up with more sarcastic humor and ironic, sadistic wisecracks. He should speak like "The Man Who Came to Dinner." He should have sarcastic and brutally funny remarks to make to everybody. But generally speaking, he comes off very well in the script. However, if Monty Woolley plays the role, you cannot have a fistfight at the finish where somebody hits this bearded old man, or the audience will hiss. . . .

Laura is a mess. She is neither interesting nor attractive, and I doubt if any first-rate actress would ever play her. As it is now, she seems terribly naive—a complete sucker. It is bad enough for her to fall in love with a glorified pimp like Shelby Carpenter, but when she tries to protect him later on I feel that she is either a very stupid person or just a puppet. Actually, she *is* a puppet. She does no thinking in the picture at all. She has no decisions to make. She doesn't try to solve anything or really think in any situation. She just acts as the scenario writer wants her to act. . . .

I can understand Mark falling for her, even falling for her picture [portrait]. But it is difficult for me to accept her falling for Mark. Their relationship is so brief. She is in a hell of a jam. It seems to me that her mind would go to anything but romance. . . .

Unless you work hard on Laura she will continue to be a nonentity. This is the most difficult problem which you have to overcome. You have to make her just as much a character as Waldo and Mark. She has to become a distinct, definite personality.

Mark is generally well drawn, but I think needs work. He shows flashes of a distinct characterization such as you might find in *The Maltese Falcon* or *The Thin Man*. But these are only brief flashes. There ought to be more of [James] Cagney about him. He also should have humor, but his humor is entirely different from Waldo's. His is the humor of the police desk, the morgue, the humor of a guy who is used to dealing with tough people. Then when he comes up against this gorgeous creature, Laura, we see that it is something new to him. There was a good thing in the book, which you have eliminated here, and that was the point that fashionable Park Avenue murders were not Mark's dish. He was a guy who dealt with gangs like the Dutch Schultz racketeers, and he hated the idea of being mixed up with these people. He should say: "How did I get attached to this kind of thing?" Thus you set the stage when Laura comes in, and you will have a Prizefighter-and-the-Lady setup.

All of the people, Mark included, should seem as if they stepped out of *The Maltese Falcon*—everyone a distinct, different personality. This is what made *The Maltese Falcon*. It wasn't the plot, it was the amazing characters. The only chance this picture has of becoming a big-time success is if these characters emerge as real outstanding personalities. Otherwise it will become nothing more than a blown-up Whodunit. . . .

When Waldo describes Laura to Mark in the early part of the story, he should build her up. He should say what a tremendous effect she has on men. Men always go crazy for her. It isn't because she is so beautiful, it is just because there is something about her. This will also help the fact of Mark becoming infatuated even by her picture. When he examines her apartment I would like to see him look at her lingerie, among other things. He looks at her shoes, her clothes, and he keeps looking back at the picture. He tries to reconstruct her. She begins to get under his skin.

The only place that I did not like the voice [-over] at all was when Laura starts to tell her own story. There is no reason for her to tell her own story. The voice did not help at all. Perhaps it can be rewritten and helped, but just to keep it in to maintain the form of the book doesn't mean a thing. It was good with the other people because you had to explain what they were thinking about, but for Laura you do not need it because then it becomes straight action.

D.F.Z.

≡

Laura's voice-over was dropped, and later on so was Mark's, leaving only Waldo's.

≡

TO: Mr. Otto Preminger [producer]   DATE: March 20, 1944
CC: Mr. Rouben Mamoulian [free-lance director]
    Mr. Samuel Hoffenstein [writer]
    SUBJECT: LAURA

Dear Otto:

As I told you in our conference today, I am pleased with the present script of *Laura*. The following points, I believe, must be taken into consideration while you are doing the rewrite. . . .

Laura's charm should be in her frankness and honesty. Where the others are Park Avenue cutthroats, she should be as fresh as a child. She should be witty but never mean. . . .

Waldo: I still think Waldo's dialogue can be improved. Some of the lines are very witty and smart but not all of them. He should be at times more sarcastic, more ironic and sadistic in his humor. But with it all, he should be likable and charming, so that Mark would tolerate having him around. As it is right now, in a couple of places, I believe Mark would throw him out the window, and why Shelby doesn't shoot him I'll never know.

Waldo should be able to say the most insulting things but at the same time know where to draw the line to preserve his own skull. We will decide in the next day or two what actor is to play this role, and of course this will influence the writing. If we decide to use [Fox contract player] Laird Cregar, you should again look at those scenes in *Blood and Sand* [Fox, 1941] in which he was so magnificent as the sardonic super-critic. And a great deal of Waldo's dialogue can have the biting flavor of *The Man Who Came to Dinner* [play and film]. . . .

The continuity should go as follows, starting on Page 71: . . . I want to dissolve to Mark in front of a little New York Newsreel Theatre. He goes into the theatre and sits down in the darkness. A newsreel is on, of course, and the woman in the newsreel dissolves into Laura. Madame Chiang Kai-shek dissolves into Laura. A girl on a surfboard dissolves into Laura, and finally the scene is filled with Laura. Mark gets up and goes out. We then dissolve back to *Scene 141*, on Page 71, and we put in the business from *Scene 116* where Mark's voice comes over as he looks at her clothes, thinks about her, and begins to realize that she has really gotten under his skin.

This logically leads into the scene where Waldo appears and accuses Mark of falling in love with the dead girl. Now I will believe it. . . .

On Page 128, when Waldo says to Laura, "With you a lean, strong body is the measure of the man," I do not believe it for a moment. This is not Laura. She is not a woman who goes for every guy with a good physique. She is nothing like this. I think this remark hurts her character terribly.

Again on Page 130, Waldo says, "It's the same obvious pattern—the muscular man." This is idiotic to me. Are we to assume that Laura has a complex for muscles on some manly torso? I can understand a certain mothering instinct making her like the worthless Shelby. He is charming and weak, but wonderful women frequently marry likable men even though they are weak. I can understand her interest in Mark because he is the direct opposite of Shelby or anybody else she has ever come up against. Mark is everything she would have liked Shelby to be. . . .

D.F.Z.

≡

The sequence of Mark in the newsreel theatre was not used. In the next scene, Mark's voice-over was dropped and David Raksin's music rose to the foreground. The dialogue referred to on pages 128 and 130 remained. Contract star Gene Tierney was cast as Laura, Dana Andrews as Mark, Vincent Price as Shelby, and stage actor-dancer-singer Clifton Webb, in his first screen role in nineteen years, as Waldo. The picture, based on the novel by Vera Caspary, started shooting with Otto Preminger producing and Rouben Mamoulian directing. On May 15, after Mamoulian had shot for eighteen days, Preminger took over as director as well as producer, and Mamoulian left the studio. The reasons were somewhat complex and differed depending upon the source. It is safe to say that Mamoulian and Preminger did not get along too well.

≡

February 16, 1944
Mr. Jack Warner
Warner Brothers Studios
Burbank, California

Dear Jack:

[Fox executive] Joe Schenck has shown me a letter from you about *The Sullivans* [Fox, 1944] and the Jewish ancestry of the mother.

First off, I want you to know that when I told Joe to go ahead and buy the original story, there was no mention in the story of any ancestry except all members of the family were clearly identified as Irish Catholics.

I can say conservatively that I had at least ten or fifteen story conferences. . . .* Not once during any of these conferences did any of the individuals present advise me of the Jewish ancestry. . . .

I can say this to you, Jack, if it had been brought up and if anyone had suggested that we put in a few lines or a scene to try and show that one of Mrs. Sullivan's ancestors was Jewish, I would have strongly objected and done everything in my power to keep it out of the story. I can imagine nothing that could be more harmful, in the present Jewish situation, than to have a scene in a typical Irish Catholic story, where you bring up any problem of race or creed. Audiences throughout the world, not knowing the true facts in the case, would immediately accuse the so-called "Jewish producers in Hollywood again trying to stuff propaganda down their throats"—and insomuch as our story has nothing whatever to do with any religious or racial matters, I cannot conceivably believe that you would want to see anything like this dragged in whether or not it is factual—and certainly if you include it at all it must be literally "dragged in for effect"—and in my opinion this is exactly the kind of crude propaganda that is far more harmful than helpful. . . .

Recently you saw *The Purple Heart* [Fox, 1944]. You saw the charac-

---

* There were several story conferences, but not "at least ten or fifteen."

ter of Sergeant Greenbaum as played by [free-lance player] Sam Le-vene. I put that character in the original story. I put him in not for propaganda purposes and certainly not as a favor to my Jewish associ-ates and friends. I put the character in because the character fitted and believe me, this is the only kind of propaganda that can ever be useful.

I once made a picture called *The House of Rothschild* [1934]—remember? If you want to produce a really worthwhile Jewish histori-cal film, why not Haym Salomon? Believe me, Jack, in my sincere opinion this is the only way to be helpful. It will not be helpful merely to drag in elements that have no significance or bearing on the subject at hand.

Best always,

Darryl

P.S. Did you know that Sergeant Alvin York's great-grandfather was Jewish?

≡

Haym Salomon was an American Revolutionary financier. Inciden-tally, Zanuck was not Jewish.

≡

The following is a blending by the editor of various remarks, articles, letters, and interview answers by Zanuck during 1943 and 1944 regarding his personal production of Wilson (1944).

≡

Originally, the idea for a motion picture based on the life of Woodrow Wilson came simply as a byproduct. For some time, I had been mulling over another idea altogether—a picture dealing with the life of the late Samuel Gompers, the great labor leader.

But as I continued to delve into the subject, with the aid of Lamar Trotti, one of the screen's most capable writers, I found myself more and more often confronted with the name of Woodrow Wilson, the record of his accomplishments and the part he played in Gompers' career. Naturally, I was familiar, rather hazily, to be true, with Wilson's achievements, but this close perusal of the man's record, his great vision and his courage convinced me that here indeed was a subject worthy of cinematic consideration.

Consequently, we dropped the Gompers project for the time being and shifted to the story of Wilson. However, our research activities into President Wilson's life had been in progress for only a short time when the nation was plunged into World War II. I became a colonel in the Army Signal Corps. While I was in the Army I made it a point to bring up the subject of Wilson and the League of Nations wherever I went and with as many people as possible, enlisted men as well as officers, and I found them almost without exception, from Africa to the Aleutians, keenly aware of the necessity for some kind of police force to regulate the world after this war.

Right now the one thought of these fighting men is to get the present job over with, so they can get back to their homes, and they want a guaranty that this war won't be followed by another. That's the big difference between now and in Wilson's day. I was a kid in the last war, and I don't remember ever discussing things like world problems, either in camps here or overseas. We just weren't interested in that stuff. But look at the difference today.

After being placed on the inactive list a year later, I plunged at once into the task of preparing the picture for production. I was determined to make *Wilson* regardless of the headaches. Here I must add that many members of the Twentieth Century–Fox organization opposed the idea as entailing too great a risk. They argued from motives which were utterly sincere. The history of Hollywood's ventures into the field of contemporary affairs had not been a particularly happy one. There are two reasons for this. We had learned, through bitter experience, that any attempt to deal realistically with the problems of the day was bound to bring down on us a flood of vituperation and criticism from special groups. It did not seem to matter how worthy or well intentioned such attempts might be. We were vulnerable in the sense that the screen did not seem to enjoy the same privileges of expression accorded the press or the radio. Reprisals were often threatened and in some cases carried out. They were carried out, for example, when a Senate committee, dominated by isolationists, called the entire motion picture industry on the carpet to accuse us of warmongering a short time before the attack on Pearl Harbor. I had been a witness at that farcical hearing and was well aware of the lengths to which some groups would go to shackle this vital medium.

We are gambling a great deal of money in an effort to prove that audiences are ready to accept something more than straightforward entertainment. It is, of course, a postwar picture. It deals frankly with the politics that crucified the League of Nations, and the stupid isolationism that caused American's disarmament. These things must not happen again after this war—that is what we are showing in our film. It will be a positive contribution to the postwar situation. By revealing, dramatically, the tragedies at the end of World War I, which led, invariably, to the tragedies of World War II, the film in its final form must, to a certain extent, affect public opinion.

I knew from experience that criticism from outside quarters would not be long in coming. I knew I would be accused of partisanship, of playing politics, of advancing the Rooseveltian cause for the fourth term or pleading for the election of my good friend, the late Wendell Willkie, a truly great man. I was not disappointed. The drumfire began almost simultaneously with the announcement of the plans for the picture. It was so funny I sent wires to both Roosevelt and Willkie asking "Which one of you gentlemen am I working for?" I could not see then and certainly cannot see now how anyone can quarrel with the projection of a man who almost literally had given up his life to the cause of peace.

The other problem was much more pressing and local. It concerned the box-office fate of pictures which had attempted to break into new and controversial ground. With a few rare exceptions, they had not done well. *The Grapes of Wrath* was a financial success but it had been backed up by a great a novel which had had a phenomenal sale. On the other hand, *The Ox-Bow Incident* [Fox, 1943], a story of mob violence and its dreadful consequences, had been a flop. In spite of its significance and its dramatic value, our records showed that it had failed to pay its way. In fact, its pulling power was less than that of a Laurel and Hardy comedy we made about the same time.

To be truly successful, to make its point, a picture must be a financial success at the box office. It must be seen by the maximum number of people. If it fails at the box office it merely means, particularly in a serious film, that the point has failed to get across. Artistically and technically, it may be perfect. But unless people wish to see it and do, it is still a failure. It has failed because it was made to be seen.

You could, of course, blame the public, but that would be self-deception. The fault, in other words, too often lies not with the public but with ourselves. We had turned out pictures of meaning and of value but we had not presented the subject properly.

Consequently, as we progressed with the planning of *Wilson*, many of the details were changed in the interest of wider popular appeal. Originally we had intended to make *Wilson* in black and white, but later, in spite of the enormous added costs entailed, we decided to film it in Technicolor. The change meant much more than simply a shift from black and white to color. It meant the automatic elimination of hundreds of feet of black and white newsreel film of the Wilson era which we had managed to obtain at great cost and labor.

Wilson was in the nature of an experiment. We felt that if the experiment were to succeed it would have to have all we could give it. Therefore, the decisions were made. They brought the cost of the picture from an original estimate of less than $2,000,000 to more than $4,000,000.

For weeks we had frantically cast about for an individual able, by training and personal force, to depict the President. It was not our intention to find someone closely resembling Wilson. That, we felt, would be caricature. What we desperately needed and wanted was a trained actor, not well known, to delineate the character of the President, to project the fervor and the idealism which animated him and the cold stubbornness which he could display whenever he felt a principle at stake. No established, big-name actor would do for the reason that his gestures and expressions, his smallest movement, would be familiar to millions of moviegoers. The essential portrait of Wilson which we desired would necessarily be distorted.

We decided to make a recording of the dialogue in the screenplay to give us a chance to judge by ear the dramatic effectiveness of what we had. To portray Wilson in this recording, we called in Alexander Knox, who was all but unknown to film audiences. That recording by Knox proved so moving and dramatic we knew we had our man.

If physical similarity to the subject was not important in the case of Knox, it was quite otherwise as regards the host of historical figures to be portrayed. They would be delineated but briefly. There was no chance of developing a rounded portrait through speech and action. And finally, these figures were familiar to millions of Americans still living. It was a gigantic job getting the consent of brilliant men and women who had gone through the Wilson regime to allow themselves to be impersonated on the screen and all these people had to pass on my story and the way each was portrayed on the screen.

Obviously, in any film dealing with the fight over the League of Nations, the conflict between [Senator] Henry Cabot Lodge and Wilson had to be paramount. Young Senator Henry Cabot Lodge came all the way to Hollywood to confer about the scenes his grandfather participated in. He wanted no favors but insisted that his grandfather be treated as an honest and sincere man. Since everything in the film is taken from official government records, there was no hitch on that, and his consent was given to the portrayal of the original Lodge.

The choice of Henry King as director was all but automatic. Time after time, he had demonstrated his ability to handle sensitively and with fine intelligence screen subjects of great sweep and power. Lamar Trotti rates far more than mere honorable mention for his contribution to the whole. A motion picture is never better than the screenplay which is its essence and foundation. For him, *Wilson* became a labor of love. It was truly a monumental job of research and writing which he accomplished single-handed. I know very few others who could have done it.

We are producing *Wilson* because we believe in it. It is, by far, the biggest undertaking of the Twentieth Century–Fox studios.

And what is true of *Wilson* is equally true of Wendell Willkie's *One World*, which we are also preparing for the screen.* Those pictures simply supplement one another. The one deals with a principle—visual proof of how the world has shrunk and how completely the nations of the world have become dependent on one another.

* It was never produced.

These pictures, I feel, have something of importance to say to the world. They cannot say it if people do not see them in great numbers. I can tell you that unless these two pictures are successful from every standpoint, I'll never make another film without Betty Grable in the cast. . . .

≡

Although critically acclaimed for the most part, Wilson *ultimately represented a record $2.2 million loss for Fox. The film simply did not capture the imagination of the mass audience. Possible reasons were the subject matter, the lack of stars, the title, the timing, an aura of propaganda and political controversy, a perceived absence of entertainment values, or a combination of some or all of these factors. To say that Zanuck was disappointed would be a considerable understatement. Years later he said the following:*

Of all the pictures I have made in my career, *Wilson* is nearest to my heart. None of my studio confreres shared my fond hope of making such a dramatization a box-office success. When *Wilson* was released their worst fears were realized. The picture was an artistic and sociological success but a financial failure.

I have always felt that if I told the story of *Wilson* through the eyes of his second wife, I would have had an enormous box-office hit. And I still would not have spoiled the basic story of Wilson, the man. . . .

≡

November 15, 1944
Mr. Jack Warner
Gideon Putnam Hotel
Saratoga Springs
New York

My dear Jack:
I wondered why you avoided me before you left for the East. . . .
I am now certain, after receiving your letter, that it had to do

with none other than our old Hungarian friend, [director] M[ichael]. Curtiz. . . .

I have not directly or indirectly made Mike Curtiz any offer to come to Twentieth Century–Fox, nor has anyone else associated with this company made him an offer.

I have heard, however, that David Selznick, Hal Wallis [by now an independent producer with offices at Paramount], and [independent producer] Bill Goetz have made Mike offers. I do not want to make a definite accusation, but nevertheless my information on this subject comes from reliable sources.

Why don't you talk to your friend [agent-producer-packager] Charlie Feldman. He is Mike's manager and he is probably very familiar with the whole situation.

In ten years I have never taken a single individual from any studio. Just examine the record for yourself and name me even a mosquito that I have taken from anyone else. What I have I developed myself or bought on the open market. Practically every personality has been manufactured here on the lot from scratch, yet I have been robbed right and left, and it was only by giving terrific increases that I have been able to make new deals with people like Tyrone Power, Betty Grable, Alice Faye, etc.

I could not hold Sonja Henie or [writer-producer] Nunnally Johnson . . . because of the fabulous and idiotic offers made for them elsewhere. [Writer] Lamar Trotti has four years to go with us, and yet he was made two definite offers last week, one from a major company and one from an independent. None of this, however, justifies me in stealing anyone from anyone else or in any unfair practice. On the other hand, if Mike Curtiz ends up with Wallis or Goetz or Selznick, what have you gained?

You should have an understanding with Mike and if you are going to sign him you should sign him now. If you fail to sign him, then he is on the open market, and I will do my utmost to convince him to come with us. In the meantime, I will neither negotiate nor attempt to negotiate in person or by telephone.

Sincerely,
Darryl

≡

*Curtiz continued on with Warner Bros. Zanuck had worked with him
at that studio from 1926 to 1933.*

≡

TO: MR. WILLIAM BACHER [producer]   DATE: December 4, 1944
        SUBJECT: LEAVE HER TO HEAVEN
CC: MR. JOHN STAHL [director], MR. JO SWERLING [writer]

There are many excellent things in the script and a great deal of great
dramatization has gone into it, but I am absolutely certain that on
several major problems we have missed the boat.

I also think that readers of the [best-selling Ben Ames Williams]
book will severely criticize us not so much because we have not followed the book as because we have lost the spirit of the story between
Ellen [Gene Tierney] and Richard [Fox contract star Cornel Wilde].

Ellen is a girl with a possession complex. She captures and marries
Richard because he represents somehow the attraction she had for her
father. She savagely monopolizes him and she kills his brother when she
feels that the brother is something of a barrier, and she kills her own
unborn child when she is afraid that it, too, may become a barrier
between her and Richard. It is now that Richard turns on her and sees
her for what she really is. When she realizes that her possessiveness has
caused her to lose Richard forever, she determines to possess him even
after death. She knows that she cannot have him so she will fix it so that
Ruth [Fox contract star Jeanne Crain] can never have him either.

Now I find many of these elements missing in this script. The
shadow is present, but the substance has been diluted.

We must be prepared to discuss the following major points:

(1) Should or should not the story be told in a frame? [Producer-
director] Otto Preminger suggests a very exciting framework which
might be effectively used. It starts with the arrest of Ruth for murder as
she and Richard are about to start on their honeymoon in Mexico.*

(2) Should or should not Richard be a partial witness to the murder of
Danny [Richard's brother (Darryl Hickman)]? Isn't this the moment

* Another frame was used, however.

that starts his growing fear which comes to a climax when Ellen destroys her unborn child and Richard then knows actually what he is up against?*

(3) The device of using the mother [Mary Philips] for a last minute ride to the rescue is highly questionable. I, for one, did not like it at all. It seemed like a prop. It took all the elements of drama away from the principals and gave them to a secondary character. It ruined all of the suspense because I knew from the beginning that the mother would eventually tell. . . .†

I am enclosing herewith three confidential memos to me—one from [writer-producer-director] Joe Mankiewicz, one from [director] John Stahl, and one from Otto Preminger. These three men encouraged me to purchase the story in the first place. These are three people who liked the story. You must read their criticisms dispassionately.

We will have a conference tomorrow afternoon and make a determination about the story.

D.F.Z.

≡

Cast with popular Fox players and photographed "in gorgeous Technicolor" against striking Arizona and California exterior backgrounds, Leave Her to Heaven *made more money than any Fox picture up to that time by a wide margin. Essentially a melodramatic soap opera, it obviously worked for postwar audiences.*

≡

TO: MR. ERNST LUBITSCH [producer]   DATE: December 6, 1944
     MR. JOE MANKIEWICZ [writer-director]
     SUBJECT: DRAGONWYCK

Dear Ernst and Joe:

Here is my note on the script of *Dragonwyck.* . . .

I read the script three times last Sunday and then I went back and read a very good synopsis of the [Anya Seton] book. . . .

---

* Richard was "a partial witness."

† The device was not used.

The script is way over length, but it is not over length because of too many sequences. . . . Practically all of the sequences are essential. What makes for the forty pages of overlength is that we have overdialogued, in my opinion, almost every episode in the entire picture. The characters talk and talk and talk, and incidentally their talk is very good, but they talk so much that there are no surprises left and there is no chance for *acting* left. They say everything they feel and there does not seem to be anything left for them to dramatically portray.

I realize that this is a first draft and that my criticisms may sound brutal, but in my opinion the major fault of the story lies *within* the individual sequences. . . .

I feel that suspense is lacking in the individual scenes. They all play themselves out too perfectly and too completely. There is just a little too much of everything within the scenes. One look and one line and a significant gesture should give the audience an impression of the drama that is impending and of the things that are to come. I find that the long dialogue passages explain everything to the audience so perfectly that I am way ahead of the story. I know what is coming or I make up my own mind in advance as to what is coming, and the story always seems to be a few pages behind me. I am not breathlessly waiting for the next page to see what has happened or what is going to happen.

I am not suggesting an obvious whodunit flavor or the technique of *Laura*, but I do feel that an application of certain parts of this technique would be beneficial, and I'm absolutely certain that almost every sequence of this picture from start to finish can be tremendously intensified by dramatization and conflict within the scenes themselves. It is too methodically pat. It is too *deliberately* right. . . .

Darryl

≡

Modifications were made. Because of a recent illness, Lubitsch functioned only as the producer on this film, rather than producer-director. The somber Gothic tale, starring Gene Tierney and Vincent Price, did well.

≡

January 20, 1945

"CAPTAIN FROM CASTILE:" COMMENTS ON [writer] JOHN TUCKER BATTLE'S MEMORANDUM OF JANUARY 19, 1945

I feel that if you do *all* the things you want to do in order to satisfy the Church and the Hays Office, we will have taken out of the [Samuel Shellabarger] book everything that makes it a best-seller. . . .

I like your idea of establishing the friendly priest at the beginning of the story. By having *him* speak for the true Church we will be able to show the Inquisitors in a way that would not be possible if we did not have a voice to speak for the Church.

You do not have to use the actual name "Inquisition." Give it some other name. Also, you do not have to mention the Catholic Church. Keep crosses and crucifixes and all such out of it completely. The Inquisitors are just the local Ku-Klux-Klanners, so to speak. . . .

I agree that the rape of Mexico should not be under the name of the Cross, but instead under the name of the greedy conquerors.

Making the Aztecs a conquering nation themselves, which they were, is good. . . .

D.F.Z.

≡

The final drafts of the script were written by Lamar Trotti.

FOUR

SEMIDOCUMENTARIES, FILMS NOIR, LITERARY WORKS, AND SLEEPERS

January 9, 1945
"NOW IT CAN BE TOLD" [*The House on 92nd Street*] CONFERENCE ON
FIRST DRAFT CONTINUITY ON JANUARY 5, 1945

. . . My first criticism is that I find it singularly lacking in personal drama. I find practically no acting scenes in the picture. . . .

In the dialogue, for instance, it is hard to distinguish one character from another. Some speeches that the Colonel [Leo G. Carroll] says could be said by either of the two women. To make this clearer: in *Laura*, for instance, nothing that was ever uttered by Clifton Webb could have been said by any other character. Dana Andrews was completely different from any other character, so was Vincent Price. Therefore, you provoked drama between these characters. . . .

We have to do what we do dramatically or it will fall into the category of documentary features, and there is just no market for them. We have to make up our minds to make an entertaining picture out of it or we should just turn the material over to "The March of Time" and forget about making a picture out of it. . . .

=

Zanuck's points were observed in the next draft.

Producer Louis de Rochemont, who had created (with Roy E. Larsen of Time Inc.) the "March of Time" series, had joined Fox as a producer in 1943 (The Fighting Lady, *1944).* The House on 92nd Street *(1945), produced by de Rochemont under Zanuck, became the initial "semidocumentary" feature film, blending at least partially true case histories, on-location filming, and a mixture of professional actors and "real people."*

≡

TO: Mr. Louis D. Lighton [producer]   DATE: March 8, 1945
    SUBJECT: ANNA AND THE KING OF SIAM

Dear Buddy:

. . . This is a great personal story which cannot help but be a wonderful film in every respect. Its simplicity is its greatest charm and by keeping the story intimate between four or five characters we achieve a much larger picture than we could achieve if we went into spectacle, which, in my opinion, would ruin the wonderful personal drama. . . .

The comedy possibilities are enormous. This picture, with all its tenderness and conflict, is basically one of the funniest stories I have ever read. It is genuine comedy because it comes out of the characters themselves and is a result of clashes of personalities. The incidents you have used for comedy purposes are wonderful. . . .

I was talking to Ernst Lubitsch about the story today, just in passing, and I told him of the treatment. He was most enthusiastic.

I still feel that the King, almost as an afterthought on his deathbed, should give Anna the raise which he would not give her for forty years.★

The banquet for the foreigners is riotous. The letter to [President Abraham] Lincoln, etc., etc., are wonderful moments.

I am afraid that if [M-G-M star] William Powell reads this treatment he will shy away, not because his part is not the equal of Anna's, but

---

★ No raise was given in the final version.

because in your first few pages you have sold it almost as a solo story for Anna. When you study the continuity you find that it is equally distributed but I would be very frightened to have him read the first dozen pages in its present form.

Powell would be sensational as the King. The Dorothy McGuire situation, however, is up in the air. Just as I anticipated, David [O. Selznick] is now asking for certain conditions that are not covered in our original contract with him for McGuire. Among many other petty things, he wants to announce that he has put her in the story; that he has thus approved the project, etc. etc. In addition, he has put other stumbling blocks in our way, and Mr. [Joseph] Schenck has definitely determined to tolerate no further nonsense.

Dorothy McGuire would be great in the role, but I want you to know we are not going to get down on our knees to get her. There are others who want to play the role who would be equally as great. As you probably know, [free-lance star] Jean Arthur is insane to do it. She is an outstanding actress. She sent word to me that she would drop anything to play the role. You know what [M-G-M star] Myrna Loy thinks about it. [Free-lance star] Olivia de Havilland personally went to Lubitsch and asked him to intercede with me for her.

I personally feel that while Dorothy McGuire would be great in every respect, Jean Arthur would give as great or even a greater performance, and of course with her name the enormous cost of the production would be completely safeguarded.

If we get into difficulties with [director Elia] Kazan, John Stahl is eager to do this picture, and it would not surprise me to have Ernst Lubitsch ask to direct it himself, providing his health permits.

We should proceed immediately with the continuity as you certainly have licked the major obstacles, and we should not worry about who is to play Anna. If David [O. Selznick] comes off his high horse we will use McGuire; if not, we will have practically the pick of the industry for this role. I forgot to mention [free-lance star] Irene Dunne, although in my opinion she is too old for it. She also wants to play it, and you cannot entirely thrust this aside when you consider that she has been in three great successes, one after another. Incidentally, [free-lance star] Charles Boyer would love to play the King. . . .

By the way, did you know that [President] Lincoln actually answered the King's letter about the elephants [from Siam to help in America's Civil War] and thanked him profusely? [Fox producer] George Jessel, who is an authority on harems, gave me this piece of information in the dining room today.

In closing, I would like to go on record as saying that this, in my opinion, will be the best picture of the year. It is something entirely original and has great quality.

Best ever,
D.F.Z.

≡

Irene Dunne and Fox contract star Rex Harrison were cast as Anna and the King. Free-lance John Cromwell directed. The picture was well received critically and commercially, and of course, the Margaret Landon book and the film were the basis for the musical treatment in the later The King and I.

≡

TO: Messrs. Robert Bassler [producer] DATE: March 22, 1945
Louis King [director]
SUBJECT: SMOKY

I see the treatment of [the Will James book] *Smoky* as follows:

We use the present story insofar as the relationship between the man and the horse is concerned. This will provide four outstanding episodes as revealed in the old [1933 Fox] picture where there are marvelous and new situations between the man and his horse.

For our personal story, we will borrow the brother versus brother element from *Western Union* [Fox, 1941] and adapt it to fit our needs. . . .

D.F.Z.

≡

TO: Messrs. William Perlberg [producer]   DATE: May 18, 1945
Jerome Cady [writer]
SUBJECT: "FOREVER AMBER" First draft continuity of May 1, 1945

. . . *How Green Was My Valley* and *The Grapes of Wrath* prove that if you are true to the *spirit* of a book and reasonably accurate with the characters, it does not matter a tinker's damn whether or not you faithfully follow the continuity or structure of the book, providing, of course, you do not leave out any of the outstanding moments of the book. . . .

In my opinion, if we were to put the entire [Kathleen Winsor] novel, as written, on the screen, it would take thirty reels and a great deal of it would be very dull. And I am sure that we must abandon any thought whatever of trying to preserve, even in a condensed form, the actual structure of the novel. . . .

The Song of Bernadette was a simple, direct story about *one thing*. All of the situations in the story evolved out of that one basic situation. *Forever Amber* is exactly the opposite and, if we are to succeed, we must adroitly select *what* we are going to tell and then devote our footage exclusively to telling it clearly, effectively, and dramatically. We cannot hope to tell it *all*. It is a hopeless task. By concentrating on these selected elements and devoting our full footage to an exposition of this chosen material, we will come out with a powerfully dramatic story of a strange, gorgeous, glamorous young girl who slept with seven men, but only loved one of them and the one whom she loved, she could never get. . . .

As a closing argument, I would like to cite two examples. *Anthony Adverse* [Warners, 1936] was a bad picture and an unsuccessful one because [director] Mervyn LeRoy endeavored to reproduce the entire book on the screen. He used a shotgun and the effect was scattered. It was a big, long, drawn-out narrative minus situations or dramatization. [*The Life of Emile*] *Zola* [Warners, 1937], on the other hand, was a very fine film and a very successful one, because they did not endeavor to tell the entire life of Emile Zola, but they picked the Dreyfus Case and concentrated eighty percent of their dramatization on this one very powerful and dramatic situation. Thus, they produced a strong drama, with conflict and climax, rather than a rambling narrative.

D.F.Z.

≡

October 1, 1945
"CARNIVAL IN COSTA RICA" CONFERENCE ON TEMPORARY SCRIPT OF
SEPTEMBER 27, 1945

. . . As far as the development of the situation is concerned, everything is A-B-C. Everything is right on the nose. It is cut and dried. All the charm has vanished.

State Fair [1945] is the most popular musical we have had in years and the business nationwide is just sensational. There are two reasons for its success: the wonderful [Rodgers and Hammerstein] score and the great charm of the piece as a whole. We could easily have gone overboard with the comedy, and we might have put into it comedy gags, which were funny in themselves but completely out of keeping with the story we were telling. We could have been obviously sentimental, too, but we avoided that. We had comedy, but it was charming comedy. We stayed away from the obvious. As a result, you believed the story of State Fair. . . .

[Carnival in Costa Rica] reminds me of things we did eight or ten years ago, which were good at the time, but couldn't compare with things that are being done today, like State Fair, Anchors Aweigh [M-G-M], Centennial Summer [Fox], etc. . . .

D.F.Z.

≡

Carnival in Costa Rica was a commercial flop.

≡

TO: [blank]   DATE: June 16, 1944
    SUBJECT: THE RAZOR'S EDGE

This is my analyzation of The Razor's Edge by Somerset Maugham. Despite the fact that to date no producer on the lot has shown any great enthusiasm for this story as a motion picture and despite the fact that no other studio has purchased it, I am inclined to believe that we should buy it.

The book was published in May, and it immediately went on the best-seller list. . . .

There must be a reason why the American public at this moment is reading this book more than it is reading any other book. The answer, I think, is simple: Millions of people today are searching for contentment and peace in the same manner that Larry searches in the book.

As I see the basic story, it is an adventure picture. It might even be referred to as a melodramatic adventure, wherein a man searches the face of the earth for the hidden key to contentment. In his particular case he finds the key is within himself, and at the end of the story he must dedicate himself in some simple fashion to an effort to give this secret to others. . . .

Incidentally, there is a marvelous opening to the picture when Larry sees his best friend killed in 1918 just five minutes before the Armistice. Although at first he does not realize it, this is the moment that changes his whole life. He returns to Chicago determined to pick up his regular routine civilian life, but he finds he cannot do it. Something is wrong—he doesn't know what. Things that he liked before the War he now finds that he does not enjoy. He thinks that perhaps if he gets away he will feel differently. Isabel and his friends humor him. They know that he has been deeply shocked by the War and they feel that his mood will change with time. But it does not, and therein lies our story. . . .

D. F. Z.

===

October 24, 1945
"THE RAZOR'S EDGE" CONFERENCE ON FINAL SCRIPT OF AUGUST 18, 1945

Our only problem now is the problem of Larry [Tyrone Power]. . . .

I put this script aside for five or six weeks in order to regain my perspective on it. And I now see very clearly what the trouble is. There are four or five spots in the script where Larry says things that I do not think any man today can say on the screen and get by with.

He says things which I am sure the average audience cannot swallow. . . .

Consider this: Why did *Going My Way* [Paramount, 1944] make such a phenomenal success—much more so than any previous [Bing] Crosby picture? It was because they told the story of a very religious man, but they never let him *be* religious at any time. He was a regular guy all the way through it and they never let the collar get in the way.

Now in our script we do just the opposite. We go out of our way to try to let Larry state his case, and in doing so he oversells it. You do not believe him. This was not the intention of Mr. Maugham, nor was it our intention, but nevertheless it comes through that way, because in our medium we have no way of taking twenty or thirty pages to explain his philosophy, or to get over what his trouble is, or what motivates him. Therefore, when we try to let him explain himself we get into trouble. . . .

Because he is the lead in the picture, if the audience thinks he is a half-baked religious fanatic or a man who does not know what he wants, all the fine writing and drama and magnificent construction will go for naught, because you will never be able to overcome the faults of your basic character. The reason people constantly say that Larry is a dull guy is because he does just the opposite of Crosby in *Going My Way*. Crosby wore a collar and talked baseball, Larry doesn't wear a collar and he talks religion. Of course, he doesn't call it by any particular name, but it is there just the same.

I think Larry can do everything he now does in the script, providing he is less articulate about it. . . .

I do not want to change the character of Larry, I merely want him throughout the picture not to talk about himself, not to explain himself; to let the audience write its own answers. Let him convey his inner convictions by deeds and actions alone. He should not stop to give the audience his motivations, and he should never voice anything that makes him look noble, holy, or sanctimonious. This, I am convinced, audiences will not tolerate. . . .

≡

November 14, 1945
Mr. George Cukor [M-G-M director]
9166 Cordell
West Hollywood

My dear George:

I have just spent three calm and peaceful days in Palm Springs doing utterly nothing but studying and analyzing the dramatization of *The Razor's Edge*, and also the contents of your letter.

Now in some respects this note is going to appear to you to be exceptionally egotistical, and you are apt to resent some of my opinions. But on an undertaking as important as this where I am gambling a very large amount of money and a number of reputations, including your own and my own, I feel that I have got to be perfectly frank and honest even at the risk of appearing highly conceited.

We worked together only once before [*Winged Victory*, 1944], and at that time I was not the producer. I served as a sort of superficial supervisor to both [playwright and occasional screenwriter] Moss Hart and yourself. Outside of setting Moss straight on the original construction and later on in editing the film, I was of little use because of my occupation with *Wilson*. . . .

I feel we can make a tremendous motion picture out of *The Razor's Edge*. . . .

Now I bought this novel and paid a phenomenal price for it when all the other major studios had turned it down. As a matter of fact, they were so uninterested that Maugham made a screwy percentage deal with an unknown "B" producer who has never made a film. I saw something in this story that appealed to me. . . . This is the only picture that I am going to put my name on as an individual producer this year. . . .

I feel justified in saying that if something goes wrong with it I will be primarily the one who is left holding the bag. They may complain about Maugham's dialogue, and they may criticize [Lamar] Trotti's adaptation, or lambast your direction, but in the final analysis if it turns out to be a dud I know that I will be the one whom the critics and the industry will pounce on and hold primarily responsible. . . .

I am conscious of all these things and I want you to be conscious of them too, so that you will bear with me and understand what may appear to be arbitrary decisions on my part. In other words, if I cannot make *The Razor's Edge* my way, I would rather not make it at all, as it is too big a gamble and there are too many chances for it to come a cropper.

I believe firmly, at this moment, that while there are differences in opinion between us on certain points, we are not too far apart. Yet at the same time I believe that these differences are almost the difference between a very good picture and a very, very great picture. . . .

I have never been lucky with stage plays but I have invariably had great success with adaptations of books, and usually they have been books that did not appeal to other producers. . . .

Now to get to the letter: You have accepted all of the technical changes and a few of the minor changes, but you have not at all accepted any of the changes which I consider to be major in importance. Furthermore, you open the door to additional changes, such as in the Sophie [Anne Baxter]–Larry [Tyrone Power] relationship, which, in my opinion, should not be opened. . . .

If you want to find the real answer to the Sophie-Larry relationship, please reread the speech at the top of Page 111, where Maugham says, "He's in the grip of the most powerful emotion that can beset the breast of man. Self-sacrifice. He's got to save the soul of the wretched woman whom he had known as an innocent child. . . ."

Now let us take up the point of Larry being a taxi driver. You suggest that he should not be a taxi driver, and you indicate that perhaps we should vaguely suggest that he is going to teach at some school or university. Honestly, George, I think this would be a tragic error that would kill the picture. I find no quarrel whatever with him being a taxi driver at the finish, and a mechanic who works in a garage, as long as we do not physically show him working at it. . . .

Larry is happy and through his happiness and goodness he probably is going to make other people happy. To infer that he is going to teach at a university or deliver lectures or anything of the sort would be, in my opinion, in complete defiance to the characterization of Larry. . . .

Now as to cast: There is an acute problem that arose over the weekend. I was with [M-G-M executive] Eddie Mannix for a few hours at Palm Springs and I told him my problem, which I will restate for you: Tyrone Power should be on terminal leave [from the Marine Corps] before this month is out, which means that by the middle of December at the latest he will have reported back to the studio. Now of course he will want a rest, but in my recent wire from him he says he is eager to resume his career.

I have checked all of the dates and I find that the latest we can start shooting *The Razor's Edge* is on Monday, March 4th. . . .

Now comes the big problem of your availability. Mannix told me that there would not be a chance of your finishing your next assignment [at M-G-M] before sometime in April, providing you get started the first week in January, and he was very doubtful about this starting date. If this is accurate—and Eddie was very definite about this point—it would be a terrible stumbling block for us as it would mean that I would have to hold off Ty's second picture, *Captain from Castile*, for an entire year. It is an exterior picture that I must start shooting no later than July, or I will have to wait until the following spring, and Ty is so eager to play it and so grateful that I have held it for him that I have no choice in the matter. In addition to this, I would miss a commitment with Gene Tierney, and this is very important to me at this time for I fully believe Miss Tierney is going to win the Academy Award this year for *Leave Her to Heaven*, and I want her name badly in our film.★

Now it goes without saying that I want you above anyone else to direct this film. While we have some difficulties as to interpretations of certain sequences, I know that you are the man for the job, and I know that on these points you will be prepared to go along with me and accept my instinctive feelings about them. After all the work you have done on the script and in the production preparation, it would be a pity if you could not do the film, but if what Mannix told me on Monday is true, then I know you are not going to be available. They have never made a picture with [Greer] Garson in under ten to twelve weeks, and you certainly cannot stop shooting a difficult picture with her on one Monday and start here the next Monday, no matter how much preparation has been done in advance. You would be a fool to attempt it and I would be exercising poor judgment if I permitted you to attempt it

★ Tierney was nominated, but did not win.

after an undertaking that will consume as much of your energy as that one will.

What, then, is the next move? . . .

I wish you would get as much information as you can on the M-G-M thing, and then come over to see me. . . . In any event, we have both certainly got to find out where we stand. If I am going to regretfully be compelled to assign someone else to direct the film, then I have got to make the decision very shortly. I sincerely hope this will not be necessary.

Best always,

≡

Because of the scheduling factor (and possibly other reasons) director Edmund Goulding was assigned to The Razor's Edge. *Regarding Cukor's wanting to suggest that Larry "is going to teach at some school or university," in the final version Larry says "I might take a job in a factory or garage. . . . I might buy a taxi." And the concluding shot shows him on a tramp steamer.*

≡

DATE: October 22, 1946

TO: Spyros Skouras [president of Fox],
    Joseph Schenck etc. etc. etc.

An additional forty-two preview cards came in the mail today on *The Razor's Edge*. This is the largest amount of cards we have ever received on any picture in the mail. To date we have a total of one hundred and twenty-four cards. This is the largest amount ever received on any of our previews.

The cards are divided as follows: fifteen are marked good or very good, one hundred and nine are marked excellent or superb.

This is the only preview we have had on any film where no cards were marked fair or bad.

Tyrone Power received eighty percent of the cards. Anne Baxter and Clifton Webb come next. There is frequent mention of [Gene] Tierney, [Fox contract star John] Payne and [free-lance player Herbert] Marshall.

The scene most mentioned on the cards is the sequence on the mountain top in India. The second most mentioned scene is the climax at the end of the film between Power and Tierney. The third most mentioned scene is the drinking scene with Baxter.

Many cards openly state that the picture, in addition to being outstanding entertainment, made a great impression upon them. The cards are truly remarkable in this respect. Tyrone seemed to represent something more to them than an actor in a role.

The only criticism is that the music and sound effects were too loud. This is not the fault of the picture but my fault as I played the fader in the theatre entirely too high.

Altogether they are the most unusual and outstanding set of preview cards we have ever had on any film.

D.F.Z.

=

October 22, 1946
Mr. Jean Hersholt [president of the Academy of Motion Picture Arts and Sciences]
Academy Award Theatre Bldg.
9038 Melrose Avenue
Hollywood 46, Calif.

My dear Jean:

I am very happy that you had the time to see *The Razor's Edge* the other afternoon. . . .

As you know, I am a severe critic of sound and projection in the theatre. I believe I personally attend more previews than any other executive. I believe my complaints are responsible throughout the years for improving both sound and projection in theatres.

I raise hell and my hell has had beneficial effects. The Fox West Coast [theatre chain] people have continually made improvements and these improvements have been reflected in other circuits. We spend millions of dollars endeavoring to obtain perfection in photography and sound recordings. The effect of all this can be spoiled by a number of insignificant things which could easily be remedied.

I have seen *The Razor's Edge* in three theatres. I have seen it in the Fox Theatre in Riverside at the sneak preview, I have seen it at a press screening at Grauman's Chinese Theatre when the house was practically empty and I have seen it in your new Academy Theatre. I have the following sincere criticisms to make. Please accept them as the honest desires of someone who is interested only in perfection.

(a) The carbons [for the arc lamps] in your projection are faulty. They are not the quality of carbons that we use at the studio. This causes a flicker and a change in density which can become very noticeable and irritating.

(b) Your auditorium is not dark enough. You should turn out the side lights on the walls of the auditorium and leave on only the tiny lights in the aisle. You will notice that these side lights cast a slight reflection on the screen which causes detraction and your blacks [in the projected images] do not go black enough because of this reflection.

(c) Your timing device must be out of gear as on two occasions during the screening of *The Razor's Edge* the operator missed the switchover from one reel to another. (This may, of course, be the operator's fault if you do not have an automatic switching device.)

(d) Heavier aisle doors would keep out a lot of extraneous street noise.

(e) This is my largest criticism and I realize that I am sticking my neck out. Your screen is not as large as it should be for the size of your throw. I am certain that you will benefit [from] the reproduction of photography on the screen if you enlarge the screen approximately four feet in each direction. I have the feeling that I am looking at the picture in an intimate projection room rather than on the screen of a theatre.

If you can get a larger screen I will be glad to donate it and pay for it personally. When I go to a threatre I want to see the picture in approximately the same size that I would see the picture if I went to Grauman's Chinese Theatre. I am certain you have ample length to your throw which will enable you to install a larger screen.

Again my thanks for your courtesies and kindest personal regards,

Darryl

≡

There seems to be no record available as to whether any of Zanuck's suggestions were implemented at the time.

===

TO: Mr. John Ford   DATE: November 6, 1945
      SUBJECT: FRONTIER MARSHAL [*My Darling Clementine*]

Dear Jack:

I have had a conference this afternoon with [producer] Sam Engel and [writer] Thomas Job and they will report to you immediately to go to work on *Frontier Marshal*. I told them all the things we have discussed as to characterizations, historical background, and that we are trying to get Henry Fonda as Wyatt Earp, [free-lance star] James Stewart as Doc Holliday, [Fox contract star] Linda Darnell as the Mexican dance hall girl and [Fox contract star] Jeanne Crain as the young nurse.

They are highly enthusiastic. . . .

                                    D.F.Z.

===

Some time later writer Winston Miller was assigned to work on the screenplay and Thomas Job, whose assignment had been to work on "notes on scenes," checked off the lot. Ford had been in the U.S. Navy since September 1941. Henry Fonda and Linda Darnell were set shortly after the above memo was sent.

===

TO: John Ford   DATE: November 6, 1945
     Sam Engel
     SUBJECT: FRONTIER MARSHAL

We should try and find a new title for *Frontier Marshal*. We don't want it to sound like something that has already been made, and besides I think the title is ordinary. If possible I would like to get more or less of a neutral title and not be tied down to *Boom Town* or *Tombstone* or anything that sounds like a typical western. Our picture is far too important for this.

D.F.Z.

≡

Frontier Marshal had been made previously by Fox in 1934 (with a different story) and in 1939 (with a similar story line to the new version). The book, Wyatt Earp, Frontier Marshal, *was by Stuart N. Lake.*

≡

TO: Mr. John Ford   DATE: January 8, 1946
     SUBJECT: MY DARLING CLEMENTINE

Dear Jack:

I am pleased that you like [Fox contract star] Victor Mature. Personally I think the guy has been one of the most underrated performers in Hollywood. The public is crazy about him and strangely enough every picture that he has been in has been a big box-office hit. Yet the Romanoff* round table has refused to take him seriously as an actor.

A part like Doc Holliday will be sensational for him as I know you will get a great performance out of him and I agree with you that the peculiar traits of his personality are ideal for a characterization such as this.

Whenever you have the tests cut let me know and we will run them together.

D.F.Z.

≡

---

* A popular restaurant of the time frequented by motion picture executives and players.

TO: Mr. John Ford   DATE: February 26, 1946
CC: Sam Engel
    SUBJECT: MY DARLING CLEMENTINE

Dear Jack:

There will be no chance for us to get Jeanne Crain to play in *My Darling Clementine*. I know she would be delighted to be directed by you but the part is comparatively so small that we would be simply crucified by both the public and critics for putting her in it. She is the biggest box-office attraction on the lot today. There is no one even second to her. . . .

                                                        D.F.Z.

≡

Newcomer Cathy Downs played Clementine.

≡

TO: John Ford
June 25th. 1946

Dear Jack,

I am typing this letter myself. In many respects I think it is one of the most important letters I have ever written to you. I am going to be frank and please believe me when I say I am going to be honest and sincere.

As far as *My Darling Clementine* is concerned I have no ax to grind. I do however have a grave responsibility to the corporation. I personally selected the subject and suggested it to you. I authorized the expenditure of more than two million dollars and I sat in on many of the story conferences. I authorized the giving to you the number of shooting days that you requested and I am sure that you will be the first to admit that I gave you every actor that you asked for regardless of whether it was a bit or an important role.

I know that in addition to being a director you are also an experienced executive and you know that I would not and I cannot shirk my responsibility in case *Clementine* does not turn out to be both the critics and box-office hit we all anticipated.

I didn't tell you the full truth last night when I gave you my reactions to the film. I did not sleep last night thinking about it and it has been on my mind all day. You have in the film a great number of outstanding individual episodes and sequences. You have a certain Western magnificence and a number of character touches that rival your best work, but to me the picture as a whole in its present state is a disappointment. It does not come up to our anticipations.

I know we can cut it down and make a number of adjustments and that these will probably represent a definite improvement but I sincerely believe that we face a major and radical cutting job. I also feel that perhaps there may be certain scenes that we will have to rewrite or in some way adjust. These are in the minority however.

My main concern lies with the construction of the continuity. I think certain elements have been already eliminated that were absolutely essential if we are going to put on the screen *all* of the story we started to tell. There are many inconsistencies that you would not personally accept in a finished picture of this calibre and quality.

Please believe me, Jack, that I do not for a moment ignore all the many moments of fine drama, characterization and simplicity that you have in this film but it is my honest conviction that these things are not enough if the picture does not live up to my own personal anticipation, it will not live up to the anticipation of a paid audience. Many of my recommendations in the Editorial handling of the film are radical. I believe we have sufficient film and that you have provided ample protection to make 95 percent of the changes possible, but there are so many things I do not understand about the continuity and development of it and so many contradictions in action that I am prompted to write this letter.

I recommend that you have a talk with Sam [Engel] and that *you* suggest that I be given the film to edit. You trusted me implicitly on *Grapes of Wrath* and *How Green Was My Valley*. You did not see either picture until they were playing in the theatres and innumerable times you went out of your way to tell me how much you appreciated the Editorial work. We won Academy Awards with both pictures and I

The original Rin Tin Tin and fledgling screenwriter Darryl F. Zanuck reviewing a scene in Zanuck's first script for Warner Bros., Find Your Man, on location in Oregon in 1924.

USC DEPARTMENT OF SPECIAL COLLECTIONS

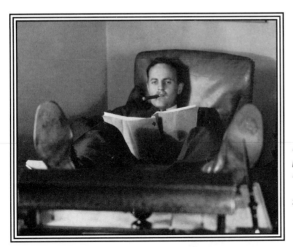

The young mogul: Chief Executive in charge of all productions at Warner Bros.—under Jack L. Warner. Circa 1930–31.

ZANUCK FAMILY

This logo directly preceding a Main Title began to appear shortly after the merger of Twentieth Century Pictures and Fox Film Corporation in 1935. Trademark of Twentieth Century Fox.

THE ACADEMY OF MOTION PICTURE ARTS AND SCIENCES

Shirley Temple, Zanuck, and his daughter Darrylin in 1935. Shirley is in costume for The Littlest Rebel.
THE MUSEUM OF MODERN ART/FILM STILLS ARCHIVE

Family birthday celebration at the Zanuck residence on Hillcrest Road in Beverly Hills. Left to right: Susan, Virginia (Mrs. Zanuck), Richard, and Darrylin. December 1935.
ZANUCK FAMILY

Shooting the climactic fire on Fox's back-lot lake in 1937 for In Old Chicago. THE ACADEMY OF MOTION PICTURE ARTS AND SCIENCES

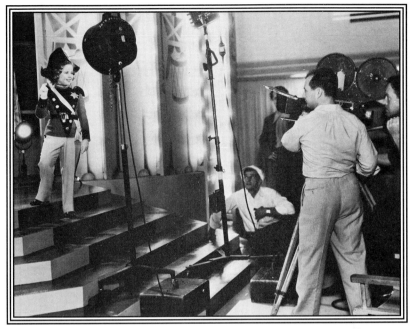

Shirley Temple filming the "Toy Trumpet" number for Rebecca of Sunnybrook Farm *in late 1937.* THE ACADEMY OF MOTION PICTURE ARTS AND SCIENCES

Fox star Alice Faye and Zanuck at the Biltmore Bowl in the Biltmore Hotel, Los Angeles, for the Academy Awards Presentation, February 1939.
THE ACADEMY OF MOTION PICTURE ARTS AND SCIENCES

Zanuck with Fox stars Loretta Young and Don Ameche during the making of *The Story of Alexander Graham Bell* in 1939. BISON ARCHIVES

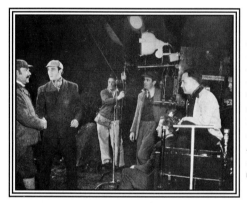

Filming The Hound of the Baskervilles *in early 1939 on a Fox soundstage set representing Dartmoor in Devonshire, England. Nigel Bruce and Basil Rathbone play Dr. Watson and Sherlock Holmes for the first time. Director Sidney Lanfield (with hat) and cinematographer Peverell Marley (with light-colored sweater) next to camera.* THE ACADEMY OF MOTION PICTURE ARTS AND SCIENCES

A set on the back lot for The Grapes of Wrath *(1940): Director John Ford (left) talks with visitor Tyrone Power, Fox's biggest star at the time, while Henry Fonda, the star of* Grapes, *listens. Above are "Joad family" cast members Russell Simpson (left) and Frank Darien.* THE ACADEMY OF MOTION PICTURE ARTS AND SCIENCES

Left to right: William Goetz, Zanuck's executive assistant; D.F.Z.; and Lew Schreiber, casting director (and later Zanuck's executive assistant), on the Fox lot, circa 1939. BISON ARCHIVES

Tyrone Power being coached by fencing master/duel choreographer Fred Cavens on a set for The Mark of Zorro (1940).
THE ACADEMY OF MOTION PICTURE ARTS AND SCIENCES

D.F.Z. dictating to secretary-in-chief Bess Bearman in Zanuck's Trophy Room, next to his office proper, in early 1941. RUDY BEHLMER COLLECTION

Contract player Anne Baxter, famed French director Jean Renoir, and contract player Dana Andrews during the filming of Renoir's first American film—and his only one for Fox— Swamp Water (1941). THE ACADEMY OF MOTION PICTURE ARTS AND SCIENCES

No, ice-skating champion Sonja Henie did not play drums in Glenn Miller's phenomenally successful orchestra, but the two did star in Sun Valley Serenade, a well-received Fox musical of 1941. Publicity photo.

THE ACADEMY OF MOTION PICTURE ARTS AND SCIENCES

Polo was one of Zanuck's
favorite participatory sports in
the 1930s. ZANUCK FAMILY

Another was skiing—which
extended far beyond the 1930s.
Zanuck's wife, Virginia, almost
always went to Sun Valley,
Idaho, with him.
ZANUCK FAMILY

Fox star Carmen Miranda rehearses the "Chica, Chica, Boom Chic" number for That Night in Rio *(1941) with dance director Hermes Pan.*
THE ACADEMY OF MOTION PICTURE ARTS AND SCIENCES

For How Green Was My Valley *(1941), a Welsh coal-mining village set was built at the Fox ranch in Malibu Canyon (now Malibu State Park). Note the camera and crew on top of the high platform at far right.* THE ACADEMY OF MOTION PICTURE ARTS AND SCIENCES

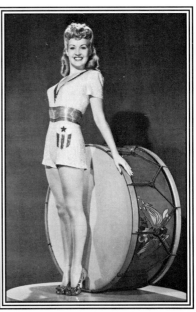

Betty Grable, Fox's most popular star all during the 1940s, in a publicity shot for Footlight Serenade *(1942).*
THE ACADEMY OF MOTION PICURE ARTS AND SCIENCES

recall your telling me that in your opinion the cutting job on *Valley*, which was a difficult subject, was the best job you had ever seen.

You will recall on both jobs I made a number of radical changes. You provided me with ample film to work with as you have done in the case of *Clementine*. As was the case then I believe that my present perspective on the film is better than either Sam's or yours. I have been practically away from it for three months. I am not going to lose any of the things that appeal to you because past performances have proven that the things that appeal to you also appeal to me.

It is my opinion that in this picture we have to be *big time* all the way. We cannot be big time only in certain outstanding episodes. The critics and the public alike have been fed up with an avalanche of Western and outdoor films. They know every gag and every cliché. The moment we let our guard down for an instant they will smack us right on the button. Anything that appears even slightly obvious or formula will look ten times as bad in this type of film. If we permit inconsistencies in continuity or characterization to exist we are going to be crossed up just as sure as I am writing this letter. Certain things that we could excuse or disregard in the average quality picture will never be accepted in this background and with the type of characters we are dealing.

Please give this your consideration and talk it over with Sam if you like. If I have sounded too pessimistic in this note I have not intended to, but sincerely I am worried. We have a tremendous investment on our hands and without taking anything away from you or Sam or Dorothy [Spencer, film editor] I believe that my perspective is such that I can benefit the whole project.

Best always,
Darryl

≡

Zanuck did modify the film in the editing room, and there was a bit of material added and/or reshot. It is difficult to ascertain Ford's true reaction to all of this. Writer Winston Miller in 1982 was quoted by Robert Lyons as saying that "Ford was very unhappy about it. He felt it was no longer his picture."

≡

TO: Mr. Lloyd Bacon [director]   DATE: July 13, 1946
    SUBJECT: MY DARLING CLEMENTINE

Dear Lloyd:

  I thought the rushes that you did for *My Darling Clementine* were excellent, particularly the scene at the grave. This should be a very effective scene.

                                                                D.F.Z.

CC: Mr. Sam Engel

≡

TO: Mr. Samuel Engel   DATE: Sept. 4, 1946
    SUBJECT: MY DARLING CLEMENTINE

Dear Sam:

  Insomuch as I am flying East in the morning I thought you should have this note in case you wish to show it to Jack Ford and Henry Fonda.

  I like the ending of *My Darling Clementine* exactly as it is. It is completely satisfactory to me from every standpoint. Unfortunately 2,000 people who saw the picture at a preview did not agree. You were present at the preview and you know what happened and you have read the preview cards.

  I would like to ridicule the mental attitude of the audience at this preview but you must remember that this is the same audience which applauded the quality of the picture in its earlier sequences. . . .

  Therefore it is difficult for me to ignore their request for a more satisfying or satisfactory conclusion to the film. Furthermore, let us be frank. This audience accepted and tremendously enjoyed every moment of the picture but they laughed *at us* at the finish.

  You will recall that the last scene was perfect up to where Fonda reaches out to shake hands with Cathy Downs [Clementine]. It was such an obvious buildup for a kiss or for some demonstration of affection that the audience felt first amused and then completely cheated. . . .

I do feel that it will be honest, legitimate and reasonable if Henry looks at the girl, smiles, leans over and kisses her on the cheek. It is a good-bye kiss and nothing more. He *does* like her. The audience *knows* he likes her. Now is no time for us to get smart.

Believe me we need the picture in New York. I detest going back for this scene as much as anybody. But I actually think that it is absolutely essential that we avoid spoiling the last moment of an outstanding picture and we certainly spoiled it for the audience that saw it at the preview.

D. F. Z.

=

The kiss was filmed and used. My Darling Clementine *was critically well received but because of its high cost was not a big money-maker.*

=

April 2, 1946
Mr. Joseph I. Breen [director, Motion Picture Code Administration]
Motion Picture Assoc.
5504 Hollywood Blvd.
Hollywood, California

My dear Joe:

You know I do not want to make trouble for you. You have a very difficult job and I believe I appreciate it more than most producers.

However, when an ad like this [for Howard Hughes's *The Outlaw*] appears in the paper after the conference we had the other day, I have a hell of a job keeping my boys in line. The whole campaign on this picture [starring Jane Russell] is a disgrace to the industry and I am on the verge of publicly attacking Howard Hughes with a blast in the newspapers. Before I do so I would like your opinion as I do not want to do anything that would adversely affect you or your organization.

I am also furious with [producer Walter] Wanger. I believe he has deliberately capitalized on the censorship trouble with [his production] *Scarlet Street* [advertising art and text] and while I don't blame him at all for making money, I think it is bad money and that in the final run he will have to pay for it; however, my main fury is at *The Outlaw* advertisements.

The major companies make many mistakes but I have never seen any major company resort to such cheap vulgarity as this.

Best always,
(SGD) Darryl

≡

The Outlaw*'s ad campaign featured a very busty Jane Russell wearing a bra (personally designed by Howard Hughes) under a blouse in blatantly exploitative sex-object poses accompanied by such copy as "Two good reasons why people should see* The Outlaw.*"*

Scarlet Street*'s artwork depicted a femme fatale (Joan Bennett) standing under a streetlamp in a lurid pose with accompanying suggestive copy.*

≡

TO: Producers, Directors, Executives   DATE: June 13, 1946
CONFIDENTIAL

I have just examined a very recent survey made on our present pictures relative to the rising cost of production. It was the most alarming report I have read at any time in the twenty years I have been producing pictures.

The cost of the construction of sets, the cost of labor, and the cost of the operating crew on the shooting company has increased to a point where it is simply staggering. . . .

We know there are certain limitations on grosses. As an example, we know that *Diamond Horseshoe* [1945], which was a hit in every theatre in the world and ran up a gross of more than $3,150,000 domestically, will still wind up breaking even or making a very insignificant profit due to the fact that it cost in excess of $2,600,000. Here we have an example of a tremendously successful picture struggling to make even a minor profit. . . .

In analyzing the report and studying the rising cost, I have come to a very firm conclusion. The responsibility of each individual film must become more than ever before the responsibility of the individual producer. Our survey shows that if we *originally* plan a film production with an eye toward economy, we usually end up by coming somewhere near the budget price. But if we go ahead on an elaborate production setup and then try to make cuts *after* the script has been written and the budget has been made, we never succeed in actually cutting anything substantial.

It is difficult to explain the numerous reasons that result in this deduction and conclusion. Nevertheless, the record substantiates the fact that unless we *start* a production on paper in the right direction you will never achieve economy by last-minute eliminations or last-minute rewrites. It just doesn't work that way.

Therefore it is the *original* design of the production that we must henceforth examine with great caution and care. Generally speaking, writers are not cost-conscious nor do they understand the actual meaning of production economy. I do not blame them in the least. It is the producer's job to guide them in these matters. The average writer writes the script as he sees it and the number of sets he uses probably never occurs to him. I believe that there are very few writers and regrettably very few producers who study the dramatization of a script from the standpoint of production economies. Yet herein lies our greatest danger. . . .

We do not want to cheat on the quality of our pictures. We have no desire to spoil our merchandise. . . .

Margie, recently completed by Henry King and [producer] Walter Morosco in Technicolor, is a production triumph. From the very beginning the picture was conceived toward certain economic specifications and the drama was built to fit these specifications. No last-minute frantic changes were necessary nor wild cuts made. The picture contained 15 sets and the picture is the only picture this year that has come in under the budget. If you examine what made this possible, even with a director who takes the care that Henry King takes, you will realize that it was made possible by the original design of the production. . . .

When we select stories like *The Razor's Edge, Forever Amber* or *Captain from Castile* we know from the beginning that we are faced with a difficult and costly production problem and the cost is no great surprise to us. I do not particularly speak of these pictures. We go into them with our eyes wide open. We know we are up against it. I speak mainly of our other top "A" pictures, not the super-specials, but our other important pictures and particularly of our musical productions. . . .

State Fair is another good example of sensible production. We conveyed the impression of a big festival but we did not extravagantly waste money. The action was condensed into a few sets. The story was dramatized to take advantage of these sets. It could have been spread all over the place. . . .

Today we have hit pictures that are not showing a profit and therein lies our greatest danger. If a hit picture costs more than it can earn, then we have come to a point where the danger line is not far away. . . .

D.F.Z.

≡

DATE: June 24, 1946

TO: Messrs. Fred Kohlmar [producer] and Philip Dunne [writer]
  SUBJECT: THE GHOST AND MRS. MUIR

Dear Freddy and Phil:

I am delighted with the script on *The Ghost and Mrs. Muir.* . . .

The script is beautifully written throughout, and my recommendations are mainly minor. . . .

Now we come to the illusion itself [of the ghost] and how to technically treat it. . . . You will probably recall that in *Sentimental Journey* [1946] we treated the vision without any technical tricks whatever. It never dissolved in or dissolved out. The little girl would hear the voice, look up, and [the] Maureen O'Hara [character] would be there. We finished in the same way, without the trick of dissolves or without any camera manipulations. As proof that audiences accept this, the picture is doing far more than we ever anticipated. . . .

Somehow or other, when you use trick devices or dissolves, the realism seems to vanish. The audience starts to wonder about the technical trick and they forget the emotions of the moment. This should not be difficult to accomplish in a script, because only the entrances and exits are involved. . . .

Someone has suggested both [ex-M-G-M star] Norma Shearer and [free-lance star] Claudette Colbert for the role of Lucy [Mrs. Muir]. Many people, including Spyros Skouras, believe that Norma Shearer has one great picture left in her yet, and that she would make the same comeback that Joan Crawford made last year [in *Mildred Pierce*, Warners]. She is certainly no deader than Joan was. . . .

Have you heard anything further from [free-lance star] Olivia de Havilland or Katie Hepburn? Richard Haydn, of course, is perfect for Coombe, and after the triumph that Rex Harrison scored in New York last week with *Anna and the King of Siam*, I think in him we have one of the biggest names in the business today. It is going to be very difficult to keep him from winning next year's Academy Award. . . .

D. F. Z.

===

Gene Tierney played Mrs. Muir; Rex Harrison played "The Ghost"; Robert Coote was Coombe. Only one "dissolve out" of the ghost was used—far into the film, after he speaks to Mrs. Muir as she sleeps, asking her to believe that he has existed only in her dreams. All other entrances and exits were handled without any effects. The script was based on the novel by R. A. Dick (Josephine A. C. Leslie).

===

September 20, 1946
Mr. David O. Selznick
The Ritz-Carlton
Atlantic City, New Jersey

My dear David:

. . . I cannot contemplate surrendering our next Jennifer Jones commitment to Metro, mainly because I believe that we possess equal or better story material than any other major studio at the present time. I do not intend to be at all modest on this claim. . . .

[Director Anatole] Litvak and his writers have come up with a wonderful slant on *The Snake Pit*. They have devised an angle which develops the strange romance between the girl, the doctor and the husband and goes a long way toward solving the obvious problems of this spectacular novel. Next to *Forever Amber* I believe that more women are reading *The Snake Pit* than have read any other book this year. . . .

You speak of wanting Jennifer to do another picture with Henry King. No one would be happier about this than I. I work closer with Henry than any other director in the business and no one holds any higher respect. You also speak of [Louis] Buddy Lighton. I brought Buddy back and there is no question but what he is one of the most capable producers in the industry today. I have complete confidence in him and I know you share my views.

I cannot, however, guarantee to deliver either Buddy or Henry on any specific story because that is not the way we operate this studio. If, as an example, [Robert] Bassler or [Fred] Kohlmar or [William] Perlberg or [Gene] Markey or any of our producers have developed a story and worked on it for many months and if that story has been assigned to [Ernst] Lubitsch or [John] Stahl or [Lloyd] Bacon, [Fritz] Lang, [Otto] Preminger, [Joseph L.] Mankiewicz, [Henry] Hathaway or [Anatole] Litvak, I know you will agree that I could not under any circumstances jerk them off of it to accommodate an individual situation. . . .

The point I am trying to establish is that once both Jennifer and you are satisfied with a story that I have submitted, you should trust me to personally protect the proposition from there on. Nothing would give me greater pride and satisfaction than to make the best picture of the year with Jennifer. I have reason to be very proud of our organization but I have long ago found out that I can only function effectively when I have *full* responsibility. . . .

I am looking forward to your return so that we can sit down and thoroughly discuss the material. I regret that Jennifer was not available for *Captain from Castile* [1947] as the role in the final version of the script has turned out superb. . . .

Henry King is directing and I am personally supervising the picture with Lamar Trotti as my associate. It is a $4,300,000 subject and will probably be one of the great productions of next year. I still have not cast the role of Catana and if there is any change in your plans please telephone me at once. King is now in Mexico and because of our Technicolor camera commitments we start shooting November 25th. But I could probably arrange the schedule to keep away from Catana for one or two weeks. . . .

Best always,
s/Darryl

≡

Newcomer Jean Peters was cast as Catana.

≡

TO: Fred Kohlmar [producer],   DATE: October 30, 1946
   Julian Johnson [story editor], Ray Klune [production manager],
   Henry Hathaway [director]

Dear Freddy:

I am very excited about the whole situation on the *Stool Pigeon* [*Kiss of Death*] story. This is an absolute natural. I hope Hathaway is as excited about it as we are. It is really a combination of the best parts of *Public Enemy* [Warners, 1931] and *I Am a Fugitive from a Chain Gang* [Warners, 1932], and if we tell it with the realistic technique of *The House on 92nd Street, 13 Rue Madeleine* and *Boomerang* it will be one of the best pictures of the year.

The idea of bringing the author, Lawrence Blaine, out here to work with the writers is wonderful as he was the Assistant District Attorney in New York City and will know all of the technique.

If we do not get [free-lance writer] Ben Hecht then we must get someone as good for the dialogue. This is the kind of script that can be written in six weeks at the outside, and Hecht would probably do it in three. . . .

I know this is bad weather usually in New York at this time, but we have a great many interiors that we can shoot there, and bad weather does not hurt in a realistic show like this.

I would want to use [cinematographer Norbert] Brodine and the camera crew that have done our other [semi] documentaries. They will be available and they know all of the tricks, and Klune can give you the same production staff.

The idea of Victor Mature for the leading role of Nick Bianco is a sensational idea. He has made a big personal hit for his performance in *My Darling Clementine*. He is the typical Italian type of hold-up man, and the fact that he is younger than Nick in the story is all on the good side of the ledger. It is the same thing that we have in *Boomerang* when we reduced the age of the State's Attorney and had Dana Andrews play it. This will be a great thing for Mature, and for once he fits the part perfectly.

I see someone like [free-lance star] Edward G. Robinson for Louis D'Angelo, the Assistant District Attorney. Robinson is great when he is cast right and this is a perfect role for him. . . .

We must strive to maintain the simplicity and honesty of the original. The people are very real and the very fact that the author based all of his situations on personal experience is the thing that we want to preserve. You feel it in the story.

The title is poor. Personally I like the title *Blind Date*. I know at first it sounds perhaps like an adolescent title, but this man certainly goes to a blind date with his destiny, and he keeps a blind date with fate. It is a great box-office title, and we own it. Let us call it this temporarily. . . .

D.F.Z.

≡

Kiss of Death (1947) was the title of the released film. Victor Mature was cast as Nick, Brian Donlevy played Louis D'Angelo, and Richard Widmark made a spectacular film debut as a psychopathic killer who extracts vengeance on an informer (Mature). Ben Hecht and Charles Lederer collaborated on the screenplay with a revised third act written by Philip Dunne (uncredited) after the film was shot and edited. The official credits read "Based on a story by Eleazar Lipsky"—Lawrence Blaine was a pseudonym Lipsky used on the submitted manuscript. Lipsky did spend several weeks at the studio as an adviser and consultant.

≡

NOVEMBER 5, 1946

TO: ELIA KAZAN, CARE 20TH CENTURY FOX UNIT, ROGER SMITH HOTEL, STAMFORD, CONNECTICUT

I GOT CAUGHT UP WITH THE LATEST RUSHES LAST NIGHT AND AGAIN THEY WERE UNIFORMLY EXCELLENT. I WANT YOU TO KNOW I AM FULLY AWARE OF ALL THE HARD WORK YOU HAVE DONE ON "BOOMERANG." YOU HAVE PERFORMED LIKE AN EFFICIENT VETERAN DISREGARDING NEITHER QUALITY NOR ECONOMY AND I AM REALLY GRATEFUL. I HAVE SEVERAL NEW STORIES COMING ALONG AND IF YOU COULD TELL ME APPROXIMATELY WHEN YOU WANT TO MAKE YOUR NEXT PICTURE UNDER YOUR CONTRACT IT MIGHT BE HELPFUL AS I COULD PUT SOMETHING ASIDE FOR YOU.

REGARDS,

DARRYL

≡

Boomerang! *was New York stage director Elia Kazan's third feature film (his second for Fox). The entire picture was shot in Stamford, Connecticut—interiors and exteriors—using a blend of actors and local citizens. It was based on a true story related in a* Reader's Digest *article by Anthony Abbot (Fulton Oursler) called "The Perfect Case."*

≡

DECEMBER 2, 1946

TO: ELIA KAZAN

167 EAST 74 ST., NEW YORK, N.Y.

DEAR KAZAN:

I DID NOT WIRE YOU WHEN I FIRST SAW [THE EDITED] "BOOMERANG" BECAUSE I WAS FRANKLY DISAPPOINTED WITH THE STORY AND CONTINUITY. THE DIRECTION AND ACTING WERE ABSOLUTELY SUPERB BUT THE STORY LINE LACKED ANY SUSPENSE OR SUSTAINED CONFLICT. I WORKED ON IT AGAIN THE FOLLOWING NIGHT AND DISCOVERED THE ROOT OF OUR TROUBLE AND IT IS EASILY RECTIFIED. BY PLANTING "CROSSMAN" [PHILIP COOLIDGE]

DEFINITELY AS THE MURDERER IN THE FIRST REEL WE ELIMINATE ALL SUSPENSE AND OUR SYMPATHIES ARE AGAINST DANA [ANDREWS] AND THE POLICE BECAUSE THEY APPEAR STUPID AND LESS OBSERVANT THAN THE AUDIENCE. BY REVISING THE EARLY CONTINUITY AND MAKING SOME DEFT ELIMINATIONS, THE TRANSFORMATION IS REALLY ASTOUNDING AND THE AUDIENCE HAS A CHANCE TO ENJOY THE DEVELOPMENTS AS THEY OCCUR AND THEY ARE FINDING OUT THINGS AT THE SAME TIME THE CHARACTERS ARE FINDING THEM OUT. EVERYONE HERE SYMPATHETIC WITH CHANGES AND I WILL WIRE YOU AFTER WE HAVE LOOKED AT THE NEXT CUT.

REGARDS,
DARRYL

≡

Boomerang! was a big success in every respect.

≡

November 5, 1946
"NIGHTMARE ALLEY" CONFERENCE ON OUTLINE OF NOVEMBER 1, 1946 (with Messrs. [George] JESSEL [producer], [Jules] FURTHMAN [writer], MOLLY MANDAVILLE [script consultant]).

It is my belief that in every story there has to be a rooting interest. You have to have one person whom the audience sympathizes with; one person whom they want to triumph at the end of the story. This is utterly essential; there is no way to avoid it. Your sympathetic character does not necessarily have to be your central or pivotal character. It is better for the story if it is your central character, but if the story is such that this cannot be, then it must be one of the other characters.

I believe that in *Nightmare Alley* our only chance to obtain this element is in the character of Molly [Fox contract player Coleen Gray]. I believe she has to be young, fresh, warm and completely sympathetic. The story itself provides opportunity for her to be this way; she is the one who is appalled at the thought of Stanton [Tyrone Power] tampering with religion, pretending to be a minister. "You can't do it!" she protests. "After all, there *is* a God! Where is this going to lead you?"

From the start we want to get out of the story any suggestion that she is a slut. She is a young girl who has been drawn into this life. Later, when we see her with her husband and her baby, we will have the feeling that faith and goodness have triumphed, and have not been smothered in the mire.

This is very important—it is a *must* for our story.

Without compromising any further in the character of Stanton, there must be some way to get a certain amount of sympathy for him. It should be the kind of sympathy the audience felt for James Cagney in *Public Enemy* [Warners, 1931]; or perhaps a better illustration would be the feeling the audience had for Lew Ayres at the end of *Doorway to Hell* [Warners, 1930], where he knew he was about to be killed. We should feel that there is a certain majesty in Stanton's decline. He reached for the moon—and he missed. In the writing of it Mr. Furthman can probably find a way to get over this feeling about Stanton, and at the same time not to lose any of the characterization which makes him the kind of man he is in the story. . . .

≡

January 29, 1947
"NIGHTMARE ALLEY" CONFERENCE ON FIRST DRAFT CONTINUITY OF DECEMBER 31, 1946 (with Messrs. Jessel, Furthman, William Gresham [author of the novel], Molly Mandaville)

Generally speaking I like the first two thirds of this. . . .

Stan: While we want to keep him a man who has this insatiable appetite for money and success, there must be a point where we feel sympathy for him. Otherwise it becomes a story of frustration and there is no audience for that. Nobody is all good or all bad, and there must be a shading in Stan's character so that once or twice in the script we see him do a decent thing.

This is an unconventional story, but it must be told in terms that will make it a popular story. It can't be a popular picture if it becomes the story of the decline and frustration of a louse. It can only be popular if it is the story of a man who has some good traits, however deep they may be buried beneath his evil traits; a man who, if he had applied himself with the same zeal could have amounted to something worthwhile. And it must be a love story between Stan and Molly. . . .

≡

DATE: February 10, 1947

TO: George Jessel, Jules Furthman, Lloyd Bacon [director], Molly Mandaville

SUBJECT: NIGHTMARE ALLEY

So that we do not have too long a conference tomorrow, I want to give you my main points of criticism on the new [February 8, 1947] script of *Nightmare Alley*. . . .

We have *almost* succeeded in making Stan a sympathetic character despite all of his evil. Now this is exactly what we intended to do and it at last gives us a rooting interest in the story.

A man sins and a man is punished, and in the degradation of his punishment you feel genuine compassion for him.

I want to give him one more good trait among all of his bad ones. He should be much more deeply affected by Pete's [Ian Keith's] death. We should know right at the moment it has shaken him and he feels terribly guilty despite the fact it was an accident.

We can demonstrate this attitude by showing that Stan cannot have anything more to do on an intimate basis with Zeena [free-lance player Joan Blondell]. In other words he does not sleep with her again. He cannot. He can work with her and do everything else, but to touch her brings up the vision of Pete—thus he goes for Molly.

The script tells us now that of course in the first place he didn't want to marry Molly, and this is correct, but we want to go a step further. He learns to *love* Molly. This is the first time in his life he has loved anyone, and he can't get over it.

From the moment he discovers he really loves Molly, he does not change any of his evil pursuits, but he does remain true to her. . . .

In *Public Enemy* I gave Cagney one redeeming trait. He was a no-good bastard but he loved his mother and somehow or other you felt a certain affection and rooting interest for him even though he was despicable. . . .

D.F.Z.

≡

Despite Zanuck's care, a first-rate production, and excellent reviews, audiences stayed away from what they sensed, heard, or read was unpleasant subject matter. Edmund Goulding, not Lloyd Bacon, directed.

≡

TO: William Perlberg [producer]   DATE: November 6, 1946
CC: George Seaton [writer-director]
   SUBJECT: THE BIG HEART (*My Heart Tells Me*) [*Miracle on 34th Street*]—(First draft continuity 11-2-46)

Dear Bill:

I read with great pleasure the first ninety-seven pages on *My Heart Tells Me*. . . .

It is excellent, fresh, exciting, and delightful.

I definitely want to use John Payne for Fred. [Contract player] Mark Stevens does not fit the part at all and in any event it is essential that we have a box-office name with [Maureen] O'Hara, as the only conceivable excuse we have for making the picture from a box-office standpoint is the combination of O'Hara and Payne who have already established themselves. . . .

I will not tell you about the many things I like but will get to the points that actually disturb me.

I feel Doris [O'Hara] is overdrawn. I feel that she is so cold, cut and dried, that an audience will have a difficult time forgiving her. Perhaps if there were a way to bring out quicker the hurt in her background and past life we might be able to understand her.

It was impossible for me to believe that any mother could be as heartless as she appeared to be. Now maybe it is only a question of toning down her dialogue or letting her chide Susan [Natalie Wood] in a lighter manner. . . .

Any man who ever heard [a mother] give her child the kind of advice that Doris does would start running in the other direction. Furthermore I do not believe the characterization is either plausible or true to life. . . .

There must be somewhere in Doris a likable spark or a trace of something that will make an audience interested in her. . . . You get the feeling that she is a bit of a fanatic on the subject of Santa Claus when actually she is merely a modern woman who doesn't believe in feeding a child a lot of silly, antiquated fairy stories.

I also think that if you make her a little more normal Fred [Payne] will automatically be more understandable. . . .

I have one other criticism. I believe we go too far with the montage satire dealing with the exploitation of [sending Macy's customers to Gimbel's and vice versa]. . . . I believe that we run the risk, for the sake of a few laughs, of jeopardizing the sincerity and honesty of the balance of the story. The very fact that you show the merchants urging courtesies is enough and very amusing but when you go into radio, moving pictures, etc. etc., then I know this has not occurred and I begin to face everything from then on with my tongue in my cheek.

This story to me is very honest and believable and with the exception of the two above points I like it immensely. I *want* to believe the story. Don't do anything that will make me lose faith in it or imagine it is a satire. . . .

I am crazy about the title *The Big Heart*.

If we can clear it, it is a natural. It is the kind of title like *Sentimental Journey* [Fox, 1946] that made such a hit previously with these two people.

D.F.Z.

≡

For unknown reasons, the title was changed to Miracle on 34th Street *in the subsequent drafts of the script. Zanuck's other points were observed.*

≡

March 22, 1948
Mr. Valentine Davies [writer]
916 Thayer
West Los Angeles, Calif.

Dear Val:

Congratulations on winning the Oscar [for best original story]. There is no question but what your story was the best original story of the year. I would have been really outraged if you hadn't received it.

Best always,
Darryl

≡

Miracle on 34th Street also won Oscars for best screenplay (George Seaton) and best supporting actor (Edmund Gwenn—who played "Kris Kringle" or more accurately, "Santa Claus"). The charming film became a popular holiday perennial.

≡

DATE: January 15, 1947
TO: Lew Schreiber [executive assistant to Zanuck]
   SUBJECT: CALL NORTHSIDE 777

We are preparing to obtain the rights to a true story which was written up in the December issue of *Reader's Digest*, 1946 and also in *Time* magazine August 27, 1945. The title of the *Reader's Digest* article was "Tillie Scrubbed On."

We will have to buy permission from the mother, the son and other members of Mrs. Majczek's family in Chicago. We will also in all probability have to buy clearances from the reporter on the Chicago

Daily Times named James McGuire. All of these people will be portrayed in the picture. . . .

Our lawyers will have to determine this. . . .

≡

The true story involved a reporter (free-lance star James Stewart) helping a scrubwoman in an office building prove her son (Fox contract player Richard Conte) not guilty of murdering a policeman.

≡

TO: Messrs. Otto Lang [producer]   DATE: March 5, 1947
Quentin Reynolds [writer]
Leonard Hoffman [writer]
SUBJECT: CALL NORTHSIDE 777

. . . I recognize that it has been rapidly written and that it is only a first draft. I do not like it. . . .

The story lacks any genuine semblance of dramatization. While it is our intention to tell a hard-hitting, factual, semidocumentary story like *The House on 92nd Street*, *13 Rue Madeleine* and *Boomerang*, we cannot ignore drama any more than these films ignored drama.

If we do not have a vital personal story and characters whom we understand and appreciate, then our film becomes as impersonal as a "March of Time." And it loses the very elements that made the aforementioned films tremendously popular. . . .

Almost like a cold, stenographic report, we tell the facts which we want the audience to know in each separate episode, but we fail to take advantage of the opportunities to dramatize these facts.

There are exceptions to the above, of course, but almost all of our episodes have a vague beginning and no climax whatsoever. We seem to suddenly stop and jump to the next episode. There is no curtain or dramatic high point and very rarely is there a blend into the following sequence.

I do not want to be overly critical, but I know that you want me to give you my frank analyzation of the problem. If I am right, then it is better that we find out now, rather than after we have invested a million and a half dollars or whatever the picture will cost. . . .

I think it would be worthwhile for you to read the scripts of *Kiss of Death* or *Nightmare Alley*, particularly in regard to the dialogue and the careful, thought-out dramatization of each specific episode. In these two scripts, the characters come to life. Without reading the characters' names, you instinctively know who is talking and you can visualize the movement and drama in each scene. In our script, I get the impression that this is a recital, a lecture, more than a drama. . . .

When Louis de Rochemont originally came to me [in 1944] with the idea of telling a story [eventually *The House on 92nd Street*] in the "March of Time" vein, I vetoed it. And, from this veto, we devised the plan of combining "The March of Time" factual technique with factual dramatization. We followed through the same plan in casting. The bits are all played by nonactors, but the featured roles are played by qualified performers. Thus, you have a blending of fact and drama. I cite this in an effort to indicate that the formula is vital if this film is to be as successful as the others.

It is not enough just to tell an interesting story. Half the battle depends on *how* you tell the story. As a matter of fact, the most important half depends on how you tell the story. . . .

D. F. Z.

≡

March 19, 1947
Mr. Quentin Reynolds
The Bel Air Hotel
701 Stone Canyon
Bel Air
Los Angeles, California

Dear Quentin:

By all means you can rest assured I will read the last half of the script [of *Call Northside 777*] with both care and interest. To be perfectly frank, there is nothing terribly wrong about the script as it stands now. If *Boomerang* were not such a highly successful and respected film, I probably would do some additional work on our present script and put it into production. . . .

Unless we top *Boomerang* by a very wide margin, we are going to take a severe beating.

We face a very stiff challenge, and it is most difficult, as you well know, to apologize later on to an audience. They just won't listen. I happen to have personally originated the so-called de Rochemont touch. It came out of my noodle and no one else's, and therefore I consider myself to be personally on a spot in this venture. I feel I must not let anything go unnoticed or unrepaired until I am positive I have a tight, well-knit dramatized version of this story. You have marshaled the facts very well and you have stated the case and presented the basic continuity line. From here on we must carry the ball to the next step.

Best always,
s/Darryl

≡

Jerome Cady and Jay Dratler were assigned; Leonard Hoffman and Quentin Reynolds were given adaptation credit. The picture did quite well, and was James Stewart's first post–World War II hit, following two commercial disappointments.

≡

TO: Lyman Munson [executive]   DATE: February 25, 1947

Dear Lyman:

Your analyzation of story costs and shifting of writers from one assignment to another is accurate and correct. However this is a peculiar business, and while I admit the practice is theoretically wrong, there have to be exceptions.

If there were enough good writers we would never shift them, or at least very rarely shift them. As a matter of fact there must even be exceptions to this rule. As an example, a writer has completed a script. It is not scheduled for immediate production. He is an excellent writer and has done a fine job. He is given a new assignment. He is halfway through the new assignment and then the first story is put on the production schedule. The director wants certain changes. They are not extensive changes, but they are changes. We are faced with a problem. If we bring in an entirely new writer to rewrite what is already a script that is eighty-five percent good the original writer gets sore as hell because he has to take a split credit, and usually the second writer rewrites much more than the director wants because he wants to be sure he gets a credit.

In a case like this it is obviously better to stop work on the second story and let the writer go back for revisions. . . .

We should avoid the practice wherever we can, but I don't see how we can eliminate it.

D.F.Z.

$=$

TO: Messrs. Robert Bassler [producer],   DATE: July 5, 1947
Anatole Litvak [director], Millen Brand, Frank Partos, Arthur Laurents [writers]
SUBJECT: THE SNAKE PIT

. . . It goes without saying that the commercial potentialities are highly questionable, in spite of the fact that it is based on a best-selling novel [by Mary Jane Ward] and has a star in the leading role [free-lance star Olivia de Havilland]. However, I have long ago crossed that bridge in connection with this subject. . . .

The silent scenes over which we use narration should be condensed and the action concentrated with footage only long enough to cover the length of the narration.

In making semidocumentary films, I have found that audiences will accept concentrated action in scenes over which there is narration. . . .

Again, my experience with semidocumentaries has taught me that the character who is going to *tell* the story should never start off by apologizing or advising the audience that he is going to tell "the whole story" . . .

D.F.Z.

===

The Snake Pit was a milestone film dealing with mental breakdowns and mental institutions. The picture was shot to a large degree at the studio with actors depicting a fictional composite of various people and situations experienced by the novelist, who had spent several months in a state mental hospital.

===

July 25, 1947
"SITTING PRETTY" CONFERENCE ON TREATMENT OF JULY 25, 1947 WITH MESSRS. [Samuel] ENGEL [producer], [F. Hugh] HERBERT [writer], MOLLY MANDAVILLE

Generally speaking, I like what you have done on this story. . . .

This story is very thin and tends to be highly repetitious because out of necessity we have to play practically the same scene over and over again. There is no big development once we play our ace card—introducing the sitter [Mr. Belvedere]. It is then a question of how amusing we can play our scenes and how long we can stretch out our ace card. Of necessity this must come very early in our story. And once it comes it is apt not to wear as well as it first appears to wear. You show one series of incidents about it, then show another series of incidents about it. No matter how funny each individual episode is, somewhere along the line the audience is going to want *something* to happen. . . .

We have a sensational character in Belvedere [Clifton Webb]—original, fresh, wonderful. This is a perfect setup, but the story of the husband and wife must be great, too. They must be interesting, honest and real, and funny in the manner of Claudia and David [the married couple in *Claudia* and *Claudia and David*—Fox, 1943 and 1946].

Let's not overdo the kids. Soft-pedal them wherever possible. Use the kids only as they affect Belvedere. . . .

Story suggestions:

When Belvedere arrives at the King home he does not say he is a writer. He merely tells them that he is a genius and must have eight hours sleep per day. He makes it very clear that he wants to take care of his own room, and would like to have the key to the room.

Try as they do, Harry and Tacey [M-G-M star Robert Young and Maureen O'Hara] can't find out what Belvedere does in the room. He makes no noise whatever. There is no sign of a typewriter (and we learn later that Belvedere wrote the entire book by hand). At first they are only mildly inquisitive then their curiosity grows and they determine to find out what goes on in that room. They sneak up the stairs, listen at the door. . . .

≡

The modest Sitting Pretty (*1948*), *which introduced the character of Mr. Belvedere, became the sleeper of the year, made a major Fox star of Clifton Webb, and inspired two sequels:* Mr. Belvedere Goes to College (*1949*) *and* Mr. Belvedere Rings the Bell (*1951*). *The original was based on* Squatter's Rights, *a comedy in three acts by Gwen Davenport, and her novel* Belvedere.

≡

TO: Mr. Jules Furthman [writer]   DATE: April 2, 1947

Dear Jules:

. . . If you have not seen *Leave Her to Heaven*, you should do so. As you know, it is an uncompromising character story of a vicious woman who murders for love. She is a woman with a possession complex. She even tries to come back from the grave to kill her own sister. The book was tremendously popular and, with the exception of *The Razor's Edge*, it is the most popular motion picture ever released by this company. It will gross more than eight million dollars worldwide.

The woman in *Leave Her to Heaven* deliberately kills her own unborn child, drowns the crippled brother of her husband and endeavors to send her adopted sister to the electric chair. And yet, despite all this, there are certain things about her that you rather like. . . .

D.F.Z.

≡

TO: Messrs. Sol Siegel [producer],   DATE: April 9, 1947
    Martin Berkeley [writer]
    SUBJECT: THE IRON CURTAIN
    CONFIDENTIAL

The Iron Curtain is a story to be written in the technique of *The House on 92nd Street*, dealing with the activities of secret foreign agents in the United States and Canada and the subversive activities of the Communists. . . .

In *The House on 92nd Street* we used parts of ten or twelve cases and we boiled them together into one specific case. I have no doubt but what our story, like *92nd Street*, will commence with the discovery of some tiny object or insignificant item which leads to the realization on the part of the FBI officials. . . .

Our personal story, as was the case on *The House on 92nd Street*, must be present but it must be held to a minimum. Of course our leading man must be placed in positions of jeopardy. . . . It must be remembered that in *92nd Street* the entire last three reels of the picture were completely fictional. No such event occurred as the capture of an FBI agent by the Nazi agents, although it was a fact that we did send an FBI agent to Hamburg where he enlisted in the Nazi spy school, graduated with honors, and was returned to the United States as a Nazi agent and operated in New York City. . . .

What we basically need from official Washington is the lowdown on three or four cases which the government, or the FBI, has already solved in America, or the lowdown on a case now existent which they are ready to break. From this we can design one major case from which the body of our story will evolve.

≡

The story used was based on the true account of Igor Gouzenko, a Russian code clerk. This was blended with other elements.

≡

TO: Sol Siegel   DATE: March 20, 1948
CC: William Wellman [director]
    Milton Krims [writer]
    SUBJECT: THE IRON CURTAIN—Letter from Spyros Skouras with
    magazine articles from *Pravda*

Dear Sol:

I am sending you a letter from Spyros together with translations from the official Russian magazine [*Pravda*] published in Moscow which has a section devoted to cinematography.

This contains the various attacks by the Soviets on *The Iron Curtain* and it certainly shows that they are petrified and frightened to death of the film and the fact that it will expose them to the world.

What disturbs me more than anything is the fact that the author of the article admits that he has read the script, and this is true because he definitely quotes certain scenes that were contained in the script. I wish there was some way we could have the FBI or somebody find out how they got the script and through what channels.

I agree with Spyros. We should be proud of this denouncement. . . . Some of the charges in the article will certainly amuse you.

If you read a little further, on the last page from this magazine you will note how scenarios are approved by the Russian government and how each scenario must come before the Ministry of Cinematography and be checked as to its political content. Can you imagine our having any such procedure in America? Can you imagine our being able to make pictures that were critical of America such as *Grapes of Wrath*, *The Best Years of Our Lives*, *Gentleman's Agreement* and hundreds of others? Can you imagine making a picture where the policeman or law enforcement officers were in the wrong? When I read this last part of the article it frightened me. . . .

                                                              D.F.Z.

≡

FEBRUARY 4, 1947

TO: ELIA KAZAN

  167 EAST 74 ST, NEW YORK, N.Y.

DEAR GADGE [KAZAN'S NICKNAME]:

WE HAVE DECIDED TO WAIT UNTIL YOU ARRIVE BEFORE [PLAYWRIGHT AND OCCASIONAL SCREENWRITER] MOSS [HART] ACTUALLY STARTS TO WORK AND WE WILL MEET AT THE STUDIO WEDNESDAY. MEANWHILE MOSS IS CAREFULLY STUDYING THE BOOK [*GENTLEMAN'S AGREEMENT* BY LAURA Z. HOBSON] AND ARRANGING HIS IDEAS. DO NOT HAVE THE SLIGHTEST WORRY ABOUT HIS INTENTIONS AS HE GENUINELY ENTHUSIASTIC ABOUT THE BOOK AND HE HAS NO IDEA OF DOING ANYTHING BUT DRAMATIZING IT AND MARSHALING THE IDEA OF THE BOOK INTO A PRESENTABLE PATTERN. . . . HE DOES NOT LIKE OUR FRAMEWORK AND HE HAS VERY SANE AND LOGICAL REASON WHICH HE PREFERS TO PRESENT TO US JOINTLY. HE BELIEVES THAT THE PICTURE SHOULD SNEAK UP ON THE AUDIENCE THE SAME WAY THAT THE BOOK SNEAKS UP ON THE READER AND THAT THE IMPACT OF THE THEME WHEN IT COMES IN THE OPEN IS TWICE AS STRONG. HE HAS NO IDEA OF GRANDEUR OR ELABORATION BUT HE DOES HAVE VERY STRONG CONVICTIONS AS TO THE FORM OF DRAMATIZATION AND HE HAS NO QUARREL WITH ANY PART OF THE BOOK EXCEPT HE FEELS THAT THE LAST FOURTH OF THE BOOK LETS DOWN THE PERSONAL STORY. . . . CONFIDENTIALLY I AM MEETING WITH GREGORY PECK TOMORROW AND WILL LET YOU KNOW THE OUTCOME.

REGARDS,

DARRYL

≣

Daring for the time, the novel and film dealt with a writer (Peck) pretending to be Jewish in order to write a series of articles and in the process discovering rampant anti-Semitism. Gregory Peck had commitments with various studios—including Fox.

≣

June 7, 1947
Mr. Moss Hart
Fairview Farm
New Hope, Pennsylvania

Dear Moss:

As I telegraphed you this morning, last night I had a long session with Kazan going over for the second time all of the new material which you sent on to us and which in the main we found very effective. . . .

First off I want to tell you of several experiences we have had on the picture. We completed the photographing of the first sequence between Kathy [Dorothy McGuire] and Phil [Gregory Peck] in Kathy's apartment before they go out dancing. It took two days to photograph it and then we cut it together and we have looked at it several times, and we are going to reshoot it entirely starting Monday.

Kazan directed the sequence beautifully but no matter how he treated it and no matter what amount of movement and business he gave to the characters, the sequence as finished seemed quite talky.

Kazan played it lightly and with a touch of romance and yet the dialogue following the reading of *Time* magazine seemed to bog down. Earlier in the day Kazan had rehearsed the next sequence between Phil and the mother [free-lance player Anne Revere] and in that particular sequence he found in rehearsal he was practically playing the same scene with the mother which he had played with Phil and Kathy. At least the content was very much the same. As a matter of fact the scene between the mother and Phil seemed much the best scene and we did not touch a line of it.

We have gone back over the Kathy-Phil scene and pruned it, only eliminating the items which might tend to be repetitious or make the scene between Phil and his mother repetitious. This involves considerable expense. As a matter of fact the retakes will run about $30,000 as we are operating at the rate of about $15,000 a day. This I do not mind at all as I would rather get it good *now* than to have to chop it up and try to trim after the picture is finished.

These things are to be expected, particularly in a film where you have eighty percent talk and twenty percent action. Rest assured that to the best of our joint abilities we will eliminate nothing that is essential or significant to either the story or the theme, but I am sure you agree that by all means we must not make a dull picture even though it be significant and important.

These things we can only find out as we go along. As an example the breakfast table sequence was played magnificently. We never had to change a comma or a period, but as we move forward into the guts of our story, we have to expect certain condensations. It always happens. The same as you change a play after rehearsal or after you take it on the road, we find ourselves in the same boat. I have been facing it consistently for twenty years and I find that the only way to do it smoothly and effectively is to do it *while* you are making the film and thus avoid the necessity of cutting into scenes later on when the cast has been disbanded and expensive retakes are out of the question.

We all consider this picture important and a great challenge. It is a double challenge to me. The subject on one side and the utter necessity for an exciting, lively drama on the other side. . . .

We are both strongly opposed on page 69 to the additional line given McAnny [Curt Conway] about the "little Jew boy from the Bronx." If we have this line then why have the dialogue about Guam, etc. One happens to be obviously on the nose and the other as now written in the script seems to be a very effective and subtle jab.

I am sure on this point as well as some of the others I am going to mention we have to rely not only on the spoken word but what you read in the actors' faces. In other words we must leave some room for performance. If we say it *all* and leave nothing to acting, then we are apt to slow the picture to a walk directly due to overemphasis. I think that both the actors and the audience are entitled to use a certain amount of imagination, particularly in a scene like this which is necessarily played in a close shot where the arch of an eyebrow is comparable to the largest span in the George Washington Bridge (all this and jokes too). . . .

Affectionate regards
s/Darryl

CC: Miss Laura Z. Hobson

≡

TO: Mr. Elia Kazan   DATE: June 18, 1947
        SUBJECT: GENTLEMAN'S AGREEMENT

Dear Gadge:

In thinking over our discussion of last night in regard to the dinner scene between Phil and Kathy, I am more than ever convinced that from the standpoint of Kathy, we have hit the scene too hard and too deliberately.

As now played there is no question that Kathy is not only frightened over Phil's being Jewish—she is horrified. And she betrays herself so completely that it is difficult to know why Phil comes back to her and forgives her.

I always visualized the scene like this: When Phil says that he is going to tell everyone that he is Jewish, Kathy first has a puzzled smile as she repeats, "Jewish?" Then suddenly for a brief second she betrays herself when she gives him a startled look and says, "But you're not, are you, Phil?" Then she quickly realizes that she has put her foot in it and she tries to get off the hook by saying that it wouldn't matter to her if he were Jewish.

From here on, she tries to cover up her original blunder but in doing so she again puts her foot in it when seeing Phil's attitude she says that she thinks it will cause a lot of confusion.

After Phil has firmly explained to her there must be no exceptions, etc., then Kathy should try to play the rest of the scene with forced lightness, doing her best to get off the spot. She does not succeed through dinner and only after dinner are they reconciled.

If Kathy has gone too far, I really doubt very much whether Phil would come back, despite the fact that he is attracted to her. He can easily forgive her original shock and her worry about confusing people and her lack of real understanding of what he is doing. These things are readily understandable, but if he feels that she has actually been horrified and deeply shocked by the thought of his being Jewish, then I doubt that he would return.

Furthermore, what about the next time the subject comes up? If she has hit it too heavily and betrayed herself too completely, then he is justified in being highly suspicious from here on and I am afraid that it may warp our future scenes. However, if he just thinks she has had a momentary shock and a lack of comprehension, then he would not be entitled to watch her like a hawk from here on, and the other clashes between them can be arrived at naturally.

I believe this paragraph is the keynote of our entire picture and the theme of our picture. Kathy is *not* anti-Semitic. Not a bit of it. *But* she makes the mistake that 99 percent of the people make by conforming to the custom and unconsciously observing the gentleman's agreement. This is not, however, the story of a woman who is really anti-Semitic and reforms at the end of the picture, and, therein lies the guide to her reactions.

D.F.Z.

≡

Apparently some modifications were made in the playing of the scene.

≡

September 8, 1947
Mr. Moss Hart
Fairview Farm
New Hope, Pa.

Dear Moss:

Thanks for your letter, even though it is a letter of disagreement.

I am not quite sure that I made myself clear in the original letter. I have no desire to hide the content of our film. We couldn't hide it if we tried and it would certainly be a weakness. On the other hand I always admire a fighter in the ring who knows how to land a counterpunch and who knows how to lead his opponent on before he lands the knockout blow. Many fighters, like many croquet players, lead with their chins and they are either flat on the canvas or dead on three balls before they even have a chance to display their skill.

If Gregory Peck were to go on the air [radio] and talk *only* about the theme of *Gentleman's Agreement*, I think this would be a disadvantage to the picture and also an incorrect presentation of the values of the picture because it would only tell *half* the story.

Why did we try so strenuously to develop an adult and interesting love story? Why did we strive to put the emphasis on personalities and warm, personal relationships? . . .

In my opinion it would be idiotic for Gregory Peck or anyone else to get up in *advance* of the picture and talk about the wonderful love story between Phil and Kathy—this wouldn't sell a ticket to anybody. I also do not believe that Peck could sell a ticket to anybody if he got up and talked *only* about the intellectual side of the picture and how much good it will do.

We have made the picture and pulled no punches. I think the sensible plan is to say nothing and let the picture speak for itself. I went to a party Saturday night at [independent producer] Sam Goldwyn's house and at least ten people came up to me and said that they had heard that *Gentleman's Agreement* was one of the really great films. I did not deny it. This of course goes to show you how one little private screening can start a chain of highly beneficial gossip.

When you hear the plans I have for New York I believe that both Miss [Laura Z.] Hobson, Gadge and you will be delighted. I am going to have a series of very small, intimate, private screenings prior to the New York opening. To these intimate screenings will be invited certain select lists of opinion-makers, publishers, critics, socialites, columnists and certain people "in the know."

As an example, one night I will probably ask Clare and Harry Luce to invite a dozen people to see the picture with them, preferably people from the editorial staff of *Time* and *Life*. Then on another evening I will ask you to invite a group of guests. These groups will not only contain certain personal friends but we will sandwich in with them selected individuals who in one way or another can do us good.

The same thing will be done one evening with Kazan and insomuch as Virginia [Mrs. Zanuck] is coming on with me I will have her invite Mrs. Reid and other of her personal friends who also are in a position to help form advance public opinion.

Goldwyn used a similar formula in handling *The Best Years of Our Lives* [1946] and, as you know, *before* the picture opened in New York it was already the talk of the town. I used the same plan twice before, once on *Grapes of Wrath* and once on *How Green was My Valley*. There are very few pictures that justify such treatment. In the case of *Gentleman's Agreement* I have every logical reason to believe that we are on firmer ground in this respect than anybody has ever been in the history of this business with any picture.

I am anxious to know what you think of the plan and if you will help me out and attend as many of these screenings as you can. We will try and limit each group to not more than twenty people and I am stopping all of my other work and will attend every screening. This, strangely enough, has a very good psychological effect. The guest feels that he is in the *one and only* private screening and until Miss Hobson writes a book dealing with anti-ego in America we will have to put up with the situation. . . .

I am sending a copy of this letter to Miss Hobson and Gadge. I hope you don't think that I am writing a circular letter but I know that they are interested and I have always considered this a joint operation. In case anything goes wrong I am getting ready to reissue *Sun Valley Serenade* with Sonja Henie.

> Best always,
> s/Darryl

≡

September 12, 1947
Mr. Elia Kazan
167 East 74th Street
New York, N.Y.

Dear Gadge:

. . . I am now working with the Advertising Department on the trailer ["preview of coming attractions"]. This is a hell of a problem because when you select individual scenes for a trailer which can run only four minutes you find that these scenes, while wonderful in the picture, do not seem to make much sense by themselves.

Therefore the trailer will be mostly narration with statistics about the book and the cast, and I am emphasizing *both* angles. I am using part of

Peck's scene with [free-lance player] June Havoc when he grabs her and says, "Look at me—only the word Christian is different," etc., etc. I am also using one of the love scenes between McGuire and Peck and also a scene with [free-lance star John] Garfield.

It is a ticklish business to know how far to go and where to stop. If you could have one trailer for the intellectuals and one trailer for the [others] . . . our problem would be simple. I still believe that nothing we can say will be as important as what the picture itself says for us.

I have had several meetings with [Fox music director] Al Newman on the music and as I told you before there will be no musical score but only source music.

Best always,

CC: Mr. Moss Hart
Miss Laura Z. Hobson

≡

Gentleman's Agreement *received three Academy Awards: Best Picture, Best Direction, and Best Supporting Actress (Fox contract player Celeste Holm).*

FIVE

THE GOING GETS TOUGH

I have held many meetings with the executives of our Company, including one with our producers, for the purpose of analyzing ways and means of reducing our production costs. The economic conditions which confront the Industry, which means *our Company* as well as others, make this subject a critically urgent one. It became clear in all of these discussions that the subject could not adequately be covered without taking into account the function of our directors. I, therefore, plan to hold a meeting with all of our directors in the very near future for the purpose of frankly discussing with them the manner in which they can importantly help us in reducing our cost. . . .

Directors should study scripts more thoroughly so that *minimum requirement* for all physical elements *is the basis* upon which work is commenced. Sets, wardrobe, and other things, must be put into work weeks before the picture starts. Sometimes a director is not yet in the "spirit" and as a consequence requests costly measures of protection as a substitute for figuring things out more in advance.

A director *is* the chief executive on the set whether he wants to be or not. Because of this, his attitude and conduct establishes the attitude and conduct of the rest of the company. He should be on the set not later than 8:30 A.M. and *earlier* most often. If the director habitually does not get in until 8:45 or 9:00 A.M. (the record discloses a great many instances where they have gotten in *after* 9:00 A.M.) the cameraman and crew gather the impression that no one is seriously interested in actually starting to shoot at 9:00 and as a consequence we never do. There have been instances where our stars have attempted to justify their own tardiness by the conduct of the director in this regard. Some directors arrive at the stage at 8:50 or 8:55 and then promptly go to the barber shop for a shave and thereafter report for shooting at 9:15. This practice requires no comment. He should not leave at night until the crew has been given a bona fide "first [camera] setup" for the following morning. A director often gives what *purports* to be the first setup, because it is a prerequisite to his leaving for the day, but knows in his heart that he hasn't figured it out thoroughly and more than likely will change it in the morning—usually after the crew has worked on it for an hour or more. The change is then made on *shooting time*. Our first shots average us 10:38 A.M. If the setup given the night before was not altered, there is no reason why our first shots should not invariably be 9:30. This in itself would account for a minimum of one full week on an average picture.

Directors should, in a larger measure, plot their shooting in advance. An unnecessary amount of shooting time is now consumed between 9:00 A.M. and 6:00 P.M. figuring out how a scene is to be staged and how it is to be photographed. As a result of this lack of Directorial preparation, time that should be spent on performance is spent on mechanics and because of the uncertainty of the mechanics under this system, several superfluous angles are shot per day. Even if *only one* superfluous angle per day is shot, this could easily add six to nine days to a schedule.

Some of our directors seem to feel that their constant presence on the set is not necessary and between setups find many reasons to leave the stage. In the case of a producer-director who may have one or more other stories in work, it is occasionally justified for him to leave the set. In other cases, it is inexcusable. The director's presence not only has a healthy moral effect on stage activities but it is essential that he be available to answer the multitude of questions that arise concerning the work of the moment. Many of them argue that it is boring to stay on the set and they become impatient. An occasional manifestation of their impatience may be just what is needed to gain one or two hours work per day. . . .

A few of our directors conduct too much of their personal business during the shooting day.

Many of our directors leave the set at 4:00 P.M. daily to view their dailies. This is "presumably" between setups and does not delay the company. This is sheer nonsense. Too often things just stop until he returns, especially since, for one reason or another, the cameraman and other key personnel often go with him. Usually from fifteen minutes to a half hour per day is dissipated in this fashion. This also adds up to a number of days on a picture's schedule. At all other studios, dailies are run for the company after six o'clock. We should establish the same practice.

Examination discloses that a moderate cost picture will be shot in from 40% to 60% the number of angles as an expensive (not necessarily big or successful) picture. Cost and number of angles (setups) are interminably related—since a setup represents time. In our studio, we average about six setups per day (five years ago the average was 9 $\frac{1}{4}$). Almost every director either occasionally or constantly shoots superfluous angles. In some instances, it is chronic and shameful. The change in angle is so slight in some cases as to be not even noticeable. In other cases, angles are shot that cannot conceivably be used as proper thought would have disclosed prior to their shooting. In still other cases, it is just a matter of gilding the lily. It is one of our costliest individual practices. One superfluous angle per day eliminated on a 60-day picture would reduce that schedule by approximately *nine days*.

Many of our directors will strive to get a perfect take "all the way through" on each angle, as if the entire scene were to be played in that one angle, even though this is almost never the case. Even when a good take has been obtained, he will go on and on trying to get a better one. . . .

Some directors have a veritable passion for "long shots" where it is doubtful if such long shot is of any appreciable value. Often they are shot because they are specified in the script. . . . It should be borne in mind that our *full* day's expense is determined by the biggest shot.

Directors constantly complain that we cannot make pictures inexpensively because of our very high overhead. Again they do not recognize that some substantial part of overhead is within their *means* to control. In addition to the normally accepted items of overhead such as Plant and Equipment maintenance, Depreciation, Taxes, Insurance, Police and Fire Protection and Administrative Expenses, a very substantial part of our overhead consists of the undistributed time of Producers, *Directors*, Players and all other classifications of Production Personnel. . . .

I am not trying, in this memorandum, to create the impression that the directors are the archvillains in the matter of excessive production costs, nor am I attempting to say that the whole solution of the problem is in their hands. I do say, however, that they are one of the *most important* keys to the solution of high costs. I believe this to be demonstrably indisputable.

The matters dealt with herein are not all applicable to all of our directors. It is certain, nevertheless, that *some* are applicable to all of them and without, in any sense, kidding ourselves and by carefully analyzing the points brought out in this memorandum, we can readily and conservatively conclude that our average shooting schedule can be reduced by a minimum of two weeks (it could very easily be more) if the indicated faults in our shooting procedures are assiduously examined and corrected. . . .

D.F.Z.

≡

DATE: July 8, 1947

TO: Mr. Preston Sturges [writer, producer, director]
CONFIDENTIAL

Dear Preston:

This note personally addressed to you is actually a copy of a note I am sending to all contract directors and producer/directors at our studio.

I have recently conducted a series of experiments. We now have six pictures actually in production, but I did not limit my experiment alone to the pictures now on the stages, but also included three recently completed films. The necessity for the experiment was forced upon me by the continuing rising cost of the production of pictures and the radically declining attendance in theatres.

During the war years and the boom period in the theatres, we were able to afford certain luxuries that must obviously be denied to us at this time. Theatre receipts are hitting a new low, both here and in England. We have made radical curtailments in overhead and all production departments have responded in this emergency by economizing.

In studying the production charts of the nine productions mentioned above, I noticed the directors appear to be making more takes, generally speaking, than heretofore. It was a common occurrence to find anywhere from ten to twenty takes being shot on certain individual scenes. Several times, as many as twenty-five takes were shot.

Now, I know very well the multiple problems that confront a director on the set and I'm aware of the many things that can go wrong through no fault of the director. My experiment took into consideration all of these elements. I did the following:

I went back and printed up [from the negative] takes that were not previously printed. In other words, if the director had printed the tenth take or the twentieth take, I blindly ordered the laboratory to print up the number one take of the same scene. If the director had selected the twentieth take, I printed up the first take, the second take, and sometimes the fifth and sixth take. They were selected at random.

The slate numbers [identifying each take before the start of the scene] were snipped off of all the takes and they were patched together with the take the director had originally selected. The screening was most revealing, and also most disturbing. While certain minor variances in action were apparent, on close scrutiny between the selected take and the takes I had printed up, the difference was frequently so slight, that we were compelled to consult the slate numbers to discover which was the selected take.

I can conservatively say that of ninety to ninety-five percent of the outtakes reviewed, an actual difference in quality was not noticeable. There were, of course, certain exceptions.

A further study of the daily production report, in association with these takes, reveals that in many instances the director had shot, let's say, twelve takes on the scene and then he had printed the twelfth take when actually the fifth or sixth take proved to be of superior quality. In this instance, the director, having shot twelve takes, I presume, felt compelled to okay the last take, when, actually, there could not have been any perceptible difference to the action after the fifth or sixth take.

Most of you, to whom this note is addressed, have worked with me for a great number of years. You are aware of my desire for quality and perfection. As a matter of fact, I have been exacting in my demands for retakes, regardless of cost, if I felt the quality of entertainment could be perceptibly improved. I do not mind paying for visible quality, but I no longer believe that any company in this industry can afford extravagance, and certainly not at this time. If we demand that all departments in the studio economize, then we cannot spare any individual or any individual department. . . .

The director on the set is the driving force of the production. Generally speaking, as the director moves, so moves the company. Therefore, his personal responsibility is a very great one. We do not have producers at this studio who make it a habit of interfering in the direction of scenes. As far as we are concerned, this has been a long established policy. The director is the director when he is on the set.

Therefore, in the interest of the welfare of our company, I ask for a careful consideration of the matter listed above. I realize fully well that there are times when it is essential to make twenty or even more takes of one scene. But all I ask is that you be certain that it is *essential*.

D.F.Z.

≡

TO: Mr. Robert Bassler [producer]　　　DATE: September 5, 1947
　　　SUBJECT: WILL JAMES' MATERIAL

Dear Bob:

In reply to your letter on the [author] Will James material and particularly on the story *Sand*, I think we should benefit by past performances and not make the same mistake which we made with *The Homestretch* [1947].

The Homestretch was basically a failure (and I am convinced of this) because we told the story of human beings and not the story of a horse.

Our basic problem dealt with human relations, and the horses were only used as very effective props to tell a human story.

The reason [*My Friend*] *Flicka* [1943], *Thunderhead* [*Son of Flicka*, 1945] and *Smoky* [1946—all Fox pictures] were tremendously successful is because the story was in each instance a story about a horse, and even in the most successful of the three pictures, *Flicka*, the basic story was completely about the problem of a horse. . . .

Smoky was loaded with drama, suspense and tears, but you did not cry because of the actors or their problems—you cried because of the problems of the *horse*.

You just cannot mix ingredients because you alienate yourself from both types of audiences. The people who want to see Cornel Wilde and Maureen O'Hara in a bedroom do not want to see the problems of a cow pony. And the people who want to see the problems of Smoky do not give a damn whether Cornel Wilde is in or out of the picture and they certainly are not interested in his problems with a society girl.

In *Green Grass of Wyoming* [1948], I think we have blended the story well. . . .

Now, we are going to make another Will James story and I definitely think we should buy one of his stories for his name and for the title and we should write a story about a *horse*. . . .

D.F.Z.

≡

Sand (1949) did poorly and ended the Fox series of horse pictures (at that time).

≡

TO: David O. Selznick   DATE: September 27, 1947

Dear David:

. . . When Jennifer [Jones] was given the leading role in *Song of Bernadette* [Fox, 1943] it was on the understanding that Twentieth Century–Fox would share in her future contract with you. There were at that time no strings attached to this arrangement and I know that it was certainly your sincere intention that we should share in the benefits should Jennifer become an important star as the result of *Song of Bernadette*.

Four years have elapsed and during that time we have only obtained the services of Jennifer for one picture, *Cluny Brown* [1946]. During this same period of time Jennifer has appeared in three pictures for you and one picture for Hal Wallis. . . .

During this period of time we submitted certain stories to both you and Miss Jones for consideration, namely, *Laura*, *The Razor's Edge* and others. They were not acceptable.

The later part of last year I sent you a group of stories which we had just purchased. . . .

You very generously suggested a number of alternate proposals which under the circumstances I found difficult to accept. This brings us up to date. I have not endeavored to cover all of the ground nor our many exchanges of telegrams and letter and various discussions. . . .

I will be in your office at four o'clock on Monday.

Best Always,
Darryl

≡

Due to intricate complications regarding Selznick's intense desire to have his future wife appear in only the most prestigious and "important" projects and with the most prestigious and "important" producers, writers, and directors under ideal circumstances, it was always a difficult situation for Fox to get a definite commitment, and she did not make any additional films for the studio until the mid-1950s.

≡

After the death of Ernst Lubitsch, Zanuck made the following comments about him in the January 1948 issue of The Screen Writer.

≡

I shall always remember with great pleasure the strong conscience which Ernst Lubitsch brought to bear on every subject or problem to which he gave his attention.

He was a man of wit, but beneath his sense of fun was a stronger sense of sympathy and understanding for his fellow men.

He always lunched with his fellow producers, and it was a custom at these gatherings to argue principles and problems in our field of work and the larger field of human relationships. Frequently in these arguments Ernst was the dissenter. And we found, on reflection, that his dissents were based on a deep sense of right. He could see the other man's side of a question.

His ability to penetrate beyond a personal viewpoint was discernible in his work as well as his everyday life. It gave human qualities to the things he created for the screen and to the direction of those creations. The actions of his characters in a play were motivated by what he could see they would think to be right. This to my mind is why they were so refreshing and different.

Added to this, of course, was his keen though always genial sense of humor. His sense of fun contained no malice; his eye, his hand and his mind were too quick and nimble for this. Where many men would let emotion guide their thought, he remembered that morals are too often a manner of thinking and of the times. His pictures and his style of direction point this up.

All of Ernst's colleagues at the Twentieth Century–Fox studio were stimulated by the association with him. The deep affection they held for him will not wane with time. . . .

≡

TO: Mr. Spyros Skouras [president] DATE: January 3, 1948
   Mr. Charles Schlaifer [director of advertising, publicity and exploitation]

Dear Spyros:

Whenever a picture does not live up to its expectations, invariably the producer or studio head has to find an alibi or someone to blame. . . .

I realize that we have a problem with many pictures to exploit and that our [advertising and publicity] campaigns are in and out and we cannot expect every one to be a gem, any more than we can expect every picture to be a perfect gem. Believe me, it is my considered opinion that we have got to use a great deal more imagination than we've used recently. Particularly, we've got to avoid copying previous campaigns, unless, like in the case of *Fort Apache* [RKO, 1948] we find a new and original approach to an old idea. I don't want to seem critical, but I want you to know that I am criticizing myself as well as Charlie [Schlaifer] and you. . . .

I believe that one brilliantly executed piece of artwork used repeatedly is more effective than a half dozen pieces of ordinary artwork. . . .

I know Harry Luce [Henry Luce, founder of Time Inc.] told me that certain covers on *Life* magazine increase or decrease the newsstand circulation, depending entirely upon the originality or provocativeness of the cover photograph. And [publisher] Bennett Cerf has told me many times that the illustrations on the jacket of a book can definitely influence the sale of the book. Particularly if the author is unknown. I believe that in the selection of titles we have frequently made a horrible mistake and the change from *Summer Lightning* to *Scudda-Hoo! Scudda-Hay!* [1948] was a classical example of stupidity on all of our parts. . . .

Our most successful titles have been provocative titles like *Call Northside 777*, *13 Rue Madeleine*, etc. And we have got to be very careful in the future in this direction. Actually, I believe *Sitting Pretty* was a poor title until after you had seen the picture and realized what *Sitting Pretty* meant. And that some of the original resistance to the box office of this picture was based on the fact that the title did not mean anything until you knew the subject matter, although it was not an out and out detrimental title.

I believe both *Nightmare Alley* and *Kiss of Death* were tremendously harmful as was *The Ghost and Mrs. Muir* and *The Late George Apley* [1947]. The first two titles limited audience appeal to the horror variety of picture. And the last two titles sounded dull and boring, in spite of the fact that they were well known by a small percentage of the public. . . . While *Nightmare Alley* might be a great title for James Cagney or Humphrey Bogart, but in association with Tyrone Power, it is contradictory and not very promising. . . .

Darryl

≡

March 18, 1948
"MOTHER IS A FRESHMAN" CONFERENCE ON ADAPTATION OF MARCH
10TH, 1948 WITH MESSRS. [Walter] MOROSCO [producer], RICHARD SALE
[writer], MISS [Mary] LOOS [writer], AND MOLLY MANDAVILLE

When I first read the outline of the story [by Raphael Blau] my
feeling was that it should be done exactly as you have done it in this
adaptation—as a farce comedy . . . but when you examine the idea
more closely I think that you will see that we have an opportunity to
make a very charming, legitimate, and honest picture. I think it can
have the humorous approach of *Margie* or *Sitting Pretty*.

If you have seen *Sitting Pretty* you will quickly realize that we could
have gone completely overboard with this picture because the central
character [Mr. Belvedere], a male baby sitter, is an extreme one to
begin with. We could have made it simply a screwball picture, but
instead of this we made a very human and honest picture which is a hit
with critics and public alike.

To get humor into the situation of Mother [free-lance star Loretta
Young] at college should be easy. But it should be humor resulting from
a normal, honest character suddenly finding herself in these circumstances. The obvious things that would occur to anybody in this
particular situation would also occur to Mother. You would not have to
manufacture anything. Things that might not be funny at all if they
were happening to a teenager student might be hilariously funny if
they happened to Mother. She faces the same problems that any mature
woman would face if she had to go back to school. . . .

≡

Zanuck's ideas were implemented.

≡

TO: All Producers   DATE: April 27, 1948
PERSONAL AND CONFIDENTIAL

We were making a very great economic production record for ourselves up until recently, but now with the last group of pictures I see

that we're beginning to be lax in one way or another and slip back into the rut.

Just because we make a picture today cheaper than we did just two years ago does not mean that these pictures will automatically be a commercial success. *Kiss of Death* will probably manage to break even in the world market, in spite of the fact that it was made at a low cost. *Nightmare Alley* will lose at least five hundred thousand dollars, in spite of the fact that it was cheaper than many of the other Tyrone Power pictures. . . .

In spite of the big accumulated story cost of *Unfaithfully Yours*, we should be ashamed of the abuses that we permitted to go on in the production of this picture. I realize that we finished on budget and on schedule. But here again, we allowed the director [Preston Sturges] at least one full week more than we should have allowed him. . . . Unless *Unfaithfully Yours* is a tremendous box-office hit, and mind you, I think it's a wonderful, wonderful comedy, we are bound to lose money or at least break even. . . .*

I have no complaint on *Road House* [1948]. Considering the cost of the cast, I believe that the picture is worth every penny that we are spending on it. It is no cheap bargain, by any means, but at least we've not obviously gone overboard. . . .

I have found out by experience that retakes are the least expensive thing that we can do. I would much rather give a director a short shooting schedule and then go back and work a few extra days than give him a schedule that is overlength. . . .

The fact that we cut out a great deal of film after the first screening of almost every picture that we make is in itself factual proof that we have not done our preparation job on the script as well as we should do it, either from a dramatic or economic standpoint. I can cite examples on this lot where we have lost less than five or six hundred feet from the first assemblage of the picture to the final release, yet I can quote many more examples where we have lost repeatedly from three to six thousand feet. True, we have improved the pictures by these editorial eliminations, but I would feel much more proud of our efforts if we had been able to do it in advance.

* *Unfaithfully Yours* did poorly in theatres.

I realize as head of the studio I must accept full responsibility and I am willing to accept it, but I cannot devote as much time to every picture as I would like to devote. As an individual producer, you in turn must face the responsibility. . . .

I realize that many times you are at the mercy of the director who may not always be sympathetic, but this has not been the greatest cause of our excessive costs. . . . If you analyze the pictures that have gone over-board, you should also analyze the amount of film left on the cutting room floor—film that has not even seen the night of the first sneak preview—film that has taken days and sometimes weeks to shoot. . . .

The trade papers today reported that last year we made a net consolidated profit of fourteen million dollars. This sounds a great deal, but have you any idea of how much came from our subsidiary National Theatres and West Coast Theatres? If you knew how little we made from our pictures last year, you would fully realize why I am writing this note. You must remember that our theatre chain plays everybody's pictures, not just our own.

This note has been written to you in confidence.

D. F. Z.

≡

In October 1948 the federal government ordered complete divorcement of production and distribution from exhibition. By the mid-1950s the major studios no longer owned theatres as a result of this antitrust action.

≡

TO: Sol Siegel [producer] DATE: May 1, 1948
   Joseph Mankiewicz [writer, director]
CC: Molly Mandaville
   SUBJECT: A LETTER TO FOUR WIVES

Dear Sol and Joe:

I have just completed my first full reading of the script on *A Letter to Four Wives* and I hasten to write you this preliminary note. I like the script immensely. It is beautifully written, the dialogue is splendid, and the starring roles are evenly divided.

In my opinion this cannot help but make a very successful picture. It is exciting, interesting, dramatic and very humorous in the right places.

But for all of this I have one violent and major criticism. Insomuch as it is quite obvious that we are never going to get this script down to proper length without sacrificing or cutting some of the excellent individual episodes, I therefore began to study the script after I had finished the first reading with an idea of not cutting from the standpoint of economy or footage but trying to cut from the angle of dramatic interest. I emphasize this point. I want to make it very clear that what I am going to recommend is a result not of economy or footage but a result of dramatic storytelling, construction and entertainment.

There is one episode in the story that by comparison bored me. It seemed entirely out of place; compared with the other episodes it was dull, and I found myself very impatient when I was reading it. I refer to the entire episode with Martha and Roger. The rest of the story is exciting, interesting, sexy, humorous. It has tempo and bounce, and you sit on the edge of your seat all the time, but when you come to the problems of Martha and Roger you start on a familiar downhill path. It seems like a second-rate *Little Foxes*.

They have no real problem. . . . The other three wives have genuine problems. By this I mean they seem original problems. They are fresh and new, interesting and exciting. But the problem of Martha and Roger seems so easily solved. Furthermore it is pretty dull stuff purely from the standpoint of entertainment. . . .

I will go on record as saying that if you eliminate Martha and Roger entirely from this script you are going to have a motion picture that is one hundred percent better than if you retain the story of Martha and Roger. By dropping them out you will give the entire picture tempo and in addition to this you will bring the picture down to a reasonable length. But my main consideration is dramatic construction and dramatic interest. I can see us now in the cutting room struggling to shrink down the Martha episode if we shoot it. . . .

Just for your own satisfaction I wish you would once read this script and eliminate Martha and Roger entirely as you do the reading. Go through the script after blocking them out and see what happens from the standpoint of construction and tempo and audience interest. . . .

Again, congratulations on a very splendid job. I will be prepared to
listen to your arguments on Tuesday.

D. F. Z.

≡

*Martha and Roger were eliminated; the picture was filmed and released
as* A Letter to Three Wives *(1949). The novel on which the script
was based was titled* A Letter to Five Wives *by John Klempner. Very
well received in all respects, the film was the recipient of two Academy
Awards, for best direction and screenplay.*

≡

June 28, 1948
Mr. Charles Skouras [president]
Fox West Coast Theatres
1609 W. Washington Blvd.
Los Angeles, California

My dear Charlie:
 . . . The purpose of a first sneak preview on a picture is to *try out* the
entertainment values, particularly the comedy values.

We do not have first sneak previews on dramas, because I feel that I
am sufficiently qualified to edit a drama in the projection room, and the
only time I preview a drama is *after* I have cut it down to footage and it is
ready for release. As a matter of fact, I never previewed *Gentleman's
Agreement, Iron Curtain, Call Northside 777, Boomerang, House on 92nd
Street*, etc., etc.

On comedies, however, a sneak preview is practically essential. And,
for this reason, we leave in many things that we would ordinarily take
out. We go to the preview expecting the picture to drag and not to
screen anything resembling a finished product.

Whenever this has occurred in a Fox theatre, I have made it my
business to personally advise the manager in advance that this is a sneak
preview that will be edited and brought down into final form, later on.

Last week [Fox producer] Georgie Jessel was in Philadelphia at the convention and he dropped by the Fox theatre and talking with the manager of the Fox theatre, he was astonished to hear the manager tell him he had received the lowdown on a couple of forthcoming 20th Century–Fox pictures, namely *Unfaithfully Yours* and *That Lady in Ermine* [1948]. He had heard that they were both "weak sisters" . . . In further discussion with the manager, he found out that the manager got his so-called "lowdown" as a result of confidential reports of the previews.

Now, it so happens that *Unfaithfully Yours* was deliberately previewed in two hours and seven minutes. The picture will be released in a length of approximately one hour and forty-five minutes, showing that twenty-four minutes have been eliminated since preview. It was previewed at Riverside [California] and, while the picture was way overlength and draggy in the middle, I have never heard greater laughter in a theatre, not even for *Sitting Pretty*. Even in the overlength, the preview cards ranged from good to excellent, with the emphasis on excellent. . . .

Sincerely,
Darryl

≡

Both Unfaithfully Yours *and* That Lady in Ermine *did poor business.*

≡

July 2, 1948
Mr. Elia Kazan
167 East 74th Street
New York, N.Y.

Dear Gadge:

Many thanks for your letter. I am in accord with everything you say, particularly with your philosophical views.

In a minute analysis I do not suppose that I am quite as far to the Left. Many things in Socialism appeal to me, probably the same instincts that made me want to produce *The Grapes of Wrath*. However, I have repeatedly seen Socialists ensnared and used by Communists and then swallowed whole. Both Communists and Fascists have used Socialists as stepping-stones. Hitler did and so did Mussolini.

Mrs. FDR [Eleanor Roosevelt] is a case in point. She was sucked in by various seemingly humanitarian groups which were later to blossom into sturdy front movements for the Communists. She found herself belonging to actual Communistic groups which she courageously and publicly disavowed. This has happened to me in the past, although not on such a public or elaborate scale. I guess what I detest more than anything is any form of regimentation or any type of suppression of the individual. So far as I can see, or as far as history will let me see, the Democratic system is the only chance for survival, and the free enterprise system (call it Capitalistic if you like) is the only form of commerce that results in general prosperity.

England is a case in point. You can no more completely nationalize industry and have it succeed than you can fly without an airplane. FDR [Franklin D. Roosevelt] failed utterly with the New Deal and this country was on the brink of national disaster when the war came along and saved us.

Competition, individual inspiration, are the human ingredients which are inevitably suffocated by State or Government domination. I am flatly against monopolies of all types whether government or individually controlled. You cannot buy prosperity, nor can you pass a law or laws to make it possible—you have to earn it the hard way as England will find out. They are now having more strikes since the Government nationalized certain major industries than they ever had under private ownership. This is mainly because management has lost competition and the incentive to be smarter than the next guy. There are times when two and two make four. [U.S. public official] Harry Hopkins found it out and told me so. The plans of the New Deal were scientifically perfect. Two and two added up exactly to four. They could not miss. They would reduce unemployment, raise the standard of living and result in national prosperity. But something happened. That thing called the "human touch" was missing. The spirit vanished. One classification went on the payrolls and another classification went off the payrolls, and by early 1939 there were more idle factories in America than there were during the great Hoover depression.

In my scheme the freedom of the individual means the freedom of *all* individuals in every classification, the right to succeed if you are capable of succeeding. And furthermore I don't believe any kind of government can run Twentieth Century–Fox as well as it can be run by Mr. Zanuck, nor do I believe that Mr. Zanuck is capable of running the *entire* Motion Picture Industry. When the Government takes over any industry it appoints a Chief. Now he is appointed primarily because he has demonstrated executive ability in that particular industry, but he is also appointed with an eye on the political side of his being. His loyalty to the Party, whether it be Labor, Republican or Democratic, is obviously taken into consideration. Therefore not always the best man is placed in charge. He in turn picks his assistants by the same standards, and they in turn pick their assistants by the same standards (ability and Party loyalty). All of this eventually results in a lack of efficiency and certainly a lack of incentive because competition vanishes. Not only does a man have to make good in the job but he has to be sure that he makes good in the Party. The trains begin to run slow.

What started me on this tirade I don't know. . . .

> Best always,
> Darryl

≡

TO: Mr. Sam Engel DATE: July 6, 1948
CC: Mr. Lew Schreiber [executive assistant to Zanuck]
    SUBJECT: COME TO THE STABLE

Dear Sam:

Over the weekend I again read *Come to the Stable*. In my opinion we are on the verge of having a very great motion picture, but when I say "on the verge" I mean exactly that. . . .

The scenes in the present script for the most part are almost telegraphic. They tell what we want to tell and they tell it clearly and economically, but all of them are "right on the nose" . . .

You can feel that in almost every sequence the potentialities are always present, yet they never come to life. I am not talking about *what* the characters say; I am talking about *how* they say it and how the individual scenes themselves are manipulated. . . .

Now let us take Sister Margaret herself: while she has a wonderful role and is better written than the other characters, she really does not have a so-called big acting scene in the entire film, and this, just between ourselves, may make it difficult for us to get a star in the role. Sister Margaret plays the same scene over and over again throughout the script. I realize that sometimes this is necessary, but here again is where expert writing, not only of the dialogue but in the delivery of scenes, could come to our aid. She can be given things to say which will not be out of line with the policy of the Church, but yet give her more color and change. . . .

Personally, I keep seeing Loretta Young in this role, more than anyone else. As you know, she is a great Catholic, she was in a big hit picture last year and won the Academy Award [*The Farmer's Daughter*, RKO]. Irene Dunne wants to do it but I am afraid that she is not at all right for it.

≡

Sally Benson was signed to polish the Oscar Millard screenplay, which was based on a story by Clare Boothe Luce. Loretta Young played Sister Margaret, returning to Fox for three films after a ten-year absence. (This time, Zanuck sent flowers.)

≡

TO: Spyros Skouras   DATE: Sept. 14, 1948
    Joseph Schenck
    Charles Schlaifer, etc. etc.
CONFIDENTIAL

. . . In this day and age, it seems to me that word-of-mouth publicity is almost the most valuable type of publicity, and word-of-mouth exploitation cannot come into being at the last moment. . . .

Two current productions from other companies, namely Howard

Hawks' *Red River* [Monterey, 1948] and Anatole Litvak's *Sorry, Wrong Number* [Hal Wallis, 1948] were "made" before they ever got into the theatres. Both films were completed long ago. Everywhere you go, you hear people talking about them, even though they have not actually seen them. Repeated projection room screenings and private screenings resulted in exceptional word-of-mouth publicity and in some unknown fashion this word-of-mouth publicity *eventually* reaches the theatregoing public. No one knows exactly how or why this occurs, but the fact of its occurrence is indisputable. . . .

On a bad picture, word-of-mouth publicity can work for a very detrimental effect. I sincerely believe I am justified in saying that [many of our] pictures . . . can tremendously benefit by word-of-mouth publicity, providing you have the *time* and the opportunity to "get them in the air."

Getting a picture in the air means more than just sending it to a booker or an exhibitor to look at on the eve of release. It means more than just fashioning an advertising campaign based on the scenario or the stills or a couple of private screenings for the fan magazines. . . .

You may very well answer me on this point by saying that I should get all of the pictures to you a great deal *sooner*. Then you would not face the problem. I am fully aware of this and in spite of the many unavoidable delays I offer no alibi because the responsibility is mine in the final analysis.

D. F. Z.

≡

TO: Alfred Newman   DATE: September 17, 1948
[general music director]

Dear Al:

Do nothing but continue to use *Street Scene* [theme] whenever it fits.

D. F. Z.

≡

This note was in response to a memo from Newman on the same day in which he said, "It seems that our correspondent has had a belly full of

'*Street Scene.*' *What shall we do?*" *He was referring to the theme composed by Newman for the 1931 Samuel Goldwyn film* Street Scene. *Zanuck loved the melody and had Newman use it in conjunction with several Fox films in the film noir, New York–based dramas and melodramas during the 1940s and early 1950s. It is not clear who the "correspondent" referred to is, but the person apparently did not want to use the theme in the upcoming* Cry of the City (1948). *Nevertheless, it was used in that picture and others that followed.*

≡

TO: Preston Sturges   DATE: September 20, 1948
    SUBJECT: THE BEAUTIFUL BLONDE FROM BASHFUL BEND

Dear Preston:

I looked at the wardrobe sketches this afternoon that René Hubert has for Betty [Grable] and I think they are wonderful, particularly the first red dress. The main reason I wanted to see them is that once when we made a picture called *The Shocking Miss Pilgrim* [1947] we did not show Grable's legs in the picture and in addition to receiving a million letters of protest the incident almost caused a national furor.

I am glad that he has given her a split skirt, at least in the opening, and that later on we see her in her panties.

Right now, I have thought of another idea that I would like to get your reaction on:

Suppose in the fight to the finish she is wearing a simple two-piece suit, something like a bolero jacket with a long skirt. Someone steps on the skirt and it tears off in the start of the battle royal. . . .

Perhaps you have some other suggestion. I know it perhaps sounds like a silly thing to worry about, but from a commercial standpoint Betty's legs are no joking matter.

D. F. Z.

≡

The situation was taken care of, but it didn't help the ultimate fate of the picture, which did poorly.

≡

November 1, 1948
Mr. Dudley Nichols [writer]
504 S. Plymouth
Los Angeles 5, Calif.

Dear Dudley:

. . . I went ahead with *Gentleman's Agreement* because I firmly believed that in spite of the controversial subject matter it was a great
movie story. . . .

The reason I have vacillated so much about *Pinky* is because in
my heart I am certain that at this point it is not a good enough
movie. . . .

I am writing in large letters on my script the following legend:

THIS IS NOT A STORY ABOUT HOW TO SOLVE THE NEGRO PROBLEM IN
THE SOUTH OR ANYWHERE ELSE. THIS IS NOT A STORY PARTICULARLY
ABOUT RACE PROBLEMS, SEGREGATION OR DISCRIMINATION. THIS IS A
STORY ABOUT ONE PARTICULAR NEGRO GIRL WHO COULD EASILY PASS
AS A WHITE AND WHO DID PASS FOR A WHILE. THIS IS THE STORY OF
HOW AND WHY SHE, AS AN INDIVIDUAL, FINALLY DECIDED TO BE
HERSELF—A NEGRESS. . . .

> Best Always,
> Darryl

≡

*Philip Dunne was assigned the Dudley Nichols screenplay and did the
revised drafts. The scripts were based on the novel* Quality *by Cid
Ricketts Sumner.*

≡

DATE: December 20, 1948

TO: Nunnally Johnson [writer-producer]
CC: Molly Mandaville
   SUBJECT: EVERYBODY DOES IT

Dear Nunnally:
   . . . Recently we made over *Love Is News* [1937] with Tyrone Power playing exactly the same role he played ten years ago. We now call the picture *That Wonderful Urge* [1948]. It has been received by the trade papers and got wonderful notices, but the strange part is that not one reviewer mentioned it as a remake in spite of the fact that we did not change any basic situation and that Tyrone was playing the same role he played before.

D.F.Z.

===

Elements of the plot were also used in a Betty Grable Fox musical, Sweet Rosie O'Grady (1943). *Nunnally Johnson recently had returned to Fox after being with International Pictures (later Universal-International) for a few years.*

===

March 22, 1949
Mr. Otto Lang
Sun Valley Lodge
Sun Valley, Idaho

Dear Otto:
   . . . I agree with your letter. You should either be a ski teacher or a film man. I cannot guarantee that you will make good as a film man. I have confidence in you and you have certain ability and certain definite experience. How far you go will depend entirely upon your development. You are not yet ready to assume full producership.
   I agree however that except in special cases you are beyond the stage

of being a second unit director. When you return to the studio I will try and find some setup for you that can eventually develop into full producership providing you continue to develop, unless of course your talents should slant off into directorship.

I agree you should step out of Sun Valley entirely, but I do not want you to blame me in case things should go wrong. This is your own responsibility and I am not in the insurance business. I will try my best to give you a proper opportunity but from there on you will have to dig.

You did a good job [as producer] on *Call Northside 777* but I had to spend more time on that story and its preparation than I have to spend on nine-tenths of the pictures. If I had to give that much time to every story with every producer I would not be up to it.

What I am saying is that I will fix some sort of a setup that will give you a chance, or a partial chance, but I do not want to be held responsible or feel that I am obligated. This would be bad for you and bad for me.

Best always,
Darryl

≡

Otto Lang was the ski school director at Sun Valley, Idaho, from 1942 to 1952. Before, during, and after this period he functioned in motion pictures as an assistant director, second unit director, director, and producer.

≡

TO: Henry King [director]   DATE: October 20, 1949

. . . It is to be our policy in the future that we keep you advised exactly of the result and the box-office fate of all of our product. As an example, *Captain from Castile* [1947] and *Foxes of Harrow* [1947] were not failures as pictures, even though they both ended up showing a net loss. They were good pictures, but our failure was that we spent more for them than the market could afford.

Thus our good judgment in making these pictures was completely nullified by our bad judgment in spending more than we should have. And the result of this is that both pictures stand on the books as failures for the simple reason that they cost more than they could take in, in spite of the fact that they both grossed enormously throughout the world.

D.F.Z.

≡

ALL ABOUT EVE

After rereading "The Wisdom of Eve," a short story by Mary Orr that had been published in the May 1946 issue of Cosmopolitan, *Fox's associate story editor James Fisher felt it should come to the attention of Joseph L. Mankiewicz. Then on April 29, 1949, Mankiewicz wrote a memo to Zanuck. He recommended purchasing the property and said that "it fits in with an original idea [of mine] and can be combined. Superb starring role for [Fox star] Susan Hayward." The rights were purchased a week later and the project was given to Mankiewicz to write and direct.*

Mankiewicz developed his treatment, dated September 26, 1949, which he called Best Performance, *and subsequently turned it in to Zanuck. Zanuck made his usual thick pencil annotations throughout the text, and on the inside back cover he noted the following casting possibilities: Claudette Colbert or Barbara Stanwyck for Margo, John Garfield or Gary Merrill for Bill Sampson, William Lundigan or Hugh Marlowe for Lloyd Richards, Celeste Holm for Karen, José Ferrer for Addison, Thelma Ritter for Birdie, J. Edward Bromberg for Max Fabian, and Jeanne Crain for Eve.*

Mankiewicz and Zanuck agreed on free-lance star Claudette Colbert for the role of Margo. Gary Merrill was selected to play director Bill Sampson. Celeste Holm was agreed upon for Karen, the playwright's wife, as was Hugh Marlowe for Lloyd, the playwright, and Thelma Ritter for Birdie. All but Colbert were under contract to Fox. Instead of José Ferrer, for whatever reason, former Fox contract player George Sanders was located in France and signed for the role of the cynical critic, Addison DeWitt. Gregory Ratoff, an old friend and associate of Zanuck's, was also brought back from Europe to take the role of the Broadway producer, Max Fabian.

For the small but important role of Miss Caswell ("a graduate of the Copacabana school of Dramatic Arts"), Mankiewicz recommended Marilyn Monroe, who had been dropped by Fox about two years earlier as a contract starlet.

Anne Baxter said that she was called to replace Jeanne Crain in the role of Eve after Crain became pregnant. Both were Fox stars at the time.

Many of Zanuck's comments on Mankiewicz's initial treatment had to do with his concern about revealing to the audience too early that Eve is a villain: "Beware of Birdie's jealousy as it will tip off that Eve is a heel," "Do we give it all away?" and so forth. Also, when Eve makes an overture to Bill Sampson in her dressing room and kisses him, Zanuck notes: "This is all wrong. She is too clever to jump in so quickly." The overture remained but the kiss was eliminated. Some long speeches were cut down to a few lines accompanied by a marginal note: "This should cover it all." And there were the usual assorted "Make clear. This can be confusing." Reacting to Karen draining the gas out of the tank of the Richardses' car to prevent Margo from getting to the theatre, Zanuck scrawled: "This is difficult to swallow."

A major concern was a series of scenes depicting Eve's calculated designs on Lloyd Richards. Zanuck wanted to cut the entire four pages that showed Eve and Lloyd spending time together—in little cafes on side streets, in Lloyd's apartment with Karen present and later without Karen, Eve's little furnished room, and Lloyd going to see Eve late at night after a phone call from a friend of Eve's. Zanuck noted: "Dull, obvious, dirty. . . . This is wrong. . . . All relationships with Eve and Lloyd [should be] played offstage by suggestion. . . . We get it by one brief scene at rehearsal." The material (other than the rehearsal scene) was subsequently dropped.

After Zanuck read the first draft of the screenplay six weeks later, he praised it highly but sent Mankiewicz some notes detailing further suggested changes and cuts. "I have tried to sincerely point out the spots that appeared dull or overdrawn. I have not let the length of the script influence me. I have tried to cut it as I am sure I would cut it if I were in

shooting script. One in particular was disregarded: "On page 32 I think the use of my name in a picture I am associated with will be considered self-aggrandizement. I believe you can cut it with no loss."
The line was provoked by Bill Sampson's impatience with Margo:

BILL

The airlines have clocks, even if you haven't. I start shooting a week from Monday—Zanuck is impatient, he wants me, he needs me!

MARGO
(*facetiously*)

Zanuck, Zanuck, Zanuck! What are you two—lovers?

The dialogue was photographed and remained in the released picture.

Remarkably few changes took place during Mankiewicz's writing of the various treatments and scripts with regard to construction, characters, or dialogue.

A few weeks before shooting was to commence Claudette Colbert ruptured a disk, was fitted with a steel brace, then put in traction. For various reasons, filming could not be postponed; it was necessary to replace her. Zanuck personally called Bette Davis, who recently had concluded her longtime affiliation with Warners, told her about the crisis, and sent the script to her. She read it and eagerly accepted.

Mankiewicz delivered his rough cut of the entire film by the end of June, two weeks or so after shooting finished. Zanuck saw it and asked for some structural changes. The shooting script (in part) had a device reminiscent of Citizen Kane (RKO, 1941): *Eve's story was presented from three different points of view, those of Addison, Karen, and Margo. In addition, as scripted and shot, one scene was repeated, as in* Citizen Kane *and in the Japanese film* Rashomon, *released in the United States in 1951. This was Eve's speech about the meaning of applause at Margo's party. The speech was shown as seen by Karen and then as perceived by Margo. Zanuck decided to eliminate some of the footage that established and maintained the interrelated points of view and the two versions of Eve's applause speech. He wanted to improve the pacing in what was then a very long film.*

The completed All About Eve *was a huge success from every standpoint. The film, Mankiewicz, Bette Davis, and others associated with the production were the recipients of many awards, domestic and foreign.*

≡

June 7, 1950
Mr. Charles Feldman [agent, producer, packager]
9441 Wilshire Blvd.
Beverly Hills, California

Dear Charlie:

. . . You are entirely wrong about my views on *A Streetcar Named Desire*. I had the story bought *before* you bought it. I worked out the deal completely with [Elia] Kazan in New York and then Spyros [Skouras] came in with his objections. He was so violent on the subject he even offered to resign the presidency of the corporation if we produced the picture. If you have any doubts on this point, talk it over with Kazan. In the face of this, I withdrew. . . .

I do not get your thinking on *Night and the City* [Fox, 1950]. After you had seen the picture you told me on three occasions that you thought it was one of the outstanding pictures of the year. You said that we had underrated it. . . . Now suddenly we have ruined the story. . . .

Moss Rose [1947] was a catastrophe, for which I blame myself. Our picture was not as good as the original script and the casting was atrocious. The property lost $1,300,000 net—but I am not asking you to assume any of this responsibility or send me your check.

You really infuriate me about *Home in Indiana* [1944]. You have a short memory. I personally rewrote your original script from start to finish. I eliminated characters, introduced new situations, gave it a box-office title and took a long shot gamble of putting three newcomers [Lon McAllister, Jeanne Crain, June Haver] in the picture in Technicolor. When you make an assertion that no changes were made in your script I just cannot believe that you are serious. Here is a statement of fact—more changes were made in *Home in Indiana* than were made in *Night and the City* and practically as many as in *Moss Rose*. The next time I see you I'm going to insist that you sit down and read your own script on this property. . . .

I am certain that you have never consciously lied to me and that you never will lie to me. If I inferred that you did, then I apologize.

You are a man of great honesty and integrity—you are also a master salesman, probably the best in the world. I also admire your courage and talent in taking on difficult stories and investing your time and money in developing them.

It is difficult for me to understand how either of us have benefited by this correspondence. With the exception of *Home in Indiana* all of our contacts on stories have proved disastrous for Twentieth Century–Fox. . . .

> Affectionate regards,
> Darryl

═

Feldman was one of two or three agents with whom Zanuck dealt personally on a regular basis.

═

TO: Mr. Louis D. Lighton [producer]   DATE: June 10, 1950
   SUBJECT: "NO HIGHWAY" [*in the Sky*] Revised first draft continuity of June 6, 1950

Dear Buddy:

. . . I am sure you will remember our original and basic problem on *Twelve O'Clock High* [1949]. . . . Six important directors had turned down the script because they thought it was too familiar. This was also true of a number of actors, including Gregory Peck. When I went to Sun Valley and combined the three different versions of the script and eliminated approximately forty-five pages, I did so only after I had discovered *what* was making intelligent people misread the script. I found out that we took about fifty pages to get our story started, or rather to get the first new idea in our script. But, by that time, the reader was convinced that he was again reading another version of *Command Decision* [novel, play, and M-G-M film of the time] or other air epics and thus the balance of the script, which was beautifully written [by Sy Bartlett and Beirne Lay, Jr.], suffered. We had lost the customer before he had ever seen the real merchandise.

The cuts in *Twelve O'Clock High* were not made by trimming some of the scenes or dropping other scenes. That was only part of it. I made the decision to eliminate certain ideas and a couple of complete situations, so that page fifty of the script would actually occur on page fourteen or thereabouts. I had to make up my mind to realistically face the problem and quit shadow-boxing with it. This meant making definite sacrifices in certain instances, but it has always continued to astonish me that the very people, including Gregory Peck, who disliked the earlier script, suddenly found themselves in love with the final version. Really. Aside from being forty-five pages shorter and having a more exciting and pictorial opening the changes made in the last version were not as drastic as they obviously *appeared* to be to the reader.

There is another remarkable thing about *Twelve O'Clock High*. We actually lost in [final film] editing less than four hundred and fifty feet [under five minutes]. We dropped only one brief sequence and the balance came out in normal trims. . . .

Now, mind you, I believe you had to write it [*No Highway in the Sky*] in full as you have done, just as you did the first script on *Twelve O'Clock High*, so that it could be evaluated. I think this was a necessary *step*, but only a step toward where we have to go. . . .

I may be screwy, but I give audiences today credit for a certain amount of intelligence or native imagination. They may not be brilliant but it doesn't take them long to catch on to what we are driving at. As a matter of fact, they would rather be a trifle in the dark, than have you spell it out for them, step by step, in a-b-c fashion. I can never remember sitting in the projection room and trying to pad out a scene to make it longer. We are always desperately trying to make a scene move, and I believe that audiences are generally much further ahead of us than we are apt to give them credit for. Especially, when you realize that fifty percent of every audience at every showing comes into the theatre when the picture is half over. These are actual figures. Apparently it does not spoil the picture for them at all, even when it is a picture where we have spent several reels at the beginning to carefully and meticulously build up character motivation.

Television notwithstanding, I believe that one of the reasons theatre business is so terrible today is because audiences are outguessing the producers. They know all the answers. In most cases, they are way ahead of us, and thus most pictures seem formula and routine. Our preview cards in the last year have emphasized more than ever one point of criticism: "Too slow . . . It drags . . . Speed it up." Now we even get these cards on pictures which are fast-paced and fast-moving. It is not the scenes, or actually the tempo, which seem to irritate audiences, but it is our generally plodding method of slow development and our failure to commit audiences to do a little thinking on their own. . . .

D.F.Z.

===

TO: Messrs. John Steinbeck   DATE: May 3, 1950
      Elia Kazan
      SUBJECT: ZAPATA Revised screenplay of April 27, 1950

Dear John and Gadg:

As I told you on the telephone, I am delighted with the script on *Zapata*. . . .

Not many pictures about Mexico have been financially successful. As a matter of fact, the only really outstanding success was a terrible piece of hoke called *Viva Villa* [M-G-M, 1934] starring Wallace Beery. This does not in the least disturb me any more than does the commercial failure of John Ford's *The Fugitive* [Argosy, 1947]. . . .

I like this story because it is a great story, regardless of background and nationality. It has guts and drive. . . .

When you first told me on the telephone that you were going to use a corrido* singer throughout the picture to sing the narration, it struck me as being a very original device. I like immensely the *way* you have

---

* A Mexican ballad or folk song about struggle against oppression and injustice.

used it throughout the script, but because I know so little about music, I am now beginning to feel a certain doubt and concern. . . .

Even though we assume that the corrido singer sings the narration in English with the flavor of a Spanish or Mexican accent, I still wonder if we do not run the risk of having it sound like something out of Gilbert and Sullivan. In the script, as it is now, a great deal of information which the audience must have to understand the story will come from the sung narration. If, later on, we find that this device does not work, we are going to be in a hell of a fix. Of course, if it does work, then we have no problem.

However, further in connection with this, I am wondering if in a hard-hitting dramatic story of this nature, which deals realistically with an historical event, if it may not seem as if we are trying to make an art or "mood" picture. The kind of thing John Ford does when he is stuck and has run out of plot. In these cases, somebody always sings and you cut to an extreme long shot with slanting shadows. . . .

I admit that I am baffled and I further admit that I know very little about music. . . .

I look forward to seeing you on May 17.

D.F.Z.

≡

TO: Mr. Elia Kazan   DATE: August 5, 1950
     Mr. John Steinbeck
     SUBJECT: ZAPATA

Dear Gadg and John:

. . . I have been associated with enough musicals in the past twenty years to know that audiences pay very little attention to lyrics if, at the same time, they are looking at a series of scenes. They will grasp the general gist of the lyrics, but I would hate to be in a position where we had to tell something by this method alone. . . .

I fought the battle of lyrics with Hammerstein and Rodgers in *State Fair* [1945], where, if you will recall, we tried to tell some of the story in lyrics. We were able to tell the mood of the scenes and the general idea, but we finally resorted to supplementary scenes in order to get over specific points. . . .

I like the ambush and the assassination. It is very effective. I also like immensely the scene in the marketplace where the townspeople inspect the body and refuse to believe it is Zapata. . . .

I once made a pretty good picture with George Arliss. The film was eight reels long, but he died in the seventh reel. At the preview, I was somewhat embarrassed to find myself sitting practically alone in the theatre during the last reel.

In *Zapata*, from the scene where the countrymen refuse to believe it is Zapata, I recommend that we have a very simple finish. . . .

D.F.Z.

===

TO: Messrs. Elia Kazan   DATE: December 26, 1950
       John Steinbeck
      SUBJECT: ZAPATA (Revised screenplay of December, 1950)

Dear Gadg and John:

Here we go again. As I told you in the telegram this morning, I think the dramatic improvements are immense so I will not stop to talk about the things I like but will emphasize all the elements that continue to disturb me. . . .

As it stands now, I think we have inadvertently told a story of pure frustration. The downbeat nature of the last act, where tragedy comes on top of tragedy, is partly responsible for this. This can be cured, but I am certain that the cure must go deeper and get into the blood of Zapata himself. There is nothing exciting, or even noble, about Zapata's assassination. To me, it is the frustrating end of a series of frustrations. . . .

I have no objection to killing a leading man or a hero in the last act of a picture. I've even killed Clifton Webb in the last act of his biggest hit, *Cheaper By the Dozen* [1950] and ended a comedy on a tragic note, but the tragic note had an upbeat to it. It seemed the right and *satisfactory* finish.

For me, at least, our finish is far from satisfactory. . . .

What is the key which Zapata finally finds? What is the thing that gave him this new and last burst of energy which makes him willing to take any chance and any gamble?

I believe he has found exactly the same thing you now have in the script: "Leaders will arise from the people, if the people are given the chance" . . .

Corny or not, I think we should make use of every possible device to give us a lift in this last act. . . .

Now, further about Zapata's *idea*: Certainly it isn't Communism, and we want to make this very clear because, frankly, in the present script there is inadvertently a peculiar air about certain speeches, which might be interpreted by the Communists to claim that we are subtly working for them. It seems that Zapata is surrounded by a couple of fairly well-informed people. Even though one of them is very misguided. I refer to Pablo and Bicho. Pablo must have told Zapata about a little country known as the United States of America. After all, Pablo went to Texas. It seems to me that Zapata must have heard about free elections and a government run by the people for the people. Nowhere in the script do we get any indication that anyone is talking about democracy. . . .

Personally, I hate pictures which show scenes of people forming their own little governments in the mountains, the kids going to school, the old people working, the women making bullets, etc. All of this is no particular novelty to moviegoers. (A recent dull example is our own *American Guerrilla in the Philippines* [1950].) However, perhaps if it can be told in terms of excitement and with the driving force of a Zapata who has suddenly found what he believes to be the *answer*, it can become suspenseful and interesting entertainment. . . .

Throughout the script, I kept asking myself, "What exactly are we trying to *say* in this story? Why are we particularly making this picture? What do we *finally* say when the story is over?" Frankly, I do not know. Unless we give Zapata a key for the last act, it doesn't seem to me that we are saying much of anything. I hope people don't get the impression that we are advocating revolt or civil war as the only means of peace. When the United States revolted from the domination of Great Britain, our founding fathers already had a nice little *plan*. They wrote an interesting and very practical Constitution. . . .

You know that I hate messages and preachments in pictures. We avoided them in *Gentleman's Agreement*, *Pinky*, etc. But the picture itself, as a whole, should be the message or the preachment. I am assuming that the things I have been talking about can be dramatized in terms of action, excitement and entertainment. . . .

Grapes of Wrath was a pretty grim picture in many respects. It could very easily have been a downbeat picture of total frustration, yet the Joads were *never* frustrated. Look at the last reel again and listen to what Pa and Ma Joad have to say. Every tragedy in the world hit them, but you went out of the theatre with an upbeat in your heart because their courage and guts set an example for you.

Now, we come to the sixty-four dollar question: Let us assume, optimistically, that you agree with my observations. Let us further assume that you can reduce these observations to showmanship terms and dramatize my ravings. Is this the right *time* to make this picture? Is this the moment to tell the story of a Mexican revolutionary hero? I do not expect it to directly apply to the world situation today, nor do I expect present-day audiences to learn any great lesson from it. But, shouldn't every historical picture have some sort of significance even though that significance be vague? Of course, I suppose if it is a very great entertainment, loaded with theatre, and if the audience sits on the edge of the seats in the last act, and if underneath it all it has a small cry for democracy, audiences will love it and not ask any questions.

We should be aware, however, of the fact that we are dealing with an historical subject and thus we have a certain responsibility which makes it doubly necessary that the entertainment features of our project be twice as effective as they would have to be if we were making a period piece like *Way of a Gaucho* [Fox, 1952], which pretends to do nothing more than deal with fictional characters during the same period in the Argentine. In *Way of a Gaucho* we have no responsibility except to entertain an audience. In *Zapata*, we have to make certain that our entertainment will carry the added responsibility of answering the question: "Exactly what is this all about? And what was the purpose in making it?"

If I knew the answer to the questions asked above I would probably still be working for Warner Brothers. Every picture presents a new gamble and a responsibility of one sort or another. I like this story, or rather I like what I think it can eventually become. If you agree with me that it can become a *show* and still remain a picture of taste and dignity, then I definitely want to go ahead with it. You have got to share this decision in the light of what I have said above, and also in the light of some of the things I have yet to say. You have to share this responsibility certainly on equal terms. We will all get kicked below the belt if it does not turn out to be a commercial as well as an artistic success. *Sunset Boulevard* [Paramount, 1950] was a masterpiece until it was released throughout the country and failed to do business. It is not so big a masterpiece today.

If they say your writing is pure genius, and the direction is inspired, and the production is faultless, all of this is splendid. But, unless we earn our way with the theatregoers we are bums. I'm not trying to frighten you or frighten myself, but I want to put it all down so that you can help me make my decisions and we can go ahead with our eyes wide open. . . .

This brings me to the question of the corridos. In carefully looking through the script I cannot find one spot where we are compelled to use the corridos. It seems to me that almost everything we want to know is told clearly in the action and the dialogue. Personally, this makes me very happy, although I doubt whether you will share my elation. . . .*

Let us think a moment about casting. While I was reading this script, I was trying to visualize the scenes and the characters and the background. And I was conscious of the fact that we must make a definite decision on the principal role. Of course, English is the language of our picture, but if we have one accent we are then going to have to have everyone in the story speak with the same accent. If we are going to contemplate casting someone like [free-lance star] Marlon Brando as Zapata, this means that we must be prepared to eliminate any thought of accent, or even the flavor of accent.

How will this look and sound? What will be the illusion when we hear a grizzled old Mexican warrior speak clear-cut English? Will we

---

* The corridos were eliminated.

find real Mexican types and dub their voices? Or, will we have to find American actors and make them up to look like Mexican types?

There are many schools of thought on this and I have had both pleasant and unpleasant experiences in this regard. On the picture we are now making in Germany, *Decision Before Dawn*, which Anatole Litvak is directing, we have used an entire German cast, with the exception of the two Americans who play G.I.s. All the main roles are played by German actors who speak English with a German accent. The illusion is very good, although we are going to have to do a hell of a lot of dubbing. While you understand everything they are saying, because of the accent you get the impression that they are speaking German and the illusion is perfect.

You are going to want to use a lot of fine actors from Mexico City. They will be able to speak English, but they will certainly speak English with a Mexican accent. Yet, unless we cast a Mexican in the role of Zapata, we are going to have to have Zapata either fake a Mexican accent or we're going to have to dub English voices for the Mexican actors. Certainly, Zapata should speak like his countrymen. In addition to this, you are going to find wonderful Mexican types for bits and the small roles, and it would be crazy not to use them if we made the picture in Mexico. Therefore, these will all have to be dubbed. This is no particular problem. The big problem lies in the man who plays Zapata. If a Mexican is used, then we should use all Mexican players and let them all speak with their own natural accent. But, if we use Brando, or any other American, we face the problem of either dubbing his voice or letting him speak with a fake accent, or dubbing all of the other Mexican actors in English. . . . The leading German actors whom Litvak used refused to be dubbed, claiming that they are stars in their own country and that their voices are well known.

I suppose we cannot actually make any decision until we decide on Zapata. The simplest solution would be if we could come up with a Mexican or a Spanish actor talented enough to play Zapata. If we do not, and use an American, then I think we should figure on using Americans in all of the key leading roles.

I would value your opinions on this point.

I am going to be here until approximately the last week in January. Then I will be in Europe for about five weeks. Will you (Gadg) come out here on the 15th? And will you (John) come with him? Maybe if you could get together for a week *before* you come out here, we could then get together and come to some sort of an understanding.

I want you both to know that I want to go ahead with the project. I don't know whether I'm right in wanting to go ahead or whether it will be a mistake. But if we do go ahead, I want to be certain that we have taken advantage of every opportunity to make a fine show as well as a fine picture. . . .

If the odds are right I will gamble on anything and I have found out that the only way you can get the right odds is to take advantage of all the possibilities.

Best always,

≡

May 2, 1951
Mr. Elia Kazan
167 E. 74th Street
New York, N.Y.

Dear Gadg:

I have been working for several weeks "behind your back." I did not want to bother you or involve you in these Mexican transactions but now I will give you the whole story.

The official Mexican Government Censor Board know that we are going to make *Zapata* and make it in the United States, therefore they got in touch with our representatives in Mexico City and said that since we were determined to go ahead with the project they would like to be of "service" to us. They also implied a threat to the effect that if we disgraced their national hero in any way they would completely ban the picture from ever playing in Mexico and might even make diplomatic efforts to ban the picture for all of South America.

This started a series of negotiations while you were in El Paso. I will not go into the details of the negotiations but we finally succeeded in getting the Censor Board to send here at our expense an official Government representative, Professor Sologuren. He is an historical authority on Zapata. We brought him here to the studio and he has been here for two weeks studying the script and having innumerable conferences with Jason Joy, Molly Mandaville and Dr. Barcia, a translator.

Finally they presented their views on our script scene by scene and line by line. They have agreed that if we accept the majority of their suggestions they will pass the picture for Mexico. This is very important financially to us.

I had a meeting on the matter today and I accepted 80% of their suggestions. Do not be alarmed. They are mainly insignificant suggestions dealing with historical and technical facts. Most of the suggestions were very helpful because they corrected some errors that were very glaring errors in our script.

I did not let them tamper with any dramatic scene. I refused flatly to incorporate any of their "dramatic" suggestions—but I did agree that in the Mexican *print* of *Zapata* we would change the subtitles to meet some of their other suggestions but this would be only for the *Mexican* prints and not affect the English version. Since this only involves cutting and subtitles I saw no reason why I shouldn't compromise. . . .

I feel that they will "buy" all of the points I have agreed to because these men have definite *authority* to act for the Censor Board in this matter and before they leave we are going to try to get a letter from them accepting the script and the picture. Later on we will "doll up" a Mexican version of the picture for them that I am sure will satisfy them.

When you get all of the notes from Molly and have had a chance to study them please let me hear from you and meanwhile do not be alarmed because nothing has been harmed.

Regards,
Darryl

≡

Viva Zapata! (1952) *featured Marlon Brando in the title role and a non-Mexican cast. It was not a commercially successful picture in the United States. Several months after its release, Zanuck told columnist Hedda Hopper: "It was a disappointment. I made a mistake in subject matter. It was alien to American audiences." However, the picture did do well in Mexico, Cuba, South America, and Europe.*

SIX

THE GOING GETS TOUGHER

We have completed our third survey of audience and box-office reaction to all pictures released during the last quarter. It is always difficult to speak in broad or general terms about the *reasons* for the success or failure of individual pictures—or even of groups of pictures—because there are always certain exceptions.

One thing stands out very clearly and that is the fact that the theatre-going public has been saturated with pictures of violence and films with underworld or "low" backgrounds. . . .

There is no such thing as a "safe" field. Theatregoers are more selective of their entertainment than ever before. Anything that is routine or formula can be expected to do that type of business. . . .

You cannot regularly depend on any so-called "box-office" cast. Such a thing is practically nonexistent. Names will add a certain amount of something to a *fine picture* but without a fine picture they add very little. . . .

We are in a "fight to the finish" in an effort to revive the box office. No company can depend on only a few successful pictures. . . .

No amount of technical skill, superb direction and production or box-office names can save a picture based on subject matter that does not have the potentialities of broad, popular appeal. Overpriced pictures where we optimistically let the cost exceed the dollar potentialities have turned a number of pictures that *could* have been successes into failures. We were right in our selection of subject matter, cast—but we spent more than the market could afford. . . .

D.F.Z.

≡

June 15, 1950
Personal and Confidential
Mr. Lewis Milestone [director]
Camp Pendleton

Dear Millie:

First off I want to tell you that I am highly pleased with the manner in which you are directing [*The Halls of*] *Montezuma* [1950]. The battle scenes have scope, authenticity and a good broad sweep of action. The intimate personal scenes are sound and effective. . . .

The second purpose of this letter is to confidentially inform you that I have another project in the very near future that might be of mutual interest. . . .

Now purely as your friend and on a personal and confidential basis I will tell you what I think about you and your work. You are a highly talented individual. Your main talent is your ability to *direct*.

I believe you can contribute business and ideas to a finished script and that you can give much in the way of characterization. I think it is *fatal* for you when you try to do anything in addition.

You have a perfect knack for picking the wrong story, and I think that more than anything else this has contributed to the "bad luck" you have had in the past four or five years. Not one of the pictures you were associated with, with the exception of *Arch of Triumph* [Enterprise,

1948], should ever have been attempted, and on *Arch of Triumph*, where you had practically complete authority as both producer and director, you made one of the worst pictures I have ever seen in my life—and there was no need for it, although I would never have picked the story for myself.

Personally, more than anything else I would love to be a portrait painter, but long ago I came to the realization that if one man has *one* talent he should be grateful and satisfied.

You were blessed with the talent of directing and the ability to enthuse a company. You know your job in this category and you know it well. You do not have to take a back seat to anyone.

Right now you will need more than the one good credit for *Montezuma* to rehabilitate yourself in the eyes of this suspicious and calloused industry. In all probability you will not listen to me and you will embark on another adventure which will end up unproduced like the last one. . . . If you listen to me you will settle down, at least for the next year or two, to the job of doing what you can do best—directing.

I am saying the above not because I am trying to encourage you on the idea of going on this next expedition but because I admire anybody with real talent and I hate to see it wasted or diffused.

Best always,
Darryl

=

At the time of this letter, Milestone's best work was behind him.

=

DATE: June 15, 1950

TO: Delmer Daves [producer, writer, director]
STRICTLY CONFIDENTIAL

Dear Delmer:

Before you go away we are going to sit down and have a talk on both the practical and creative phases of *Bird of Paradise*. . . . I am content and confident that this will emerge a success, but only if you are completely honest with yourself and *recognize* the faults and excesses of *Broken Arrow* [1950].

Let me give you an example of something that happened on that picture. I saw from the very beginning that your tempo in the dialogue scenes was hopelessly slow and that we would have to find ways and means of speeding it up, cutting dialogue, etc. I made this decision *after* I looked at three cut episodes. I sent [film editor] Watson Webb down to the location to talk to you on this point because I knew perfectly well we were going to have to go through murder. You were very gracious and polite with Watson, but you told him in no uncertain terms that you were playing the scenes exactly the way that you thought they should be played and that you had deliberately timed the action in this fashion. Watson saw there was no point in sticking around so he came home.

The very scenes that disturbed me were the scenes that you yourself in the cutting room months later realized were overdrawn and dragging. You yourself urged me to make cuts more drastic than those I knew were necessary.

Now we are all genuinely happy with the final result on *Broken Arrow*. We have nevertheless edited a triumph in spite of everything. Whether it remains to be a box-office hit is another matter because the picture has to gross over $3,250,000 to break even. I don't believe any picture on this lot in many years has benefited by editing as much as did *Broken Arrow*. I know that I sweated night after night and I also know that we had to sacrifice a certain number of very valuable and good moments in an effort to give the picture as a whole the benefit of tempo and movement.

The best scenes in the picture were Jimmy's [James Stewart's] death scene and the scenes in the tent between [Jeff] Chandler [loaned by Universal-International] and Jimmy. In practically every large-scale scene we tried desperately to "cut around" guns that were lifted in the wrong places, certain awkward movements, and a few just downright poor scenes such as the barroom, the lynching, etc. I remember that you, when you were in the cutting room with me on various occasions, shared my views about these scenes—however, in the main *Broken*

Arrow was blessed with an amazing script, a powerful story, spectacular scenery, a great human quality and, in the final version, by several outstanding performances.

I make many mistakes and some of them are most serious. I honestly try to keep from kidding myself. I am aware of my lack more than anyone else is. I try, however, to benefit by every mistake. If I get by with a mistake I consider myself very *lucky* and try not to make the same mistake again. . . .

Rehearse your actors every moment you can spare. One of the criticisms on the other picture [*Broken Arrow*] was the fact that several of the actors themselves mentioned that frequently they did not feel they had had sufficient rehearsal before they were pushed into the scene and the cameras clicked. Whether this is true or not, you yourself must be the judge. I am passing it along because I want to lay *everything* on the line, and you know that my only reason is to help *insure* the getting of a great picture.

≡

Broken Arrow, *based on the novel* Blood Brother *by Elliott Arnold, was extremely well received critically and commercially. The screenplay, credited to "front" Michael Blankfort, was actually written by black-listed Albert Maltz, who was imprisoned for refusing to cooperate with the House Committee on Un-American Activities. Daves did several more films for Fox.* Bird of Paradise *did reasonably well.*

≡

TO: Delmer Daves   DATE: June 16, 1950

Dear Delmer:

. . . I do not claim that Kazan is the best director in the business but after making five highly successful films with him I am willing to bet that he puts more *responsibility* on the key men of his crew than any director that has ever operated on this lot. He invests them with authority and genuine responsibility and while he keeps the final word for himself he nevertheless repeatedly follows their recommendations to the letter. Anyone in the Production Department will substantiate this. . . .

D.F.Z.

≡

July 10, 1950
"TAKE CARE OF MY LITTLE GIRL" CONFERENCE ON FIRST DRAFT CONTINUITY OF JULY 3, 1950 (with Messrs. [Julian] Blaustein [producer], [Julius J.] Epstein and [Philip G.] Epstein [writers], Molly Mandaville)

. . . Despite Liz's [Jeanne Crain's] parrot-like mouthing of her mother's beliefs, we must know that . . . her instincts are against snobbery as exemplified by the Greek letter society system [in universities and colleges]. It is vitally necessary that we get this into the script, otherwise her turning against Tri-U is going to seem like an overnight conversion. . . .

All her life she has looked forward to being a member of Tri-U, and now it is thought to have it indicated that this is not the be-all and end-all of existence.

In her arguments with Joe [Fox contract player Dale Robertson] about Greek letter societies, Liz should be given some arguments in favor of same. Gentlemen, you'll simply have to find some credible arguments, because as it is now in the script you wonder why any idiot could be taken in by the hocus-pocus. Here are a few suggestions:

(a) "Sororities are a part of college life. You have to live somewhere; therefore, why not among people who share your likes and dislikes, etc."

(b) "You form friendships which endure for life. You may marry and live far from your own family and friends, and if you belong to a sorority you will find a circle of friends no matter where you go" (even in darkest Africa, no doubt).

(c) "Suppose colleges decided to disband all Greek letter societies? Suppose everybody had to live in dormitories? Inevitably groups would form; people with similar tastes would gravitate together and thus you would have the same 'evils' you now complain about. If groups are going to form, why not have your own house and your own life together?"

(d) "According to your theory, a person shouldn't belong to *any* organization. If you believe this, then in this same category you would have to put the Masons, the Knights of Columbus, etc. All these organizations are based on a wish for companionship of people with mutual likes and dislikes, etc. . . ."

Liz should sincerely believe these things; she has heard them from her mother all her life. It is only when she is forced to think for herself that she begins to realize the fallacy of her thinking. . . .

═══

The film was based on the novel of the same name by Peggy Goodin.

═══

July 13, 1950
Mr. Nunnally Johnson
20th Century–Fox Productions, Ltd.
Shepperton, Middlesex
England

Dear Nunnally:

Here is the story to date on *The Gunfighter* [Fox, 1950]. It did miserable business at the Roxy Theatre in New York where, with the exception of *Yellow Sky* [Fox, 1949], no Western has done well in New York. It did ordinary business here in Los Angeles. It has done much better however in most places in the rest of the country.

It will be a profit-making picture, but in spite of its sensational reviews it receives everywhere, and the unstinted praise, we will be lucky if we do seventy or seventy-five percent of the business we did on *Yellow Sky*. Perhaps, in the outlying districts and western areas it will eventually come up to anticipation. As I said, in any event, it will be a profit-making picture but certainly nothing like we had every right to anticipate.

It is unquestionably a minor classic, but I really believe that it violates so many true Western traditions that it goes over the heads of the type of people who patronize Westerns, and there are not enough of the others to give us the top business we anticipated.

By way of passing, [Fox executive] Al Lichtman showed me a report from the ushers at the Roxy Theatre [in New York City]. As you know, they have more than 100 ushers and floor employees and they are trained to talk to patrons whenever there is a gracious opportunity. What do you think the complaint is on the picture? I will list them separately:

a.) Why do they cast Gregory Peck in this kind of role and then put a walrus moustache on him and hide his face?★ If they wanted an ugly man, why didn't they take an ugly actor? Why waste Peck? This comment occurred hundreds of times, particularly from women and young girls.

b.) Why didn't they let him live at the finish? After all, he had been reformed. He could have been wounded, if they wanted to shoot him. But he should have been allowed to live.

The only thing I can say is that we live and learn. Sometimes, you wonder why classic pictures like *The Snake Pit, Twelve O'Clock High* and *Pinky* are enormous box-office hits and other pictures that belong in the same category do not do fifty percent of the business. *Yellow Sky*, in my opinion, is not half the picture that *The Gunfighter* is. Yet it went into a more formula mold and obviously had broader popular appeal. But, on the other hand, there was certainly no formula mold about *The Snake Pit* and look what it did. . . .

Best always,
Darryl

≡

The Gunfighter was based on a story by William Bowers and Andre de Toth.

≡

★ Zanuck was quoted years later by director Henry King as saying, "I would give $25,000 of my own money to get that moustache off Peck."

TO: Henry King [director]   DATE: November 7, 1950
     Billy Gordon [casting director]
     Philip Dunne [writer]
     SUBJECT: DAVID AND BATHSHEBA

. . . Practically all the screen tests were overacted so badly it was difficult for me to like any of them. I have never seen more scenery chewed up more thoroughly. The minute you put even a good actor in a biblical costume he starts to read the scriptures instead of his role. . . .

Somehow or other they always seem to get very "majestic" the moment they get into costume.

D.F.Z.

===

TO: Julian Blaustein [producer]   DATE: August 10, 1950
CC: Edmund North [writer]
   SUBJECT: FAREWELL TO THE MASTER [*The Day the Earth Stood Still*]

Dear Julian:

Herewith is my comment on *Farewell to the Master* [based on a story by Harry Bates]. I think it has great possibilities. . . .

I do not like the title. We must have an exciting, provocative title that will tell an audience what to *expect*.

I do not like Episode #1 in the spaceship. When you open a picture on something that does not "exist" you have great trouble in capturing your audience. And, to me, this opening completely spoiled the start of the film.

You should open with the second sequence and treat it as realistically as you possibly can. You should suddenly hear radio programs being interrupted with startling flash announcements from Washington, New York, Los Angeles, etc. The whole nation is "listening in." This should be dramatized like the opening of a documentary film. . . .

My whole point here is that if you give Gnut [renamed Gort] or Klaatu [Fox contract player Michael Rennie] too much supernatural power, then Klaatu will never be in any real physical danger. In the hospital, by letting him see through walls, you put him automatically beyond harm from human hands and thus, the entire chase at the finish of the picture will not have any suspense because you believe that at any moment he can press a magic button and float away or make himself immune.

It is okay to have him "disappear" from the hospital mysteriously as long as you don't actually show it—but merely find him gone.

I feel strongly that by avoiding the more fabulous "tricks" such as Gnut's ability to paralyze the soldiers and the guards, we will help an audience "accept" our entire project. If we go into elements that are so radical or so fantastic, the whole thing will actually get out of the realm of science-fiction and will look like a total fantasy.

I believe you can do most of the things that you want to do and yet compel the audience to completely *accept* this story as something that could possibly happen in the not too distant future. Every effort should be made to avoid anything that will destroy the illusion.

On this point, we should also know immediately there is a difference between Gnut and Klaatu. Gnut should have some sort of mechanical appearance.★ He is the "force" and Klaatu is the human.

I believe we have stressed from here on entirely too heavily on political problems. I don't mean to avoid them because that is an entire issue of the story, but I believe that if we try to preach or propagandize too obviously we will defeat ourselves. . . .

I do not like the idea of Klaatu being able to cure himself with some mysterious salve. This again takes him out of any future danger. Why not just let him have a superficial flesh wound in the arm? . . .

Also, I was disturbed by putting *too much* emphasis on the point that we must now turn entirely to scientists for the salvation of the problems of the earth. . . .

It seems to me that the whole last situation can be made more logical and valid if before Klaatu is shot and killed, he gives Helen [free-lance player Patricia Neal] something that will serve as a password† to get her into see Gnut. Perhaps it is a strange ring or something that he wears. Thus, when Helen goes to the spaceship she will at least have some-

★ Gort (Gnut) is a robot in the final version.

† The password became "Klaatu Barada Nikto."

thing tangible to prevent Gnut from instantly killing her and to make Gnut *believe* her story. . . .

On the last half of page 33, you state the case *perfectly*. Klaatu doesn't give a hoot how Earthmen run their own planet. He's concerned about the behavior of the Earth with regard to the other planets. This bears out the contention that I expressed earlier in this note.

I do not like the destruction of the Rock of Gibraltar. I certainly do not believe that Klaatu has to give any further visual demonstrations.

I think it can be a very exciting picture. . . .

Has the title *The Man from Mars* been used?

D.F.Z.

═══

Virtually all of Zanuck's suggestions were followed. The Day the Earth Stood Still *was directed by Robert Wise.*

═══

TO: Henry King [director]   DATE: October 12, 1950
CONFIDENTIAL

During my recent trip abroad and during my consultation with distributors and exhibitors in New York, I've come to certain conclusions regarding the present "appetite" of the theatregoing public. Since my return, I've had an opportunity to study and analyze theatre receipts and box-office grosses on all pictures, including those from our competitors. . . .

Audiences today, particularly in America, do not want pictures of violence or extreme brutality. In spite of the high quality of such pictures as *Panic in the Streets* [Fox, 1950], *Asphalt Jungle* [M-G-M, 1950], *Where the Sidewalk Ends* [Fox, 1950], etc., etc., these films and all films in this category have proved to be a shocking disappointment. . . . Particularly, if they are "downbeat" in nature or deal with sordid backgrounds, unsympathetic characters and over-emphasized "suffering."

Pictures dealing even remotely with sickness or disease are not wanted. An exceptional picture of this nature manages to squeeze by occasionally. *The Men* [Stanley Kramer, 1950] is a disappointment and *No Sad Songs for Me* [Columbia, 1950], despite it being a good picture, is an absolute washout. I actually believe that the indication of disease in *Panic in the Streets* is one of the elements that contributed to the poor returns on this fine picture, which received unanimous praise from the critics. . . .

Pictures dealing with psychopathic characters have also outlived their usefulness *at this time*. There have been twenty-three pictures released in eighteen months in which one or more characters are motivated by psychopathic or psychiatric disorders. It has gotten so that this has become the standard motivation for practically all evildoers. Of course, again, there is always an exceptional picture that for other reasons may be able to survive at the box office in spite of this handicap. But you cannot with any sense of security depend on this. Pictures in this category are certainly a very high risk. . . .

D.F.Z.

≡

November 7, 1950
"OPERATION CICERO" [5 *Fingers*] CONFERENCE ON STORY REPORT OF NOVEMBER 6, 1950 WITH MESSRS. OTTO LANG [producer], MICHAEL WILSON [writer], MOLLY MANDAVILLE

. . . The great value of any semidocumentary picture, such as *The House on 92nd Street*, *Call Northside 777* and *Street with No Name*, lies in the fact that while the story need not be true in every case, it must be presented in such a way that the audience *thinks* the whole story is true. This is . . . something you simply must have. If you can't make the audience believe your story is an actual happening or based on an actual happening, you're in trouble.

You can dramatize and take certain liberties and licenses as we did in the pictures mentioned above provided you start out with a convincing opening. If you start out with a feeling of authenticity you immediately have the audience on your side and they tell themselves that while this seems an incredible story, it must be true. . . .

I see this as a "Raffles"* type of story. "Raffles" was a thief and a robber, yet he always had the audience pulling for him because of his daring exploits, his willingness to take risks, etc. Also, "Raffles" committed his crimes purely for gain. He was not out to save the world or to get revenge on anyone—he simply wanted to make a few bucks. . . .

The idea originated by this studio in such pictures as *House on 92nd Street, Street with No Name*, etc. of having a man, usually someone on the side of the law, masquerade as someone else in order to accomplish a certain end was a very good one, but unfortunately it has been copied now in too many pictures. Therefore, in order to give freshness and originality to this idea, we should drop the idea of having the man who tells this story be on the side of the Allies. The "hero" of our picture should be Cicero, the spy [free-lance star James Mason]. At the end, we want the Allies to be chasing him and the Nazis chasing him, and it is possible to devise it so that the audience will be rooting for him to escape. . . .

Cicero is an apolitical character. He has no hatred of Germany; no love either. He has no brief against anybody. We must keep all animosity, all frustration, all desire for revenge, out of his character. He has only one feeling, one ambition: to get enough money to retire. . . .

D.F.Z.

≡

TO: Otto Lang [producer] DATE: December 5, 1950
SUBJECT: OPERATION CICERO [5 *Fingers*], WHITE WITCH DOCTOR

Dear Otto:

. . . I am convinced that the outline I wrote on *Operation Cicero* [5 *Fingers*] is the absolutely correct approach to the entire project. I did not solve all of the dramatic problems but it should not be too difficult for a capable writer to construct the story on the structure presented to him. . . .

The same is true, in less detail of course, in connection with *White Witch Doctor* [1953].

D.F.Z.

* The hero of a series of novels by E. W. Hornung.

≡

The screenplay of 5 Fingers *was written by Michael Wilson, follow-*
ing Zanuck's notes and the autobiographical source material, Operation Cicero *by L. C. Moyzisch.*

≡

TO: Otto Lang   DATE: September 11, 1951
Joe Mankiewicz
SUBJECT: 5 FINGERS

Dear Otto and Joe:

I read the final script again this morning on *5 Fingers* and after
thinking a great deal about the last act I am absolutely convinced that
we can make, without danger to the quality of our picture, a number of
eliminations.

I want to follow in this instance the same procedure that I followed
with Kazan on *Viva Zapata!* and with [Henry] King on *David and
Bathsheba.* We held in abeyance several "questionable" sequences. They
were sequences that had always been in the script but as the picture was
drawing toward a close it became doubtful as to whether or not these
sequences were essential. In the case of *Zapata* we actually held three
entire episodes in abeyance. Now that I have worked on the cutting of
Zapata I find that I need none of the episodes.

In the case of the other picture I found that I did need the opening
sequence and thus after the picture was finished we went back and
photographed it.

The eliminations that can be made in *5 Fingers* are simple and clean-
cut. If we need them after the picture is finished we can make them.
These sequences save three or four days' shooting time and when you
take into consideration the *fact* that we are tremendously overlength
from the standpoint of footage and that we are now running slightly
behind schedule and that the picture is certainly costing a great deal
more than we originally intended, I have no other decision to make in
the situation. . . .

Mainly because I am now editing nine completed pictures, I have decided not to look at any of the rushes on this picture and will wait to see it when you have it put together in first assembly. From all I hear the quality of the merchandise is excellent.

D.F.Z.

≡

TO: All Directors   DATE: November 25, 1950

This note is directed primarily to directors under contract to or working for 20th Century–Fox. As you know, I do not make a habit of going on the sets. I try to keep off the stages, so that I may view the rushes each day with some sort of perspective. This has long been my policy and it will continue to be my policy.

I realize that there are no specific rules or regulations that can be set down for directors. Every picture, every scene presents its own individual problem. . . .

I believe that as a general rule we use entirely too many closeups. They have the effect of cutting down the tempo, rather than speeding it up. It is needless for me to tell you what you save from a standpoint of time and money if you design your master scene that avoids too many subsidiary angles.

I think the two best examples are *Twelve O'Clock High* [Fox, 1949] and *Father of the Bride* [M-G-M, 1950]. They contained minimal [camera] setups and practically no closeups, yet you always had the feeling that the people were close to the camera and that everything that should be seen, could be seen. I realize that this calls for a skill and a real knowledge of your profession. I also recognize that there are circumstances where you cannot always achieve this sort of perfection. . . .

I believe *Father of the Bride* holds the record as having the lowest number of camera setups in any feature picture. I understand the sequel [*Father's Little Dividend*, 1951] was photographed in nineteen days.

Today we are continually fighting the battle of costs. A new box-office slump, which is the most drastic since the war, has compelled us, and will compel us further, to devise ways and means of economizing without affecting basic quality. . . .

If you get a chance, look at *Twelve O'Clock High* again. You will be amazed that at least sixty percent of the picture is told in master scenes, without closeups. . . . To me, this is as much of an art as the art of getting the right expression on the actor's face and the proper sound to his voice. I believe that is why you are called *directors*, and that it is an integral part of your profession.

The idea of "punching it up" here and there with a closeup is in most cases quite old-fashioned. I realize that if you are stuck with a poor actor, or if you have an action picture that has to be told in quick cuts, you cannot always follow this recommendation. But when you do have a story or a scene that can sustain itself with proper staging and use of the camera, you should certainly strive to take advantage of these possibilities. . . .

D.F.Z.

≡

TO: Joseph L. Mankiewicz   DATE: December 20, 1950
PERSONAL AND CONFIDENTIAL

Dear Joe:

This is a confidential note. Regardless of who finally plays the role in *Dr. Praetorius* [*People Will Talk*, 1951], I want you to know that I am not going to take any screen credit as producer. I will of course function in exactly the same way that I functioned on *No Way Out* [1950] and *All About Eve* [1950] and give you as much of my time, energy and attention as I have given you in the past.

My reasons for avoiding screen credit on your assignments are purely personal and selfish reasons.

When you are both the writer and director on a film the producer is inevitably subjected to a forgotten or completely secondary role. I am experiencing this now on *All About Eve* and it is the first time I have ever experienced it. Usually I give a director a finished script to work with. That script is the result of my collaboration with the writers. It is my job. . . . As a matter of fact, it has always been true, including *Twelve O'Clock High, How Green Was My Valley, Grapes of Wrath*, etc. I gave the script to Henry King on *David and Bathsheba* after the entire script had been completed to the last detail, sets designed and the picture cast.

I am saying this to you because I don't want you to feel that later on I am ducking out. You completely deserve all of the credit you are getting on *All About Eve*. By the same token, when I put my name on a picture as the producer I have my own conscience as well as my own reputation to consider. In *Dr. Praetorius* you will again make the major contribution and if the picture is a hit you will get the major share of the credit since you will serve in two capacities.

On *David and Bathsheba* [1951], Phil Dunne is the writer, Henry King is the director and D.F.Z. is the producer. Both my conscience and my reputation will survive or fall on the result of my work and good or bad, I will not be lost in the shuffle.

D.F.Z.

≡

Zanuck ultimately did take producer credit on People Will Talk. *It did very well commercially in the domestic market, but only fair in Europe.* David and Bathsheba *did spectacular business in the U.S. and foreign markets.*

≡

TO: Philip Dunne [producer-writer]   DATE: February 16, 1951

Dear Phil:

. . . Work closely with Henry [King] on [*Way of a*] *Gaucho* [1952]. He is inclined to want to make many location excursions and you can only bring this picture in for a price if we concentrate our locations as much as we possibly can. Discuss this thoroughly with [production manager] Ray Klune and he will brief you further on Henry's adventurous spirit for exploration.

As a producer you take on another dimension. You have got to stop being so damn polite and agreeable. You must stick up firmly for your point of view if you *really* believe you are right.

I do not have to give you any advice about ulcers—as they will come in the normal course of events without any assistance.

D.F.Z.

≡

Philip Dunne had been a contract writer at Fox since 1937. This was his first opportunity to produce.

≡

February 16, 1951
Mr. Clifton Webb [Fox contract star]
1005 N. Rexford Drive
Beverly Hills, CA

Dear Clifton:

Many thanks for your note. In the first place they should never have given you the fifty pages [of script] until they had corrected and approved them. . . .

I insist that you read the next script [of *Mr. Belvedere Rings the Bell*] when it comes out in a couple of weeks from now and have an official conference with all of the boys and that you express your honest opinions. . . .

I cherish Belvedere [played by Webb] as much as you do but I believe that we are both inclined to write things into Belvedere that the theatre-going public is not completely aware of. Audiences like Belvedere because he does things that they would like to be able to do. This is his main charm plus the fact that he thinks highly of himself and that he is a very remarkable man. . . .

Let us analyze the present Belvedere situation directly in relation to Mr. Belvedere himself. He comes into a poorhouse with no intention of remaining except temporarily. . . .

You will recall that in *Sitting Pretty* [1948] he managed to reunite two people who were on the verge of divorce. In the college picture [*Mr. Belvedere Goes to College*, 1949] he reunited a young couple who loved each other but were separated by what seemed to be an impossible barrier. In our story Mr. Belvedere brings youth to old people. He lifts their spirits and when he goes over the hill at the finish he has left behind him a group of people who now have something to live for.

None of this is told in mushy or sentimental terms. He doesn't do it by reading the gospel to them or asking them to "see the light."

He does it in true Belvedere fashion. . . .

I think our opening should be brief. I think we are putting entirely too much emphasis on *why* Mr. Belvedere wants to go to the poorhouse in the first place. No one in *Sitting Pretty* questioned the preposterous idea of Mr. Belvedere taking a job as a baby-sitter in order to earn a few bucks and be able to write a book on the side. The premise was pure screwball farce. Yet Mr. Belvedere carried it through because he is an incredible gent. Audiences expect the *impossible* from him and they will *accept* without question the impossible.

Another example is in the campus story when we arbitrarily invented the preposterous idea that Mr. Belvedere had to have a college degree before he could accept a literary award. In the whole history of literature, including the present Pulitzer Prize, no such condition has ever existed but we were delighted to see Mr. Belvedere go to college and we accepted at face value that this was a fact in spite of the fact that we knew that it was not a fact.

Once we open our picture and *sell* the idea of the incredible Mr. Belvedere to an audience it is my firm belief that the audience will be delighted and eager to accept his entrance into the poorhouse as another of his fabulous excursions. Of course we need some sort of a half-baked reason to get him there in the first place, but to waste reams of words and footage on this problem is totally unnecessary and delays us from getting into the meat of the play.

The wonderful thing about Mr. Belvedere is his superior attitude, his sureness, and it is amazing that an audience will completely *believe* whatever he tells them. He can tell them that he taught jujitsu in Tokyo, that he was at San Juan Hill with Teddy Roosevelt or the South Pole with Byrd or that he taught Houdini how to get out of a straightjacket—whatever it is, the audience is willing and eager to accept. . . .

In my book the success or failure of a human interest comedy lies, not in the rigid plausibility of the plot or the profound character motivations, but in one simple device, to wit, "You must only ask the audience to enter into the spirit of the fun with you." If they like you they will go along with you and accept even the improbable. The whole essence of Mr. Belvedere is that he does the improbable and the impossible.

I don't know if Mr. Belvedere really went to the South Pole with Byrd but when he tells me that he was the only member of Admiral Byrd's expedition that did not get the flu I *believe* him—and so does the audience. I laugh at what he says and even though it sounds idiotic and improbable I go along with it.

Long live Belvedere! . . .

s/Darryl

≡

Mr. Belvedere Rings the Bell, *based on the play,* The Silver Whistle, *by Robert E. McEnroe, was the last in the series. It did only fair business—in contrast to the two previous films. However, Clifton Webb's popularity in other roles continued for several years.*

≡

DATE: July 20, 1951

TO: Elia Kazan

SUBJECT: Letter to Jack Warner [from Kazan] re *Streetcar* [*Named Desire*, directed by Kazan at Warner Bros.]

Dear Gadg:

. . . We did our best to fight them on *Forever Amber*. Mr. [Spyros] Skouras issued a statement to the public in which we challenged the "C" rating the Legion of Decency gave us. In other words we went directly to the public and asked for support.

The Legion of Decency enlisted the aid of the Knights of Columbus in every city in the country and they put the pressure on the exhibitors and actually put every theatre "out of bounds" for one year that dared to play *Amber* without accepting their cuts.

This meant that we lost practically one-third of the United States, and so, like Howard Hughes and his problem with *The Outlaw*, we finally cut the picture.

The exhibitors wanted to support us as they wanted to play the picture, but when you gang up on a man and picket his lobby and threaten him with undermining the morals of youth, he finally gives in. . . .

Undoubtedly the picture [*Streetcar*] will do enormous business in the uncut version in a small New York theatre—but what the hell happens to you when you try to book it in the 10,000 or 12,000 other American theatres. Maybe I am pessimistic because of my experience with *Amber*.

I told Charlie [Feldman] and you this before you made the picture. This is the *only* reason Spyros urged me not to make the picture. It is my opinion that you should do everything you can to try and get a "B" instead of a "C" classification.

D.F.Z.

≡

The Legion of Decency had been established by Catholic churchmen and lay members in 1933 to impose standards of morality and to implement the then new industry Production Code. A "C," or condemned rating, would mean that members of the Roman Catholic faith would be instructed not to see the film. A "B" rating meant "objectionable in part for all," which is what Streetcar *ultimately received. Kazan had asked Zanuck's advice on the problem, which at the time was exceptionally serious.*

≡

OCTOBER 19, 1951
MR. CHARLES EINFELD [IN CHARGE OF ADVERTISING AND PUBLICITY, FOX, NEW YORK]
25 WEST 55TH STREET
NEW YORK CITY

DEAR CHARLIE:

I HAVE JUST SEEN BOSLEY CROWTHER'S FULL REVIEW ON "THE DESERT FOX" [IN *THE NEW YORK TIMES*] AND FROM A STANDPOINT OF COMPANY

PUBLIC RELATIONS I DO NOT THINK THAT WE CAN LET IT GO UN-CHALLENGED AS THIS IS NOT A REVIEW OF A PICTURE, IT IS AN ATTACK ON THE INTEGRITY, JUDGMENT AND PATRIOTISM OF AN AMERICAN COMPANY AND THE CREATIVE WORKERS WHO ARE RESPONSIBLE FOR THIS FILM. CROWTHER BEGRUDGINGLY ADMITS THAT THE PICTURE HAS BEEN EXPERTLY MADE BUT HE DISAPPROVES OF THE SUBJECT; THEREFORE THIS GREAT SO CALLED INTELLECTUAL LIBERAL IS GUILTY OF ADVOCATING THE WORST SORT OF POLITICAL CENSORSHIP. HE IS SAYING IT IS A FINE PICTURE BUT YOU CANNOT MAKE IT BECAUSE I DO NOT LIKE THE SUBJECT MATTER. FURTHER-MORE HIS REVIEW IS FILLED WITH INACCURACIES AND FALSEHOODS. IT ACTUALLY IS A HYSTERICAL REVIEW WHICH REMINDS ME VERY MUCH OF THE PERFORMANCE OF LUTHER ADLER [AS HITLER] IN OUR FILM. . . .

AFTER ALL, WE ARE ONLY SAYING ABOUT [FIELD MARSHAL ERWIN] ROM-MEL EXACTLY WHAT HISTORY SAID AND IN THIS INSTANCE WE ARE IN PRETTY GOOD COMPANY, NAMELY, BRIGADIER GENERAL DESMOND YOUNG, GEN-ERAL AUCHINLECK AND WINSTON CHURCHILL. CROWTHER IS SAYING THAT WHILE A BOOK PRINTED ON THE SUBJECT MAY BE PUBLISHED WITHOUT CRITICISM WE CANNOT PICTURIZE THAT BOOK. EVERY MOVEMENT IN OUR PICTURE CAN BE AUTHENTICATED BY EXISTING DOCUMENTS AND TESTI-MONY AT THE NUREMBERG TRIALS. . . . REGARDS,

DARRYL

≡

OCTOBER 22, 1951
CHARLES EINFELD
NEW YORK

DEAR CHARLIE:
. . . I BELIEVE YOU SHOULD TELL CROWTHER THAT WE HAVE DECIDED AGAINST ANSWERING HIS HYSTERIA BECAUSE HE IS CONVINCED THAT HE KNOWS MORE ABOUT ROMMEL THAN THE HISTORIANS AND WE ARE CON-VINCED THAT THERE IS NO WAY THAT WE CAN CONVINCE HIM OF THE TRUTH. YOU MIGHT ALSO TAKE HIM UP AND LET HIM SEE THE LINES IN FRONT OF THE GLOBE THEATRE. I CANNOT FOR THE LIFE OF ME UNDER-STAND WHY CERTAIN PEOPLE INADVERTENTLY INSIST ON PLAYING THE COM-MIE GAME. REGARDS.

DARRYL

≡

The Desert Fox, starring James Mason, was a critical success (for the most part) and an outstanding commercial success. It was based on the Rommel biography by Brigadier Desmond Young, M.C.

≡

December 10, 1951
Miss Marilyn Monroe [Fox contract player]
611 N. Crescent Drive
Beverly Hills

Dear Marilyn:

Your request to have a special dialogue director [Natasha Lytess] work with you on the set is a completely impractical and impossible request. The reason we engage a director and entrust him to direct a picture is because we feel that he has demonstrated his ability to function in that capacity. Whether the final performance comes out right or wrong there cannot be more than one responsible individual and that individual is the director. You must rely upon his individual interpretation of the role. You cannot be coached on the sidelines or the result will be a disaster for you.

In *Asphalt Jungle* [M-G-M, 1950] you had a comparatively simple part, in which you were very effective, but it did not particularly call for any acting as compared to the role you are going to play at the present time [in *Don't Bother to Knock*]. It is more than ever important that you therefore place yourself completely in the hands of the director—or ask to be relieved from the role.

Either Mr. [Roy] Baker is capable of directing you as well as the rest of the picture or he is not capable of directing anything, but since he is the director we must place our responsibility in him.

I am sure you realize how ludicrous it would be if every actor or actress felt that they needed special coaching from the sidelines. The result would be bedlam, and whatever creative ideas the director might possess would be lost or totally diffused.

I think you are capable of playing this role without the help of anyone but the director and yourself. You have built up a Svengali and if you are going to progress with your career and become as important talent-wise as you have publicity-wise then you must destroy this Svengali before it destroys you. When I cast you for the role I cast you as an individual.

Best always,
Darryl Zanuck

≡

Despite this letter, Monroe continued to rely on the services of Lytess— until the completion of The Seven Year Itch *(1955). After a period in New York, Monroe returned to Fox for* Bus Stop *(1956) with a new acting coach, Paula Strasberg, the wife of Lee Strasberg, artistic direc-tor of the Actors Studio in New York where Monroe had recently studied. At the time Monroe and Lytess first met (in 1948), Lytess was Columbia Pictures' drama coach and Monroe was under contract to Columbia.*

≡

March 31, 1952
Mr. David O. Selznick
Selznick Releasing Organization
400 Madison Avenue
New York 17, New York
PERSONAL AND CONFIDENTIAL

Dear David:

I feel compelled to write you about the role in *My Cousin Rachel.* [Director] George Cukor and others have told me of their discussions with you, and our good friend [agent, producer, packager] Charles Kenneth Feldman has been bombarding me daily with everything from bouquets to bombshells. Somehow he seems to feel that you hold him personally responsible for our failure to see "the light" in connec-tion with the role of Rachel.

I am not going into a lot of nonsense about how much I admire and appreciate Jennifer's [Jennifer Jones—Mrs. Selznick] talent. It would be stupid of me to be unaware of it. I just want to tell you how *we* feel about the role of Rachel.

When I say we I mean [producer-writer] Nunnally Johnson, George Cukor and me. From the very beginning when we purchased the story [novel by Daphne du Maurier] we thought of it in terms of an English actress or a foreign-born actress. We felt that this was absolutely essential. The perfect combination would be a woman who spoke with an English accent and was able at the same time to think "in Italian." Furthermore Rachel cannot be younger than forty years of age unless we destroy the whole premise of this odd love story. It is the love story of a twenty-five year old boy with a woman fifteen years older. It seems to us that if we eliminate this factor or compromise with it we will destroy the most unique premise in the book. This is exactly what makes it, we hope, "different."

This was my thought when I purchased the book. Independently it was Nunnally Johnson's thought. And when George Cukor came on the assignment it was also his viewpoint. Now I grant you that we may all be entirely wrong. Time will tell. When I suggested Jeanne Crain to play the Negro girl in *Pinky* Kazan thought I was nuts. When Kazan suggested Marlon Brando to play Zapata I thought he was nuts. It turned out in both cases we were both nuts in the *right* way.

The reason I wanted to write you directly is so that you would get the story straight and not feel for a moment that any other motives or considerations were involved.

Best always,
s/Darryl

≡

Olivia de Havilland (age thirty-six), whose parents were British, played Rachel, Richard Burton (age twenty-seven) made his American film debut as the "twenty-five year old boy," and Henry Koster (under contract to Fox) eventually directed.

≡

April 9, 1952

"WHITE WITCH DOCTOR" CONFERENCE ON FINAL SCRIPT OF MARCH
12TH, 1952 WITH MESSRS. [Julian] BLAUSTEIN, OTTO LANG, [Ivan] GOFF
AND [Ben] ROBERTS [writers], MOLLY MANDAVILLE

When you put a title *White Witch Doctor* [1953] on a screen, the
public expects to see a picture about a white witch doctor. They expect something with the excitement and interest of *King Solomon's
Mines* [M-G-M, 1950]. They do not expect to get into the problems, epidemics, droughts, suffering, or any downbeat, heavy-handed
problems.

A picture based on this script could well be called *The Woman Missionary*, and then the public, if they even went into the theatre at all,
would get exactly what the title promised.

If we made this story as written, no matter how many other things in
the way of thrills and excitement which we added to it, I believe the
audience would leave the theatre disappointed and unsatisfied because
they had been misled. . . .

You have to leave room in a picture of this kind for physical action,
à la *African Queen* [Horizon, 1951] and *King Solomon's Mines*. The plot of
these stories could be told on a postage stamp. It is the physical action
which makes them box office.

We do not want a picture based on the "exploits of an African
missionary." We do not want a picture of a woman "struggling for
courage in the African jungle." We want a picture about two interesting, exciting people, a story full of physical excitement, physical violence and sex. We do not want a picture about a woman's struggles to
cope with sickness and locusts and other depressing things. We want a
story of sex attraction and conflict between a man and a woman, against
the background of this exciting country. . . .

≡

*Compromises were made. The picture did reasonably well in the world
market.*

≡

July 9, 1952
Mr. W. D. Maxwell
Managing Editor,
Chicago Tribune
Tribune Towers
Chicago, Illinois

Dear Mr. Maxwell:

The Chicago *Tribune*, dated Thursday, July 3rd, 1952, on page 4 of Part I, published a false, untrue and libelous attack on my character in both my private, professional and military life. The article states that I have been "long friendly to internationalist and Leftist causes." The true record reveals that on October 11th, 1939, I publicly attacked the Union of Soviet Socialist Republics and made public a letter I had written to the Communist Vice Consul at Los Angeles, Mr. A. L. Timofeev. My letter attacking Communist aggression in 1939 was published in the *Congressional Record*, a photostat of which I enclose.

I have been for more than fifteen years continually attacked by *Pravda* in Moscow and by the *Daily Worker* in New York. Particularly at the time when in 1947 I produced the first anti-Communist picture made in Hollywood, namely *The Iron Curtain*. The Chicago *Tribune* incidentally praised me for this particular film. Does it not seem strange that the Chicago *Tribune* should now classify me as a sponsor of Leftist causes when every official Communistic publication has branded me repeatedly as a "vile reactionary." I have never, at any time, belonged to any organization or group that has been branded subversive by the Attorney General of the United States Government.

Your article states that I appeared at the Writers' Congress in Hollywood in 1943. You failed to state that I was invited by Dr. Robert Sproul, the President of the University of California. In the course of my address to the Writers' Congress I announced that I intended to produce a film based on the life and career of that distinguished American, Captain Eddie Rickenbacker. This announcement, to my astonishment, was greeted by boos from a large portion of the audience. This was my first intimation that any part of the audience had Left-Wing tendencies. In spite of many written protests and the threat of boycott, I nevertheless produced the film based on Rickenbacker's life [*Captain Eddie*, 1945].

I was not then, nor have I ever been, identified or affiliated with any "subversive or Left-Wing" organization.

Your article calls me one of the "Hollywood strutting colonels." Let us examine the facts, which can be easily obtained from the War Department. I served in World War I as a private and went overseas when I was only fifteen years old. I can be guilty only of falsifying my age in order to volunteer. I served two years in the Army including eight months in France with the American Expeditionary Forces. . . .

In August, 1941, I was commissioned a Lieutenant Colonel on the Advisory Council to the Chief Signal Officer of the Army. . . . I went on active duty at various times whenever the Chief Signal Officer desired my services. I wish to call to your attention at this time that I was above the draft age and the father of three children. . . .

In January, 1942, I again returned to active duty on the staff of the Chief Signal Officer and applied for overseas duty. I served in England as a special military attaché assigned to the American Embassy and later on assigned to the British Commandos to study combat film tactics. Later on in the same year I was sent to the Aleutian Islands where I established a film base of combat cameramen. Later in the same year I served in England and Gibraltar and I landed on D-Day in Algiers where I produced for the War Department a series of combat and training films.

For my service in this regard I was awarded the Legion of Merit in General Orders #18. I quote: "Disregarding personal dangers and physical hardships Colonel Zanuck secured outstanding front line motion and still pictures of our combat operations against the enemy. Colonel Zanuck participated in both ground and aerial combat activities against the enemies of the United States. These films have been of great value to the training of combat troops" . . .

I call your attention further to an article appearing in the New York *Times*, Thursday, May 22nd, 1947, under the signature of General Mark W. Clark. "I had a small party of officers with me including Colonel Darryl Zanuck who had come along to take pictures but was immediately pressed into service as Courier Intelligence Agent and intermediary in a dozen ticklish situations which he invariably successfully ironed out."

Your article further states that I was personally attacked by President Truman when he was a United States Senator. I would like to call to your attention a letter dated October 2, 1944, and signed by Harry S. Truman, U.S.S.

"Dear Colonel Zanuck:

I have been intending to write you for some time regarding your connection with Twentieth Century–Fox Pictures and the sale of films to the Government. After studying the record I have come to the conclusion that there was no intention to do any wrong on your part and I have also been informed by others in the military services that you have done a most excellent job for them in the education of the soldiers in military tactics. I appreciate it and I know that the Government officials in the War and Navy Departments do too.

Sincerely yours,

Harry S. Truman."

Your article states that until my appearance at the [Dwight D.] Eisenhower rally in Denver I have not made any public speeches or put out any publicity regarding my endorsement of General Eisenhower's candidacy [for president of the United States]. This is another example of irresponsible reporting. I have been constantly making public speeches endorsing General Eisenhower's candidacy wherever and whenever an opportunity to speak presented itself.

As an American citizen do you dare to deny me the right of freedom of speech?

Your article further states that as a supporter of the late Wendell L. Willkie I endeavored to "get America into World War II long before Pearl Harbor." If you infer that I was aware of the menace of Naziism and Fascism then you are certainly correct. It is a tragedy that more Americans were not aware of this threat at an earlier date as this in itself might have prevented World War II. I recall vividly that only two weeks before Pearl Harbor one of the present candidates for the Republican nomination stated that it was fantastic to think that the Japs would ever attack us.

I am proud of my past association with Wendell L. Willkie. I am similarly proud of my participation in the Committee for the Atlantic Union. I detest Communism as much or more than I detest Naziism and Fascism. The fact that I never even inadvertently or accidentally joined or affiliated myself with any Left-Wing movement is a matter of public record. . . . I worked closely in association with the Federal Bureau of Investigation both before and after World War II in an effort to combat the spread of Communism. For my record in this regard I refer you to [F.B.I. director] J. Edgar Hoover.

Your article states that after World War II "Zanuck proposed international control of German films in order that they might be used to propagandize the defeated Germans. He said he would like to be put in control of such films." This is sheer nonsense. I advocated the production of training films to educate the youth of Germany so that they would not again grow up to threaten the peace of the world. Does the Chicago *Tribune* disagree with such a policy of education designed toward world peace?

Your article further states that I "was found to be still taking $5,000 a week from the film firm, Twentieth Century–Fox Film Corporation," while I was in the Army. I refer you to the minutes of the Board of Directors of Twentieth Century–Fox Film Corporation. The facts are as follows: When I went on active duty in 1942 I requested and received from the Corporation a leave of absence and a suspension of my employment contract. I did not receive one penny of compensation from the Corporation during the time I was on active duty. For your information this was one of the reasons why President Truman sent me the letter mentioned earlier in this communication. It may further interest you to know that in addition to receiving no salary whatever from Twentieth Century–Fox Film Corporation I also refused to accept any pay from the War Department for my services in the Army.

There is no excuse, even in the heat of a political battle, to attack or damage the character and integrity of any individual just because he happens to disagree with your policy of Isolationism or with your selection of a candidate [Robert A. Taft—for the presidential primary]. By direct statement and inferences you have assailed my character as an American citizen, as a soldier of two wars and as an individual who has devoted a great portion of his lifetime toward defending the true ideals of Democracy. I demand an immediate retraction.

Sincerely yours,
Darryl F. Zanuck

≡

It is not clear if a retraction was printed or not. It could have been in one or more editions on a given date, but it is not in the edition preserved on microfilm.

≡

July 1, 1952
Mr. Elia Kazan
444 West 56th Street
New York, N.Y.

Dear Gadg:

I am dictating this note in the presence of [producer] Bob Jacks as he has been following your lead and has also been putting the pressure on me to give careful consideration to producing *Man on a Tightrope* in Germany—in spite of all of the difficulties encountered by ourselves as well as M-G-M when they made the Gene Kelly Autobahn picture [*The Devil Makes Three*, 1952].

In this business sometimes when we strive for perfection we overdo it and sometimes while we achieve perfection we do so at an exorbitant cost. In this case the so-called perfection ends up being of no value except to our own egos. If the picture loses money because it cost too much then we have failed in our mission. . . .

I mention price because every picture has a price on it. The price is dictated by the content, the subject matter and the showmanship values.

As an example take our own unfortunate experience on *Panic in the Streets* [1950]. We made the picture entirely on location [in New Orleans]. You did an outstanding job of directing. A couple of the scenes I thought were almost the best scenes I have ever seen you direct—but all of this added up to nothing because we lost money on the picture in spite of the fact that we made an excellent picture.

Why did we lose money? Because we made a subject that cost us $1,400,000 when it was a subject that should have been made for $850,000—or not at all. At $850,000 it would have shown a profit but we blew up the story into proportions which cost us more than the content and subject matter deserved to cost.

I fought with John Ford on *Pinky*. He insisted at first that he could not make the picture unless he made it on location. When I finally convinced him to make it at the studio he blew the job. You came in on the assignment and made a sensational picture which was an enormous box-office hit—and you never went out of the studio except for a street scene in the valley. I never heard anyone complain about the lack of Southern atmosphere, flavor or local color. The subject matter was right and we did not blow it up out of proportion. Therefore the picture made a spectacular profit. And even if the picture had not been well received it would still have made a minor profit because the cost was in the right bracket.

For my money you did an enormous job on the location of *Viva Zapata!* But here again apparently the subject matter did not have the appeal that we anticipated. It came out at a time when audiences were reaching for pure escapist entertainment and not willing to listen to any messages or historical lessons even about an exciting and colorful Mexican bandit. . . .

I rely upon you to do a wonderful workmanlike job as you always do. But I am not going to have you accidentally get into a situation that is beyond control through no fault of your own. . . . Every time we have gone on these expeditions we have convinced ourselves that we are not going to duplicate the previous mistakes of other expeditions. We have fortified ourselves and protected ourselves yet invariably we have got into situations of one kind or another beyond our control.

This may very well be the exception but none of us has the right to be convinced of this without a thorough analyzation of the possibilities. If we can achieve 75 percent of the pictorial value by second unit then there should be no argument on our decision. However, this can only be ascertained by a study and conference.

When are you coming?

Affectionate regards,
Darryl

≡

The decision was made to shoot the film in Germany.

≡

DATE: July 29, 1952

TO: Mr. Elia Kazan
CC: Messrs. Robert L. Jacks [producer]
Robert Sherwood [playwright and occasional screenwriter]
SUBJECT: MAN ON A TIGHTROPE

Dear Gadg:

. . . I can best start out by saying in a general way that I have tried to analyze *why* every anti-Communist picture made so far has proven to be a box-office flop. The only exception was *The Iron Curtain*, which was the first one and the reason it made a profit was because business was a hell of a lot better than it is now.

All of these anti-Communist pictures have come a cropper, because they were so violently anti-Communistic that they emphasized these elements rather than emphasizing entertainment and showmanship values. In addition to this, they all managed to turn themselves into "message" pictures. In most instances, they failed also because they were "obvious" . . .

More than ever before people are going to the theatre today to escape lectures, propaganda, politics and the constant talk, talk, talk which they get on television and the radio. I doubt very much whether *Snake Pit*, *Gentleman's Agreement*, and *Grapes of Wrath* would be successful if released today. Like everything else, audiences change. I can remember the day when musicals disappeared [in 1931]. The public became so fed up that I actually cut musical numbers out of three or four of our finished [Warner Bros.] pictures and tried to turn them into straight comedies, because you just could not book a musical. . . .

I cannot think of a picture on the market today which deals with a "thinking problem" and which is also successful. . . .

≡

Sherwood's script was based on a story by Neil Paterson.

≡

August 9, 1952
Mr. Elia Kazan
c/o Herman Blumenfeld
Movietone
Turkenstrasse 89
Munich 13, Germany

Dear Gadg:
. . . First off, I want to give you the benefit of some experience I have had making pictures on location with "experts" and technical advisors. This experience covers a period of almost twenty-five years. When I first started with Rin Tin Tin [in 1924] and suggested that the dog escape from the cabin by climbing up the chimney everyone including the dog experts said that was the most idiotic idea ever conceived in Hollywood, but in the finished picture it made a dog star out of Rin Tin Tin and a dog producer out of me. . . .

When [Anatole] Litvak was shooting the river crossing in *Decision Before Dawn* the military experts were so indignant that they refused to come on the set. They said that no man could possibly swim the river in daylight under the guns of the enemy. Tola argued with them and explained that we could not get any excitement out of the episode if we did it at night. I think you agree that this was one of the most exciting episodes in the picture and yet it violated every tactical military rule. Tola listened to reason from the experts throughout the picture but

Mr. and Mrs. Zanuck dining out in late 1944. ZANUCK FAMILY

Looking over a preliminary script in late 1944 of The Razor's Edge, adapted by the book's author, W. Somerset Maugham (left). George Cukor (right) was scheduled to direct. The eventually realized film (1946) was written by Lamar Trotti and directed by Edmund Goulding.
THE ACADEMY OF MOTION PICTURE ARTS AND SCIENCES

Joseph L. Mankiewicz in a rather unorthodox directorial position discussing a scene with Fox stars Rex Harrison ("The Ghost") and Gene Tierney ("Mrs. Muir") in early 1947. THE ACADEMY OF MOTION PICTURE ARTS AND SCIENCES

Richard Widmark made his impressive debut as a psychopathic killer in one of Fox's most important post–World War II pictures in the film noir and/or semi-documentary genre, Kiss of Death *(1947).*

Academy Awards Presentation in March 1948 at the Shrine Auditorium, Los Angeles. Zanuck (Best Picture: Fox's Gentleman's Agreement*), Edmund Gwenn (Best Supporting Actor: Fox's* Miracle on 34th Street*), Loretta Young (Best Actress:* The Farmer's Daughter*), Ronald Colman (Best Actor:* A Double Life*), Celeste Holm (Best Supporting Actress:* Gentleman's Agreement*). Not shown in this photo—Elia Kazan (Best Director:* Gentleman's Agreement*).*

The Fox studio in 1948. The back lot (the top third or so of this photo) has been gone since 1961, when Alcoa purchased the property and built Century City, a high-rise office, entertainment, and residential complex. BISON ARCHIVES

Left to right: Industry moguls Samuel Goldwyn, Joseph M. Schenck, Zanuck, Jack L. Warner, and Louis B. Mayer attending the March 1948 testimonial dinner for Hollywood columnist Louella O. Parsons at the Cocoanut Grove in the Ambassador Hotel, Los Angeles. USC DEPARTMENT OF SPECIAL COLLECTIONS

Zanuck, veteran Fox director Henry King, and Gregory Peck at the world premiere of Twelve O'Clock High. *Grauman's Chinese Theatre, December 1949.* ZANUCK FAMILY

Conference in D.F.Z.'s office, early 1950. Left to right: script coordinator and consultant Molly Mandaville, supervising art director Lyle Wheeler, producer-director Anatole Litvak, producer Julian Blaustein, production manager Ray Klune. RUDY BEHLMER COLLECTION

June 12, 1950. © COPYRIGHT 1950 TIME INC.
REPRINTED BY PERMISSION.

Bette Davis and Zanuck attending the Los Angeles premiere of All About Eve at Grauman's Chinese Theatre in Hollywood, November 1950. NATIONAL FILM ARCHIVE, LONDON

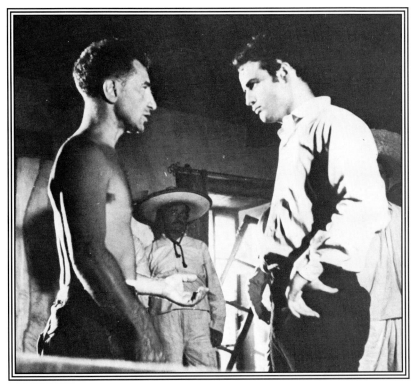

Director Elia Kazan and Marlon Brando on location in Texas for Viva Zapata! in 1951.
BISON ARCHIVES

Film editor Barbara McLean and D.F.Z. watching a rough cut of Viva Zapata! in Zanuck's private screening room on the Fox lot, January 1952.
RUDY BEHLMER COLLECTION

Fox star Marilyn Monroe.
Wardrobe test for Niagara
(1952). THE ACADEMY OF MOTION PICTURE
ARTS AND SCIENCES

Left to right: supervising
art director Lyle
Wheeler, Zanuck, and
art director George W.
Davis discussing a model
of some of The Robe's
sets, which were revised
to accommodate the
proportions of
CinemaScope in early
1953.
BISON ARCHIVES

Zanuck, with Mary Pickford, presenting the Academy of Motion Picture Arts and Sciences' prestigious Irving G. Thalberg Memorial Award to producer-director Cecil B. DeMille at the Academy Awards ceremonies in March 1953. Zanuck was the only person to receive three Thalberg Awards (1937, 1944, 1950). The Academy changed the ruling in 1962 so that a person could be given only one Thalberg Award.

Party in 1953 at an unidentified locale. Left to right (standing): Betty Grable, Zanuck, Marilyn Monroe. (Seated): Lucille Ball, composer Jimmy McHugh.

The September 1953 Los Angeles premiere of The Robe, *the first feature in the CinemaScope process, at Grauman's Chinese Theatre. Note that CinemaScope gets top billing.* USC DEPARTMENT OF SPECIAL COLLECTIONS

Preliminary read-through of The Egyptian *script in early 1954. Left to right: writer Philip Dunne, director Michael Curtiz, D.F.Z., Jean Simmons, Gene Tierney, and Marlon Brando. Behind: Victor Mature and Bella Darvi. Brando bowed out of the title role shortly afterward and was replaced by Edmund Purdom.* THE ACADEMY OF MOTION PICTURE ARTS AND SCIENCES

At the Hotel du Cap d'Antibes in the south of France, circa the summer of 1954. Left to right: Zanuck, Tyrone Power, Sonja Henie, and Linda Christian, Power's wife at the time. THE MUSEUM OF MODERN ART/FILM STILLS ARCHIVE

whenever there was a case of losing something of value he did what he thought was best for the entertainment value of the picture. . . .

I am only writing this as a warning for the future. These guys are all alike. They do not understand drama or entertainment or showmanship. They will whittle away at you and you may accidentally or inadvertently "pull your punches." It is not this particular item concerned with the escape that disturbs me; I am worried about how they will try to work on you on every point.

We want to make an authentic picture wherever authenticity does not rob us of showmanship values. Nobody buys tickets to see authenticity; they go in to be entertained. . . .

Love,
Darryl

CC: Mr. Robert Sherwood

≡

September 27, 1952
"GENTLEMEN PREFER BLONDES" CONFERENCE ON TEMPORARY SCRIPT OF SEPTEMBER 25, 1952 (with Messrs. [Sol C.] Siegel [producer], [Howard] Hawks [director], [Charles] Lederer [writer]

I like this very much. I think it is a great idea to give the love story to Dorothy [Jane Russell, loaned by R-K-O]. . . .

There are two things which I consider vital to the telling of the story, and which I want to emphasize in the script. These are: (1) The love story between Dorothy and Malone [Elliott Reid]; (2) Dorothy's genuine affection for Lorelei [Marilyn Monroe].

This is not a satire. It is a solid and honest comedy in the same terms as *I Was a Male War Bride* [Fox, 1949], for instance. In *War Bride* the audience knew that our people had a very real problem, and they never lost sight of that no matter how ludicrous the comedy seemed at times. . . .

We must be completely sold on Dorothy's love for Malone, or we won't be able to accept her taking him back. And we must be sold on her real affection for Lorelei or we won't be able to understand her sticking her chin out for her in the courtroom scene.

In order to accomplish these two things we must be willing, if necessary, to sacrifice comedy in these particular scenes. . . .

≡

Gentlemen Prefer Blondes *was based on the 1949 stage musical version of the novel by Anita Loos.*

SEVEN

CINEMASCOPE AND STEREOPHONIC
SOUND TO THE RESCUE

July 25, 1952
"THE ROBE" CONFERENCE ON FIRST DRAFT CONTINUITY OF JULY 18TH,
1952 (with Messrs. [Frank] Ross [producer], [Philip] Dunne [writer],
Molly Mandaville)

. . . I have been bombarded by letters from our people all over the
world who have learned that we are going to make *The Robe*. They are
delighted, but they take this opportunity to beg me not to make the
same mistake I made in *David and Bathsheba*. They send me letters
from exhibitors telling of their efforts to cut some of the "talk" out of
David and Bathsheba, so as to make it more entertaining and interesting
for their foreign audiences. They tell of the disappointment their
patrons have experienced on sitting through a picture where there was
talk, talk, talk through some of the biggest scenes of the picture. I'm
sure you can understand the disappointment of people who have to
depend on titles to tell them what's happening in the climax of a
picture. . . .

=

TO: Frank Ross   DATE: December 29, 1952
CC: Henry Koster [director]
    Philip Dunne
    Molly Mandaville
    SUBJECT: THE ROBE

Dear Frank:

Over the weekend I once again went through the script on *The Robe*. . . .

It seems that sometimes we write our scripts to be *read*—rather than to be seen and heard. . . .

Although we have now punctuated the script with three or four good violent action sequences, this, nevertheless, is a talking picture. It relies mainly on the spoken word. There was no way to change that entirely but I believe that you boys should once again go through the script page by page, word by word and eliminate any line or speech that may even be halfway superfluous.

We have a wonderful and spectacular pictorial background. I am sure that many things will visually tell themselves. . . .

I do not believe that even the most brilliant speech or phrase is good enough to stay in any picture if it is a superfluous phrase or speech. To break even and make a profit on this very costly undertaking we have got to have an enormous foreign gross. Anything that gives our picture tempo, pace and drive will be of enormous benefit, not only in Europe but here also. . . .

                                        D.F.Z.

≡

During all the preproduction work on The Robe *it was planned to be produced as a standard 35mm color feature. CinemaScope came later. The novel by Lloyd C. Douglas had been a top best-seller all during the war years.*

≡

JANUARY 27, 1953

SPYROS SKOURAS
NEW YORK
DEAR SPYROS:

AM ABSOLUTELY CONVINCED THAT OUR BIG SCREEN FRENCH SYSTEM [TO BE CALLED CINEMASCOPE] WILL HAVE AN ENORMOUS EFFECT ON AUDIENCES EVERYWHERE AND THAT IT IS A MAJOR DEVELOPMENT FOR THE INDUSTRY. I THINK ITS MAIN VALUE LIES, HOWEVER, IN THE PRODUCTION OF LARGE SCALE SPECTACLES AND BIG OUTDOOR FILMS SUCH AS "THE ROBE," "TWELVE MILE REEF," "THE STORY OF DEMETRIUS," "HELL AND HIGH WATER," "PRINCE VALIANT," "KING OF THE KHYBER RIFLES," "SIR WALTER RALEIGH" AND "RIVER OF NO RETURN." IN TIME WE MAY FIND A WAY TO USE IT EFFECTIVELY FOR INTIMATE DRAMAS AND COMEDIES BUT AT THE PRESENT TIME SMALL, INTIMATE STORIES OR A PERSONAL DRAMA LIKE "MY COUSIN RACHEL" WOULD MEAN NOTHING ON THIS SYSTEM.

[EARL] SPONABLE [FOX TECHNICAL DIRECTOR] AND SOME OF THE OTHERS BELIEVE THAT OUR SYSTEM HAS AS MUCH AUDIENCE PARTICIPATION VALUE AS CINERAMA* BUT IT IS MY OPINION THAT WE HAVE APPROXIMATELY NINETY PERCENT OF THE AUDIENCE VALUE OF CINERAMA, BUT THE LOSS OF TEN PERCENT IS MADE UP MANY TIMES BY THE CLEAR FOCUS OF OUR PICTURE AND OF COURSE BY THE PRACTICAL CONSIDERATIONS SUCH AS USING OUR OWN CAMERAS AND PROJECTION MACHINES AND ONLY ONE NEGATIVE. WE MUST REMEMBER THAT THE VALUE OF CINERAMA IS ALSO LOST TO A CERTAIN DEGREE UNLESS YOU HAVE PHOTOGRAPHED THINGS THAT HAVE SCOPE OR ACTION AND THIS WILL BE TRUE OF ANY SYSTEM.

PERSONALLY I BELIEVE THAT OUR SYSTEM WILL PUT EVERY OTHER SYSTEM OUT OF BUSINESS AND OUR MAIN DIFFICULTY NOW LIES IN GETTING SUFFICIENT LENSES AND JUGGLING OUR PROGRAM OF STARTING DATES TO FIT THE SITUATION WITH THE AVAILABILITY OF THE LENSES. WE ARE MEETING AGAIN ON THIS TODAY SO THAT WE CAN OFFER A PLAN WHEN YOU ARRIVE WHICH WILL VISUALIZE MAKING A COUPLE OF PICTURES ON THE POLAROID [3-D] SYSTEM AT THE SAME TIME TO KEEP GOING A MORE OR LESS EVEN FLOW OF RELEASES DURING THE PERIOD OF CONVERSION. REGARDS.

DARRYL

* A three-camera, three-film, three-projector system used for *This Is Cinerama* (1952) and subsequent films.

≡

The "big screen French system" anamorphically squeezed a horizontally wide angle of view onto regular 35mm film. In projection, a corresponding lens unsqueezed the image, spreading it out across a screen that was, in 1953, roughly two-and-a-half times as wide as it was high. The standard screen ratio that had been in use for decades was 1.33 to 1 (width to height).

≡

TO: Elia Kazan   DATE: February 4, 1953

I have struggled with the problem of the waterfront story as this means a decision of great importance to the company. I like the basic material enormously, as I told you when I read the treatment, but I continue to be worried about the labor support.★

We must not hit everything on the nose and get up on a soap box. If we do that, we will certainly have a failure. We must stick to the personal story and permit the picture to speak for itself as far as theme goes. . . . I am certain that the picture as a whole, by what it shows, not by words, will reveal the corruption on the waterfront. We don't have to make speeches about it. I believe that the evil of the waterfront situation should be the background . . . and that the personal story must predominate.

There is no use in making a wonderful picture like *Zapata* which nobody comes to see except the intelligentsia.

I recommend that Budd [Schulberg, the writer] and you come out here next week for one or two days. I believe I have some valuable story contributions which will help the girl from looking like an amateur detective who is out to right the wrongs of the world.

This is an important undertaking and if we are to go ahead with courage, we have got to know conclusively that we understand each other. . . .

★ According to Kazan, Zanuck wanted to secure the backing of George Meany, the president of the American Federation of Labor.

≡

Schulberg (but not Kazan, who was directing Tennessee Williams's play Camino Real *in New York) did come out for conferences with Zanuck.*

≡

DATE: February 12, 1953

TO: Elia Kazan
Budd Schulberg
CC: Lew Schreiber
SUBJECT: THE WATERFRONT STORY
CONFIDENTIAL

Dear Budd and Gadg:

I am dictating this in the presence of Budd at the conclusion of our second meeting. As I understand it we have solved all of the story differences between us with the exception of whether or not we keep Terry's son in the picture.

I have previously expressed my opinion on this point but I would like to make a further observation which resulted from additional study that I did this morning.

Forgetting everything else, we have the following emotionally dramatic story. A young girl sticks her nose into a situation as a result of a personal desire to see her brother's death avenged. A young man tells her that she is nuts but as the story between them develops he finds himself not only emotionally involved with the girl but he also finds that he has become involved in the same problem that she faces. At a certain point in the story he is willing to pick up the torch that she has dropped and carry it even further than she now feels that he should carry it.

In other words their positions are reversed. He carries the torch the full length which results in the desire of the girl to run away. Now she is playing the role that he played in the first half of the picture. He refuses to run and determines to stick it out and she finally determines that the only way they can ever have peace within themselves is to stick it out together. The picture ends with their decision to face it together.

The above is a brutal skeleton outline of the mere bones of the story. It does not pretend to take into consideration any of the real emotional involvements and conflicts between them nor does it pretend to show any phase of the development of his character and growth or the development in her character and growth. . . .

If we cannot develop within Terry and in his scenes with Edie the basic ingredients of our last act and if we have to resort to an "outside influence" in the form of the son or anything else, then I feel that we are avoiding the possibilities of great playing scenes between Terry and Edie and that we will be dropping the story of Edie and be telling a story of a father and a son and that we will lose emotionally from both artistic and commercial possibilities. Furthermore, I believe that putting a son in the story is in the same form as putting a prop or a gimmick which you carry along only to save you in the last act. I believe it is cheap, but more than ever I think that it is dangerous because it will eventually shift the focus of interest from Terry and Edie to Terry and his son and I am sure that you can preserve the growth of Terry's character by scenes involving Terry and Edie.

His realization that he is no longer handcuffed to the old code and that it really is not a valid code but a sort of hangover from his youth is something that should come from inside him and we should not have to use any outside device to dramatize it.

Furthermore, I just cannot visualize Marlon Brando with a 13- or 14-year-old son. It takes all of the bite out of it. To me it is a different kind of story than you started out to tell. It may be a very good story but it isn't what I expected from the Terry who was a prizefighter, tough guy, knocked off dames, vital, lusty, a product of the waterfront. It domesticated him. I don't care how clever you devise why or how he has a son. The very fact that he has a son makes him a parent. He has certain responsibilities as a parent. It tames him down and somehow in some peculiar way which I can't explain it seems to hurt his love story with Edie.★

★ The son was eliminated in subsequent drafts of the script.

Now let me explain the business ramifications of this situation as they affect me personally. We have never previously negotiated a [profit] participation deal on this basis. The only participation deals have always involved a package that included a big star or they have been participation deals with Irving Berlin or others where an accepted box-office piece of property was involved. There has always been an "excuse" for me when I negotiated for Irving Berlin's *There's No Business Like Show Business*—or even for *Gentlemen Prefer Blondes, Call Me Madam*, etc.

On these deals I have never been questioned or criticized even though not all of them have turned out successfully. When I negotiated the deal at least I was buying something that had a presold value.

If I had in my possession today a completed first-draft script on this story then it would be simply a matter of our getting together on certain dramatic points and the only decision that I would have to make is as to whether or not I felt this finished piece of property was worthy of a participation deal.

On the other hand I would buy this story in a minute and buy your services on a flat deal arrangement without ever fear of criticism. However, we have passed up any such arrangement, but now I am asked to make a decision strictly on a treatment of a story where we must all agree that there is a great deal of work to be done and particularly some great decisions to be reached in the last act.

If you could deliver me Marlon Brando; if I were assured that I had Brando in this story then I would have a little more guts and justification than I have now for authorizing this type of participation deal. You have got to give me *something* that explains why on this particular picture I give you a different deal than I gave you on *Man on a Tightrope* or any other picture that you made for us. If you come to me with a best-selling novel, *East of Eden*, or whatever it happens to be, which is a big best-seller, then I go before the Board of Directors and explain that if I want this property and you with it, here are the terms that I have to make.

Or if you come to me with this story in its present state and you say, "I have got Marlon Brando set for this picture," then it is a clear-cut and simple decision for me to make.

I know you are busy but for God's sake you have got to help me in this situation and I think that the answer lies in Brando. I think he will do the picture and that you can get him, but you have got to get him for me.

There is one other alternative which I think is unfair to Budd as well as to you. That is, let me delay my decision until you show me a script and then Brando or no Brando I can justify my position, not based on the fact that I have a presold book, but that I have a finished script which excites me to the degree that I am willing to make a deal on terms that we have not heretofore made at the studio.

I think that if you can get Brando on the phone and fly him to New York that Budd and you can sit him down and convince him in one hour. And if he says, "Yes," there is no more argument about it—we have a deal. If I owned the company I could act differently but while Spyros has great affection for you, he told me that I should only conclude this participation deal if I were convinced that I had a story that I was absolutely certain about as a box-office attraction and if I had personalities that would justify a top production. At this moment I do not have either of these two items. I have a story that I like very much, although it is in unfinished form. I have the possibilities of a cast but certainly nothing definite.

This is a personality picture if we want to get the maximum results. If the background dwarfs the two people then we are in a semidocumentary classification and this classification in today's market is very dubious. As a matter of fact you would be better off getting your regular salary and making a deal with Budd to get a flat price. If you end up with Richard Widmark or Dana Andrews and people in this classification you may be wasting your time. The only other person that I could put in the Brando classification for this role would be Burt Lancaster but, as you know, he is involved. And while we are investigating further on his availability in May or June his situation with [Hal] Wallis is terribly complicated.

D. F. Z.

≡

July 15, 1954
Mr. Elia Kazan
Warner Bros. Studios
Burbank, California
Personal & Confidential

Dear Gadg:

Thanks for your letter of June 28th. I just returned from Europe and only received it today. . . .

The only thing in your letter that disturbs me is when you say that I let Budd and you come out to California on the *Waterfront* story and then gave you a cold turn-down—and that a telegram would have served just as well.

You have a short memory, Gadg. Budd came to see me more than once. I spent many hours on many days working with him and trying to develop and alter the script. He accepted all but one of my major suggestions. You accepted them. Four of them are a part of your finished picture, or at least I have been told so by those who have seen the picture and who also had read the original treatment and script and had also read the conference notes.

I am not asking for screen credit but I am asking of both Budd and you that you treat me fairly and that you recognize the facts. I have just reread my conference notes and my various communications on this story. I think both Budd and you should read them again and think of them in the light of your finished picture. I think you should also remember that I am the one who insisted in writing that only Marlon Brando should play the role and that I first suggested him in a telegram to you.

I have just seen an article in last Sunday's New York *Times* [July 11] written by Budd in which he does not mention me by name but in which he indicates that I lost my courage and ran out on a "touchy" subject.

I am really astonished that Budd should write anything such as this. Even more than this, he knows how I sweated and worked with him in a conscientious effort to improve the dramatic construction of the story, and particularly the love story, etc. etc. The last day I saw him he shook my hands and told me that no matter how it turned out he had received valuable assistance and that working with me had been a "unique and exhilarating experience."

Actually the advent and debut of CinemaScope was responsible more than anything else for my final decision against the property. At that time I felt that since we had overnight committed ourselves to a program of CinemaScope "spectacles" I had no alternative but to back away from intimate stories even though they were good stories. I have since changed my mind as one of our most successful CinemaScope pictures [*Three Coins in the Fountain*, 1954] is based on an intimate story.

I understand your picture has turned out to be wonderful. I am happy because every great picture is helpful to the best interests of our industry.

I am taking the liberty of sending a copy of this letter to Budd. I just cannot accept the idea that I lost my courage or gave you a quick brush-off. I spent more time on your project than I do on some of the pictures that we actually produce. In addition to this I invested $40,000 in the property. If this is a brush-off then I have a wrong interpretation of the phrase.

You and I are due for a hit next time we get together. . . .

I look forward to seeing you. Come over when you finish [*East of Eden* at Warners].

Best always,
Darryl

≡

On the Waterfront (1954) *was produced by Sam Spiegel (with Kazan and Schulberg) and released by Columbia Pictures. It was a big critical and commercial success and the recipient of many awards.*

The New York Times *Schulberg article referred to by Zanuck recounted the long, troubled history of the picture. Schulberg said in part: "The head of the studio [Zanuck] had changed his mind; Waterfront didn't fit in with the program of costumed horse operas he was lining up. . . . The picture was still too controversial, we were told. Too grim, too shocking. And, would the people care about the struggle on the docks?"*

≡

FEB. 5, 1953

TO: SPYROS SKOURAS

DEAR SPYROS:

LIKE THE IDEA OF "CINEMASCOPE" AS TRADEMARK. . . . WE NEED ADDI-
TIONAL SETS OF [CINEMASCOPE] LENSES AS QUICKLY AS WE CAN GET THEM
IN ADDITION TO THOSE ALREADY PROMISED AS YOU MUST REALIZE THAT WE
HAVE TWO PICTURES STARTING IMMEDIATELY [THE ROBE AND HOW TO
MARRY A MILLIONAIRE]—WE NEED AT LEAST TWO SETS OF LENSES FOR
EACH PICTURE AND I WILL NEED SEPARATE SET TO MAKE SHORT SUBJECT FOR
EXHIBITION TO EXHIBITORS AND PRESS. . . . AND THIS MAKES NO PROVISION
FOR SPARE LENS IN CASE OF TROUBLE OR FOR LENSES TO OBTAIN BACK
PROJECTION, PROCESS SHOTS AND SECOND UNIT EXPEDITION FOR BOTH
PICTURES. BON VOYAGE.

DARRYL

≡

*Only three of the original lenses designed by Henri Chrétien were
considered acceptable, so each of the first three Fox pictures in Cinema-
Scope (produced concurrently) was restricted at first to the use of just one
lens. The third picture, overlapping the first two, was* Beneath the
12-Mile Reef. *New, improved lenses by Bausch & Lomb were rapidly manufactured and introduced in April.*

≡

March 5, 1953
Mr. J. L. Warner
Warner Bros. Studios
Burbank, California
Personal

Dear Jack:

Last night after the premiere of *Call Me Madam* [Fox] someone from
another studio mentioned to me that you had stated that you were not

overly impressed by what you had seen of CinemaScope and also that you had the same invention in your possession for fifteen years. Since both you and I know this is not a fact I do not think either you or I gain anything for the motion picture industry if CinemaScope is discredited.

By your own admission to me, you lost out on the French invention by one day. Joe Hummel [head of Warners' Paris office] was just one day late. Dr. Chrétien [inventor of the anamorphic lens] has also shown us the communications he has received from your representative concerning these negotiations. As a matter of fact when I say that you "lost out by one day" I am only quoting you.

As you know, we have every intention of making CinemaScope available to the industry and will shortly announce the signing of a contract with one of the other major production companies. It is my sincere belief that eventually all of us will be using CinemaScope entirely, and as a matter of fact, to quote you again, when you last talked to me on the telephone you were of this opinion also.

I agree that we may further develop CinemaScope, but when you see the completed sequences on *The Robe* . . . and the new New York sequences we have made for *How to Marry a Millionaire* you will be more than ever convinced that the medium of CinemaScope has really given us a new and *useful* dimension which is far more superior to the original test which you saw than is imaginable.

I am not trying to sell you as you told me you were already sold. I merely felt that it was not quite fair for you to express views about CinemaScope which were contrary to the views you had expressed to me.

I am now looking each night at flat [nonanamorphic] rushes, 3-D Polaroid rushes and finally the CinemaScope rushes on *The Robe*. Honestly, Jack, the superiority of CinemaScope is almost unbelievable. From the standpoint of "audience participation" alone it is like looking at the first talkie and trying to compare the sound with what we have in pictures today.

On a temporary basis I think you will clean up with *The Wax Museum* [*House of Wax* in 3-D], and we will probably clean up with our Polaroid [3-D] version of *Inferno*, but you and I know that this industry cannot exist if we have to depend on trick effects and stunts such as throwing objects at the audience. For lasting effect we have to have a medium that makes it easier for us to bring the audience into the realm of the drama. Instead of depth and narrowness we need width and scope—or at least these are my honest convictions after looking at almost three weeks of rushes.

We are holding our new demonstrations the week of March 16th. These will include about 4,000 or 5,000 feet of film demonstrating every phase of the possibilities of CinemaScope. If you would like to see the new scenes you and your associates are certainly invited.

Best always,
Darryl

≡

Fox president Spyros Skouras was the driving force behind Cinema-Scope. He knew that something extraordinarily important and dramatic was necessary to rejuvenate the industry, and he put everything into CinemaScope. Zanuck got behind it 100 percent. The Robe *had started testing in standard-ratio 35mm, but just when shooting was about to commence, Zanuck—and probably Skouras—decided to make it the initial picture in the wide-screen anamorphic process named CinemaScope by Fox. The studio had a major investment in the format and wanted to sell the industry on licensing CinemaScope, thereby preventing the development of similar systems by other studios. It is generally acknowledged that Skouras's vision and promotion of CinemaScope represented a major highlight of his career.*

≡

TO: All Producers and Executives   DATE: March 12, 1953
PRIVATE AND CONFIDENTIAL

Upon completion of the production of the several standard 35mm films now in production and two other pictures scheduled for production in the very near future (namely, *Be Prepared* [*Mr. Scoutmaster*, 1953] and [*On the*] *Waterfront*, Twentieth Century–Fox will concentrate exclusively on subjects suitable for CinemaScope.

Effective now we will abandon further work on any treatment or screenplay that does not take full *advantage* of the new dimension of

CinemaScope. It is our conviction that almost any story can be told more effectively in CinemaScope than in any other medium but it is also our conviction that every picture that goes into production in CinemaScope should contain subject matter which utilizes to the fullest extent the full possibilities of this medium.

This does not mean that every picture should have so-called epic proportions but it does mean that at least for the first 18 months of CinemaScope production that we select subjects that contain elements which enable us to take full advantage of scope, size and physical action.

This certainly does not mean that every picture has to contain a roller coaster or an underwater sequence or be an outdoor film or contain sets the proportions of the sets in *The Robe*. As a matter of fact Cinema-Scope unquestionably adds a new dimension to the production of musical pictures. . . .

For the time being intimate comedies or small scale, domestic stories should be put aside and no further monies expended on their development. The day will undoubtedly come when all pictures in this category will probably be made in CinemaScope. But in the present market we want to show the things on CinemaScope that we cannot show nearly as effectively on standard 35mm film. We have a new entertainment medium and we want to exploit it for all it is worth.

If CinemaScope does nothing else it will force us back into the moving picture business—I mean moving pictures that *move*.

D.F.Z.

≡

TO: Frank Ross [producer]　　　　　　　　DATE: March 25, 1953
　　　Henry Koster [director]
　　　Sid Rogell [executive production manager]
　　　Sol Halprin [camera department head]
　　　Earl Sponable [technical director]
CONFIDENTIAL

Here is further detail on the five reels of rushes I saw last night on *The Robe*. I have great praise for all of the acting and all of the directing. I continue to be concerned about several spots where we appear to be definitely soft or out of focus. I believe that these scenes can be corrected, perhaps here and there with an additional close shot or a "covering angle" . . .

The scene where Diana [free-lance star Jean Simmons] crosses over and goes out the door from the throne room appears to be very soft and should probably be covered with another angle.

Part of the scene where Marcellus [Fox contract star Richard Burton] attempts to burn the robe appears to be very soft and out of focus. I don't exactly know what we can do about correcting this. . . .

In studying five reels of rushes as well as six reels of rushes on [*How to Marry a*] *Millionaire*, I am now more than ever convinced that the *greatest value* in a camera angle is to try and keep the people spread apart if there are only two or three people in the scene so that the *entire scene* is constantly filled.

If we do use a closeup it should be like the closeup of Demetrius [Victor Mature] when he looked up and saw Christ on the cross or it should be one like the one I saw in last night's rushes when Marcellus was standing at the doorway with the candelabra on the left side of him. This was a phenomenal closeup. . . .

The greatest kick I get is when one person talks across the room to another person and when both of them are in the scene and near enough to be seen without getting a head closeup. . . .

D.F.Z.

═

DATE: March 25, 1953

TO: Nunnally Johnson [producer-writer]
Jean Negulesco [director]
Sid Rogell
Sol Halprin
Earl Sponable
SUBJECT: HOW TO MARRY A MILLIONAIRE

I see an enormous improvement in the rushes of *How to Marry a Millionaire*. I am not speaking of the acting but of the handling of

CinemaScope. In practically every instance of the six reels I ran last night you have perfectly sharp and clear photography with amazing lighting effects and in some instances with genuine 3-dimensional effect.

Almost in all instances the composition has been vastly improved over previous material. The full figure shot of [free-lance star Lauren] Bacall on the bed and the big closeup filling the screen of [Marilyn] Monroe were unique examples of the new medium.

I am still opposed to too much camera movement. I fully believe that while we have to occasionally move the camera we should put the emphasis on moving the actors.

CinemaScope gives you a certain freedom of movement. Practically everything is lost if two people are huddled together in the center of the screen with nothing but wide open spaces on each end of the screen.

If the people are spread out filling the screen then we are putting on film an effect that we cannot get on the old 35mm. . . .

We must not forget the illusion of depth comes at least 25 percent from the stereophonic sound. Stereophonic sound is not effective when two people are face to face, unless of course they are in big closeups or a big 2-shot. The full value of stereophonic sound comes from the *distance* between the two people who are talking. If one person is planted at one end of the set and the other person is on the other side of the set then the sound has a opportunity to add to the illusion of depth. . . .

D.F.Z.

≡

Stereophonic sound was a strong part of the package Fox was attempting to sell to theatre owners.

≡

May 7, 1953
Mr. Jack Warner
Warner Brothers Studios
Burbank, California
PERSONAL

Dear Jack:

I am happy to see by your new production announcement that you too are showing interest in wide-screen motion picture production. . . .

I know one thing for sure—the "flat" picture is over or will be over by the time CinemaScope hits the theatres. Our audience demonstrations in New York, Philadelphia, Chicago, Detroit have convinced us beyond a shadow of a doubt that the audience is set to see the screen open up—not by mere enlargement but by photographic design. Incidentally, we now have 2,964 contracts signed for theatres in the United States and they are coming in at the rate of about 300 a week. We will have a minimum of 500 installations completed by October 1st and they will go in at the rate of about 500 a month from there on.

Now that the sales talk is over I am compelled as an old friend and employee to register surprise and disappointment that you have selected the name WarnerScope for your process. I believe that the name CinemaScope has already become a very familiar trademark to the industry as well as to the general public. Instead of adding further confusion by using the word "scope" for your device I think you might have found some other satisfactory word. What about WarnerDimension? I would appreciate it if you would give consideration to this suggestion. We have spent a lot of money and effort in publicizing CinemaScope on a world-wide basis. It means as much to us as Vitaphone once meant to you and Movietone once meant to Fox.

I will appreciate hearing from you.

Best always,
Darryl

≡

On May 7, 1953 (the date of the above letter), Warners announced that they would film in WarnerScope, which was a wide-screen approach.

However, after The Robe *and CinemaScope proved to be outstanding successes Warners abandoned WarnerScope for CinemaScope in October 1953. By early November every major studio in Los Angeles was licensed by Fox to make CinemaScope pictures—with the exception of Paramount. That studio had developed a different approach to the big screen called VistaVision.*

≡

TO: Philip Dunne   DATE: May 7, 1953
PERSONAL AND CONFIDENTIAL

Every once in a while I write a note to certain of the producers, but actually it is more than a note—it is a memorandum to myself. This note falls in the same category.

I have analyzed and studied the box-office results of recent pictures. What I am going to say is not exactly new or startling but it is certainly worth *remembering*. . . .

What exactly do they [the public] want? It is certain that they do not want every excellent picture. It is also certain that every excellent picture is not a box-office hit. Many excellent pictures have been defeated by unsatisfactory or unpopular subject matter. In this regard we have had our own bitter experience with pictures like *Viva Zapata!*, *My Cousin Rachel*. . . . Other studios have had similar and even more bitter experiences with pictures I thought contained wonderful entertainment values.

Moulin Rouge [Romulus, 1952] is a downbeat story. In many respects it has some of the downbeat ingredients of *A Streetcar Named Desire* [Charles K. Feldman, 1951] and *Come Back, Little Sheba* [Hal Wallis, 1952]. They all have one thing in common—sex. . . .

You do not have to explain the success of *Ivanhoe* [M-G-M, 1952]. It was showmanship and adventure. Nor do you have to ask the reason for the success of [*The Snows of*] *Kilimanjaro* [Fox, 1952], as it certainly combined ingredients of showmanship, sex and adventure. . . .

This report does not necessarily prove that a picture must have sex to survive or become a big hit. It indicates, however, that more pictures with this content are successful than any other type of picture. It indicates that even a heavy, downbeat, depressing story can be lifted if it contains a really strong, violent sex situation. . . .

Another observation—*Call Me Madam* [Fox, 1953] is probably a better picture than *Gentlemen Prefer Blondes* [Fox, 1953], but I predict that *Gentlemen Prefer Blondes* may very well double the gross of *Madam*.

Another observation—*Moulin Rouge* is not a success because it deals with Toulouse-Lautrec and his paintings. This is all part of a wonderful, colorful background, but the main item is the story of a prostitute and the other women in the life of a little cripple. . . .

Another observation—if you feel the urge to make a "message picture" or if you feel the urge to take an "intellectual splurge," be sure that it can be told in terms of adventure, showmanship, and certainly in terms of sex. . . .

Darryl

≡

Gentlemen Prefer Blondes did indeed almost double the gross of Call Me Madam.

≡

TO: Casey Robinson [writer]　　　　　　　DATE: April 29, 1953
　　Molly Mandaville
　　SUBJECT: THE EGYPTIAN Revised temporary script 4/15/53

Dear Casey:

I think that in spite of everything we accomplished a great deal today on *The Egyptian*. . . . [Director] Mike [Curtiz] did not always make good sense, particularly in his selection of words, but he did point out some of the weaknesses that we both know of in the present script. . . .

This is what seems to bother people most in reading the script: They call it "flowery language." In trying to figure out the meaning of the words apparently the readers fail to understand exactly what we are talking about. . . .

≡

Michael Curtiz was now free-lancing after twenty-six years at Warner Bros. The Egyptian *was adapted from the best-selling novel by Mika Waltari.*

≡

"THE EGYPTIAN" CONFERENCE ON SECOND REVISED TEMPORARY SCRIPT OF JUNE 22ND, 1953 (with Messr. Robinson, Molly Mandaville) DATE OF TRANSCRIPT: JUNE 29TH, 1953

. . . In the scenes involving Nefer [Fox contract player Bella Darvi], go through the script and delete such descriptive lines as "We play this as frankly as decency permits" . . .

≡

"THE EGYPTIAN" CONFERENCE ON SHOOTING FINAL SCRIPT OF JANUARY 14TH, 1954 WITH MESSRS. [Philip] DUNNE, CURTIZ AND MOLLY MANDAVILLE. DATE OF TRANSCRIPT: FEBRUARY 10TH, 1954

. . . Re the Breen [Hays] Office request for changes: (1) Page 48, Scene 94: Nefer's line, "The greatest gift a man can bring to a woman is his innocence—which he can give only once."

I *absolutely refuse* to change this line in any way. . . .

≡

The line remained.

≡

DATE: April 15, 1954

TO: Alfred Newman [general music director]
SUBJECT: THE EGYPTIAN

Dear Al:

As you undoubtedly know, we have a unique situation regarding the editing and scoring of *The Egyptian*. I am now commencing to cut the picture sequence by sequence even though we do not finish photography until sometime in May.

The world premiere on *The Egyptian* is set for September 1st. We can meet this date but what is more important than that—we are compelled to meet the date because of this fixed commitment.

Undoubtedly *The Egyptian* will be a big important musical score. More than anything I would like to have you do it but I do not conceivably see how you can do it at the same time you are doing [*There's No Business Like*] *Show Business* and the other many things that you have to do.

Actually I would like to have the musical director [composer] go to work in about two weeks. I would bring him back each night with me and he would follow the cutting of the picture right up to the finishing date. During this period of time he could develop his themes and understand thoroughly the problem. . . .

I hope to have the picture practically cut, at least a complete first cut, in a few days after we have got the last rushes.

Who do you suggest to do the job? I have been thinking of both Franz Waxman and Bernard Herrmann. I actually favor Waxman for this particular assignment. Let me have your suggestions as I would like to have him actually start looking at the film with me episode by episode two weeks from next Monday. I believe that Waxman also has a record with us of being reasonably fast.

D. F. Z.

===

Franz Waxman was unavailable at the time and Bernard Herrmann was signed. Then there were delays in the filming and the release date was moved up by one week. Herrmann already had been under a tight schedule; now it was impossible. Newman and Herrmann solved the problem by dividing the extensive scoring between them. This was probably the first time in America two composers of such esteem "officially" collaborated on a single score, and the first time both composers conducted their own contributions.

≡

TO: Michael Curtiz   DATE: April 29, 1954

Dear Mike:

Last night I ran practically all of the cut material and assembled material on *The Egyptian*. . . .

Even on my personal productions I do not make a habit of screening without the director being present but I am sure you know that in the case of *The Egyptian* we, *confidentially*, face a very difficult situation. Two rival companies are trying to beat us out with stories in an Egyptian background. Jack Warner has given orders on *Land of the Pharaohs* to cut and score the picture as they go along and you know that it is a story with our background dealing with the building of the pyramids.

We probably cannot beat out [M-G-M's] *The Valley of the Kings* but I do not care about this so much as it is a modern story but the Warner picture disturbs me as they have their own color process and can make prints much quicker than we can.

Therefore, in this case I have to gamble and disregard protocol and have the picture cut so that we can get it into music shortly after you have finished final photography. I know you will bear with me as I think you remember I am a pretty good cutter. . . .

If there is anything that I have done that you violently object to I will either "argue you" out of it or let you "argue me" out of it.

D.F.Z.

≡

Curtiz had worked with Zanuck at Warner Bros. in the late 1920s and early 1930s.

≡

TO: Philip Dunne   DATE: August 1, 1953
STRICTLY CONFIDENTIAL

This is another one of my monthly reports on box-office grosses. This report, like some of the previous ones, deals primarily with the foreign market as it stands today.

We must realize that no company could exist without the foreign revenue. We have no television competition to speak of, outside of England, and new markets are opening up around the world.

Of course the most important foreign territory remains England. Next comes Italy, Japan, Central and South America, West Germany on certain pictures and a grouping of France, Belgium and Switzerland. They are treated as a unit.

The loss of the foreign market to an American picture can be enormous and can turn a successful picture in the domestic market into a failure. By the same token, certain pictures that have failed in the domestic market have been turned into profitable ventures because of an extraordinarily large foreign gross. . . .

Let us examine the musical situation. . . . Because of the sex angle in *Gentlemen Prefer Blondes* it is anticipated that it will be by far our largest foreign grossing musical. In this case it is a question of the two personalities being big enough to overcome the foreign objection to most musicals. The objection is based on the fact that, outside of England, all pictures are dubbed in most of the important territories—but you cannot dub the songs as this would mean redoing a complete musical job and it would cost a fortune. Therefore you dub the dialogue with one voice and when the singing starts you have to use the songs in English and in the original voice. . . .

It might appear that I have put too much emphasis on big-scale action and adventure stories and outdoor spectacles. While it is true in numbers they are in the preponderance, I am convinced that when we consider the entire world as one market our decision to emphasize action and scope will prove to be a wise decision. These subjects not only complement CinemaScope but CinemaScope complements them. We have tried to select varied foreign locales as a plus value. . . .

I do not mean to imply that unique scenery or spectacular monuments can turn a bad story into a good story but at least for the first year of CinemaScope we have the distinct advantage of being able to work these picturesque and exciting backgrounds into our stories. . . .

D.F.Z.

≡

TO: Sol Siegel [producer]　　　　　　　DATE: August 21, 1953
　　Richard Murphy [writer]
　　Molly Mandaville
　　SUBJECT: BROKEN LANCE

Dear Sol and Dick:

. . . [The] revised version of the Dick Murphy script on *Broken Lance*: What I mainly did in this version was to eliminate and boil down the dialogue. . . .

I feel that we have the opportunity here for an offbeat Western story and that it is certainly worth further work and study. In many respects this is a very skillful adaptation of the original [*House of Strangers*—Fox, 1949], but I think it calls for a great deal of further consideration. While it is really a better story than the original version, I think we have inherited too much of the original and that we have adhered too closely to some of the elements that made the original picture a box-office disappointment—even though it was a fine picture. . . .

The main problem has always been the father against son theme and the brother against brother theme. The basic motive of revenge within the confines of a family circle invariably turns out to be depressing. Somehow or other, family feuds and family hatreds leave a bad taste in the mouth. When sons turn upon father and disregard the mother, and when brothers turn against brother and fight each other for money and lust, it always produces a sort of sickening feeling in the pit of the stomach.

For the same reason, "happy family" stories generally are enormously successful. . . . This does not rule out *Broken Lance* as far as I'm concerned and as long as we recognize the problem and try to cure it or treat it in such a way that the whole picture will not be just a picture of hatreds, feuds, revenge, etc. There must be some way of overcoming this problem and yet retain all of the splendid elements from the script and story. . . .

I think we have got to do with the three brothers what [producer-director George] Stevens did so well in *Shane* [Paramount, 1953] with the old villain [Emile Meyer]. You hated him. But suddenly halfway through the picture, they gave him a big speech in which he justifies his position and his villainy. His position was wrong, nevertheless he was no longer just a villain. He had understandable motivations that anyone could accept, even though you knew his viewpoint was wrong. We must do this for the three older brothers. It is something we failed to do in the original version. . . .

The following thought occurs to me, and it might take the risk and the curse off the *family* feud and hatred. . . .

Matt [M-G-M star Spencer Tracy] met the Indian girl, White Flower [free-lance player Katy Jurado]. He married her. A year later she gave birth to a son—Joe [Fox contract player Robert Wagner].

The boys now are only half brothers. Joe is the only half-caste. Matt is the squaw man.

The three older sons from the beginning look upon Joe as an "outsider" . . .

It is the old story of the son by the second wife who invariably becomes the favorite.

This may be a fine distinction but it should be given careful analysis. It seems to me that I will be able to better understand the rift between the half brothers as well as their lack of regard or respect for White Flower and their eventual hatred for Matt. . . .

D.F.Z.

≡

Zanuck's suggestions were followed. The picture did much better commercially than House of Strangers, *which was based on the novel* I'll Never Go There Anymore *by Jerome Weidman.*

≡

February 16, 1954
Mr. John Ford
6860 Odin Street
Hollywood 28, Calif.
Personal and confidential

Dear Jack:

This is a personal letter. You and I have had many minor differences but we have never had a major difference. I think I am the only guy in the business you have let edit your pictures without interference. I believe I am also the only guy in the business you have let prepare a script in advance of your being assigned to the project. So much for the past.

Now we come to a major point of disagreement. I understand that you are resisting CinemaScope. Six months ago I went on record as saying to a group of people that in my opinion John Ford would do more with CinemaScope than any living director. You are a long shot master. In some strange way you have always amazed me by what you can do with what might be just an ordinary long shot. If any medium was ever devised especially for you, it is CinemaScope.

I have met similar resistance before from directors, notably George Cukor who now is so completely sold on CinemaScope that he thinks he invented it. I have had the experience of cutting thirteen Cinema-Scope pictures. We are just beginning to learn how to use the medium.

What I have seen in our unreleased pictures is really unbelievable.

Directors whom you respect have one by one told me of the "freedom" they have enjoyed with CinemaScope. I see examples of it daily on the screen. If you have a chance, I would like to have you come over one night and I will have them set up in our big projection room one or two of our unreleased pictures for you. Particularly, I would like you to see *Hell and High Water* [Fox, 1954]. I believe you will be amazed at what this camera can do in intimate quarters inside a submarine.

You have always been progressive and I believe I can convince you.

Affectionate regards,
Darryl

≡

Ford directed The Long Gray Line *(1955) for Columbia in Cinema-Scope and co-directed* Mister Roberts *(1955) for Warners in that process, but apparently was not a big fan.*

≡

Feb. 23, 1954
Mr. Jerry Wald [vice president in charge of production]
Columbia Pictures Corporation
1438 No. Gower Street
Hollywood 28, California

Dear Jerry:

In answer to you questions, here are the best answers that I can give.

The production of *The Robe* was certainly not hampered by the [Production] Code. . . .

I have been associated, as you know, with many controversial pictures and I have had many fights with the Breen [Hays] Office and with other outside censorship groups. It is my belief that the Code protected me far more than it ever harmed me. . . .

It seems to me that instead of all this fuss about the Code that you should start worrying about "outside" censorship groups both here and abroad.

I defy anyone to name me ten best-selling novels or ten successful stage plays in the last ten years that could not be put on the screen because of Breen Office refusal. Frankly I do not believe that there were five in ten years. Of course there were a lot of things that none of us wanted to put on the screen because they did not look like good motion picture material. But I would like to know where any of us had to pass up anything really worthwhile because of Code restrictions.

When you can get by with *From Here to Eternity* [Columbia, 1953] and *A Streetcar Named Desire* and have them both turn out to be box-office hits then I fail to see what all the furor is about.

What infuriates me is the pressure groups and censorship groups both here and abroad. This is where we should carry our fight.

Regards,
Darryl

≡

Wald was inquiring whether Zanuck felt hampered by what he (Wald) regarded as an increasingly obsolete production code.

≡

TO: Sam Engel [producer]   DATE: April 14, 1954
CC: David Brown [story editor]
    SUBJECT: THE QUEEN OF SHEBA

Dear Sam:

The title *The Queen of Sheba* does not lead you to believe you are going to see a so-called religious or Biblical subject. The Queen of Sheba, like Salome and Cleopatra, and perhaps Helen of Troy, has been associated to a certain degree with the elements of sex, glamor and seduction. To me this is the key to this story if we are going to make a big successful commercial picture out of it.

In a nutshell, this should be the story of a glamorous but evil temptress. . . .

As you know, confidentially, I have even flirted with the idea of Marilyn Monroe as Sheba. I think it might be one of the biggest box-office combinations of all time—but like everything else it depends on the story we create and the showmanship we employ. The potentialities are certainly present for box-office dynamite. . . .

D.F.Z.

≡

The film was not made, but Solomon and Sheba *with Yul Brynner and Gina Lollobrigida was released by United Artists in 1959.*

≡

TO: Mr. Charles Brackett [producer]   DATE: October 26, 1954
   Messrs. Ernest Lehman [writer]
   Oscar Hammerstein [lyricist]
   Richard Rodgers [composer]
   SUBJECT: THE KING AND I

Dear Charlie:

. . . Here are some interesting figures which we must take into consideration.

The old [nonmusical] film version of *Anna and the King of Siam* [1946], when it was first cut together and assembled, ran two hours and forty-one minutes. . . . In two hours and forty-one minutes, the film was dull and we had the enormous job of eliminating surplus material.

Finally, after weeks of effort, we managed to get the film down and it was released in a length of two hours and eight minutes. This meant that we had eliminated three reels of finished film.

Now we must remember that this cut-down version did not contain any songs, dances or ballets. It was purely the book. . . .

The [musical] play version of *The King and I* was two hours and forty-four minutes long. This included sixty-five minutes and twenty-four seconds of songs and musical numbers.

If our picture is going to run two hours and forty-four minutes, then I know from experience that we are in trouble. We are in exactly the same kind of trouble that another more or less celebrated musical is now facing [*A Star Is Born*, Warners]. They have opened the picture, they are recutting it and taking out somewhere between twenty-eight and thirty-five minutes. . . .

While I believe that every musical number was unquestionably essential in the stage version [of *The King and I*], I believe that we must realistically recognize the fact that no successful musical picture, to my knowledge, has ever run longer than two hours and twenty minutes.*

* *The Great Ziegfeld* (M-G-M, 1936) in its original release ran two hours and fifty-six minutes.

And that, actually, since the beginning of the motion picture industry, I do not believe that there have been more than twenty-five pictures which have run more than two hours and a half. And these included some of the big epics.

I certainly do not want to cut just for the sake of cutting, but we are in a practical business as well as a creative business and it would greatly disturb my sense of showmanship and craftsmanship if once again I had to see thirty minutes of hard-earned film land on the cutting room floor.

I believe, without a question of doubt, that without harming quality, this version can be brought down to a total footage length of not more than two hours and fifteen minutes or two hours and twenty minutes. . . .

The ballet on the stage ran slightly under fifteen minutes and I am sure that we are all aware that fifteen minutes of celluloid is a hell of a lot different from fifteen minutes of the theatre, watching a live show.

I may be naive, but it has always been my belief that when you go to the theatre to see a celebrated musical, or a celebrated drama with music, that you go there expecting a great deal of music as well as dances, etc. It is my belief, brought on by bitter experience, that too many numbers or too many reprises in a motion picture musical frequently have the effect of spoiling the very things that were so very good on the stage.

In the last three weeks, since what happened at Warner Brothers [with *A Star is Born*], I went back to work with [director] Walter Lang on *There's No Business Like Show Business* and we cut practically twenty minutes out of the picture after it had already been turned over for final recording. I believe we have improved the picture, which was already a very great picture. I hated to lose some of the musical things which we lost, because they had a certain quality. But, for the best interest of the picture as a whole, I felt compelled to make these last-minute cuts.

Wherever possible, I would like to avoid a similar situation on *The King and I*. I have great respect for all the material. It is a case of just too much of too many things, even though most of them are very good things. . . .

≡

The King and I (1956) in its initial release ran two hours and thirteen minutes and was a huge success.

≡

TO: Nunnally Johnson   DATE: December 4, 1954

Dear Nunnally:

I want you to know that I am delighted with your new [writer-producer-director contract] deal [at Fox], not only because you have earned it and deserve it but because you have, particularly during the last three years, relieved me of a lot of headaches and extra work.

When you are on an assignment I just sort of mentally dismiss it as I always know that you are not trying to write a script or do a job just to please me but because you are sincerely functioning as a creator should function. We may lay an egg occasionally but the average has been very high.

D.F.Z.

≡

With the exception of a few years in the 1940s, Johnson had been with Zanuck since 1934 writing, and/or producing, and/or directing.

≡

TO: All Producers   DATE: December 24, 1954
    Directors
    Writers
    Editors
SUBJECT: STEREOPHONIC SOUND

Al Lichtman, our General Sales Manager, informs me that he has received many complaints from exhibitors whose theatres have full stereophonic installations. They claim that there are far too few sound effects, both musical and otherwise, on the 4th or surround track, and they ask us to provide more of these effects which they say are very effective with their audiences.

As you know, our company is committed to the use of stereophonic sound with surround effects. We believe that the added production value and technical improvement in sound reproduction enhances considerably the presentation of our pictures. Furthermore, both the exhibitor and the public will pay more for a CinemaScope picture with full stereophonic [magnetic] sound than for the same CinemaScope picture with [monaural] optical sound.

I find that we have been using stereophonic sound conservatively rather than in its full potential. This is partly due to the fact that we are still learning, and partly to the fact that some of our people are opposed to it.

In the course of production, from writing through editing, I would like each of you to have an awareness of this new tool and to use it more freely, in a constructive manner. The Sound Department can only add effects which are fitting to the edited picture and, therefore, it is up to the creators to supply scenes and situations which will result in better story telling and better pictures. . . .

I am sure you realize that we are not just talking about added noise or added sound effects, we are talking about the skillful handling of sound and sound effects and by this, obtaining an added dimension to our films.

D.F.Z.

≡

January 27, 1955
Mr. Elia Kazan
Newtown Productions
1545 Broadway
New York, N.Y.

Dear Gadg:
 Over the weekend I had a chance to again study . . . properties which you submitted to us. . . .

Oedipus Rex. Honestly Gadg . . . this of course is a great subject and this is no news to you or to me. Personally I am so fed up with material of this sort that it is difficult for me to become interested. In rapid succession we have had *Quo Vadis*; *David and Bathsheba*; *Samson and Delilah*; *The Robe*; *Demetrius and the Gladiators*; *The Silver Chalice*; *Sign of the Pagan* and now they are coming along with *The Ten Commandments*; *Joseph and His Brethren*; *Attila the Hun*; *Alexander the Great*— and I understand they are to do *Homer* in Europe or planning to do it, etc.

As you know, I have been working for more than a year on Fulton Oursler's *The Greatest Story Ever Told*. . . .

I know *Oedipus Rex* is not exactly a duplicate of anything above, but it gets into the same general category. As a matter of fact, they are all beginning to look alike. In addition to the above, our friend, Charlie Feldman, also has *The Song of Solomon* and *The Story of Ruth*. If I am stalling and hesitant about proceeding with a project as gigantic as *The Greatest Story Ever Told*, then I believe you will thoroughly understand my hesitancy on this recommendation. . . .

I do not know the Budd Schulberg story you mention, but frankly, the way I feel about Budd, I want no further association with him. From my standpoint he can continue to enjoy his "independence." . . .

Best always,
Darryl

≡

Oedipus Rex *was not made. Kazan had contractual commitments with Fox; hence his submission of possible subjects.*

≡

TO: All Executives   DATE: October 26, 1955
STRICTLY CONFIDENTIAL

In analyzing the motion picture production situation today, we are all aware that it is practically impossible to obtain the services of top people in all of our pictures. The same situation exists at every studio.

Occasionally you can grab a top name if it is something that they desperately want to do but this does not happen frequently.

The independent deals have come to the point where they are practically "untouchable." We have gambled with new personalities and we will continue to gamble but we cannot sit around and wait for top names. . . .

We have got to meet this problem by once again emphasizing our determination to acquire as many presold properties as we can. . . . Starting with a best-seller or a hit stage play does not guarantee a box-office success but at least you begin with something of importance and something that is presold. You have a chance of attracting top actors and top directors. . . .

We have got to take more gambles than we have taken in the past in the purchase of material. There is always a way to "solve" what appears to be forbidden material. We turned down *Streetcar Named Desire* because we thought it couldn't be licked. Usually when you finally manage to lick one of these difficult problems you turn out to have a very successful picture. The fact that the story is censurable or difficult or unorthodox usually means that it is something off the beaten track and not in the usual formula groove—this means that it is something "different" and when you have something different, in most cases it happens that you end up with a hit. . . .

D.F.Z.

≡

TO: David Brown [story editor]   DATE: November 9, 1955
CC: Buddy Adler [producer]

Dear David:

. . . The purpose of our New York conference is not to defend ourselves, it is to study and analyze our problems in acquiring material under the present competitive system.

I called the meeting because I feel that at times I am getting too much resistance from the New York Office. We very nearly lost *Anastasia, Bus Stop, Man in the Gray Flannel Suit* because of hesitancy or lack of enthusiasm in New York. . . . Spyros himself stopped me on such properties as *Streetcar Named Desire*, *Guys and Dolls*, *Mister Roberts*, etc. Sometimes this was because of the price but sometimes it was because of lack of enthusiasm by the New York group. . . .

D.F.Z.

≡

TO: Mr. Nunnally Johnson   DATE: November 25, 1955
   [producer–writer–director]
   SUBJECT: THE MAN IN THE GRAY FLANNEL SUIT

Dear Nunnally:

I spent an hour and a half with Jennifer [Jones], going over in detail her "recommendations and suggestions." She, too, is in love with the [Sloan Wilson] book. She has practically memorized great sections of it, and many of her ideas closely parallel ideas expressed the other day by Gregory Peck.

I explained to Jennifer why we had to make certain changes and I told her the outline of the new script. She was very pleased with the outline, but what seems to be disturbing her more than anything else is where her dialogue or her viewpoint inside certain scenes has been changed from the book. . . .

To be specific:

(1) Jennifer feels that from the very beginning Betsy [Jones] is too pat and sure of herself, and that she seems to place all the blame on Tom [Gregory Peck] instead of feeling that she, too, is somewhat at fault. She feels that there is a real danger of audiences disliking Betsy if she is so damned positive and so damned sure of herself.

(2) Jennifer feels there should be a little more progression in the characterization of Betsy, even if it comes inside the scenes of the existing continuity. . . .

(5) On page 55 of the script, Jennifer thought Betsy was entirely too positive when she told Tom about war: "I don't believe men can go through what some of them had to go through and then just walk away from it like walking away from the polo grounds." Jennifer thought that speech made her look foolish because Tom had been a soldier and he certainly knows more about war than she does. She thought that this

speech of hers should be cut, and that there was a better speech on page 71 of the book, covering the same points. As written in the script, she thought she became too much the "nagging" wife. . . .

(8) Jennifer thought the seduction scene . . . was too light and frivolous, and at times somewhat cute. If possible she would prefer a more serious approach like it is in the book. . . .

I gave Jennifer's marked copy of the book to Molly [Mandaville], and she incorporated into this note the parts in the book which Jennifer underlined.

D.F.Z.

≡

The suggestions were included in the revised script. Jennifer Jones had signed a three-picture contract with Fox in 1954. The Man in the Gray Flannel Suit *was the third picture.*

≡

TO: David Brown [story editor] DATE: December 12, 1955
CC: Buddy Adler [producer]
  Spyros Skouras

Dear David:

Whenever possible I have been trying to get caught up on some of the recent "outside pictures." I have been particularly interested in seeing pictures which we rejected at the studio when they were originally submitted to us. This is why I have been asking you recently for the original Producer Reports on some of these properties.

I have seen *Picnic* [Columbia, 1955]. It is not, in my opinion, a truly great picture but I believe it definitely has the possibilities of being a box-office attraction. We made a mistake in rejecting it.

I note that one of the reasons we turned it down is because the Breen Office told us that they had flatly rejected it and had turned down Paramount. . . .

I finally rejected the play on the basis that the price was exorbitant and particularly because of the Breen Office ruling. I repeat, I am sorry we lost it as, while it is not as great as I heard, it still certainly has box-office elements, in spite of the fact that William Holden, in my opinion, is terribly miscast.

I also looked at *I'll Cry Tomorrow* [M-G-M, 1955]. This is a very interesting solid, downbeat story and, while it has an outstanding performance by Susan Hayward, I considered it to be overrated. Here again it did not quite live up to my expectations from the standpoint of quality but also here again I believe we made a mistake in passing up this property. . . .

We turned down *I'll Cry Tomorrow*, frankly because we were all afraid of the subject matter and of the fact that Lillian Roth was not a really famous personality. [Producer Julian] Blaustein wanted it but only if he could get Marilyn Monroe for the role. . . .

I also looked at *Desperate Hours* [Paramount, 1955] and I am pleased that we did not get it. I am not being influenced by the fact that the picture is doing poor business. It is a very well made picture with great performances and direction but it is the same story that we have seen on the screen and television at least 20 times. I believe I made it at Warner Brothers at least three times. I do not have my files but I believe that we finally rejected it based on the fact that the material was "too familiar" and that the asking price was too high. . . .

I have also seen *The Court-Martial of Billy Mitchell* [United States, 1955]. This is one of the worst directed, worst produced and worst acted pictures I have seen in a long while—but I hasten to add that the patriotic theme of the story is great enough to carry a strong impact. It may even be great enough to make this a box-office attraction. It is practically a documentary film but the trial itself is very interesting. . . .

I think it is a good policy for us to always review our previous decisions and not be afraid to admit our mistakes. We will probably make the same mistakes again or similar ones but it does no harm for us to go back and analyze our initial reactions.

D. F. Z.

During 1955, and probably earlier, Zanuck seriously thought about asking Fox to revise his contract so that he could step down as vice president in charge of production in order to become an independent producer. By March 1956 an agreement was worked out for him to leave by the end of June, with his independent pictures to be released by Twentieth Century–Fox. (Zanuck's outstanding success as an independent producer would be *The Longest Day*—1962.)

When asked by columnist Hedda Hopper on November 12, 1960, why he left Hollywood in 1956 to produce pictures independently in Europe, Zanuck replied:

"Anyone who thinks I'm over here [in Europe] to make a tax gain is out of their mind. I am a resident of Santa Monica; my corporation is a California corporation. I pay my American Income Tax and the State of California Taxes. I have never made one gain by being over here. I've never taken out a phony residency or that kind of thing. There's no gain for me.

"I just got well fed up with being an executive and no longer being a producer. That's what the job became. Actors are now directing, writing, producing. Actors have taken over Hollywood completely with their agents. They want approval of everything—script, stars, still pictures. The producer hasn't got a chance to exercise any authority! . . . What the hell, I'm not going to work for them!

"Now, I've got a great affection for Duke [John] Wayne, but what right has he to write, direct and produce a motion picture? What right has Kirk Douglas got? What right has [Richard] Widmark got? My God, look at [Marlon] Brando with *One-Eyed Jacks* [Brando's one directing job thus far—Paramount, 1961]. My God, he's still shooting! . . ."

Philip Dunne in his 1971 American Film Institute oral history with Tom Stempel spoke about other factors behind Zanuck's decision to leave the studio: "[Zanuck] started telling me how much money [producer] Frank Ross had made and kept on *The Robe*. He'd kept it because he got a capital gain on the whole thing because he'd developed the project and sold it [to Fox]. Zanuck figured out that on this one picture Frank had made and kept as much money as Zanuck had made and kept in ten years. Made and kept is the thing. He said, 'I'm in the wrong business' . . . I also think he was tired. . . . I think that at the rate he had gone, he had to burn himself out sometime. . . . You would notice it in the meetings. He'd begin to lose a little of that enthusiasm. . . . I think he was just bored with the whole thing . . . and not able to drive himself as he had in the beginning. He was very young when he started. . . ."

In February 1961, while still functioning as an independent producer, Zanuck wrote to Dunne from Paris:

"As I see it today, the boss of the Studio is actually no longer a boss— he has a title but that is all. He is the slave of agents and actors with their own corporations and insane competition from independent operators and promoters who are willing to give away 100% of the profits just as long as they get a distribution fee.

"I am afraid that to a great extent the industry swept out of our reach and all that is left is a struggle for survival. I do not mind a struggle, but I am afraid that the pattern has changed and that the odds are too great. They are even too great for independent producers who like to work on a creative basis.

"I, too, have memories of the Studio when it was at its peak. . . ."

Then in 1962 Zanuck responded to an appeal by members of the board of directors of Fox and was elected president of the company. He appointed his son, Richard, vice president in charge of production. In 1969, Zanuck became chairman and chief executive of Twentieth

Century–Fox and Richard was named president. In May 1971, Zanuck resigned as chief executive.

A short while before he was elected president, in a January 20, 1962, letter to Jack L. Warner, Darryl Zanuck said: ". . . When I last talked to you, I said that I was ready to go back to Hollywood. I still am ready but I am beginning to weave and wobble. . . .

"I am not bitter, but I just have reached the age and the point where I cannot spend my days with people I would not like to have dinner with at night. . . ."

After several years of retirement, Darryl Zanuck died on December 22, 1979.

ABOUT DARRYL F. ZANUCK

1902 September 5, birth of Darryl Francis Zanuck, the second child of Frank and Louise (Torpin) Zanuck, in Wahoo, Nebraska.

1917 September 4, having not told the truth about his age, enlists in the Omaha National Guard; eventually going to France as a Private First Class during World War I. Honorably discharged from the Army in August 1919.

1920 Sells his first story to *Argosy* magazine.

1922 Sells his adaptation of the play *Storm* to Universal Pictures.

1923 His first book, *Habit and Other Short Stories* (Times-Mirror Press), published. Shortly after becomes a gag writer at Mack Sennett's Studio, followed by writing assignments at other studios.

1924 January 24, marries screen actress Virginia Fox (no relation to William Fox, founder of Fox Film Corp.). Children: Darrylin (1931), Susan (1933), and Richard (1934).

Hired by Warner Bros. to write scripts for dog superstar-to-be Rin Tin Tin. Later, produces as well as writes a wide variety of scripts for Warners.

1928 Associate Executive in charge of Warner Bros. Pictures.

1931 Chief Executive in charge of all productions of the combined Warner and First National studios, in association with Jack L. Warner.

1933 Forms Twentieth Century Pictures with Joseph M. Schenck (releasing through United Artists).

1935 Named Vice President in Charge of Production when Twentieth Century merges with Fox.

1942–43 Colonel on active duty in the Army during part of World War II; then resumes at Fox.

1943 His book, *Tunis Expedition* (Random House), published.

1956–62 Independent producer releasing through Twentieth Century–Fox.

1962–69 President of Twentieth Century–Fox.

1969–71 Chairman and Chief Executive of Twentieth Century–Fox.

1979 December 22, dies in Palm Springs, California.

INDEX